MARKET FORCES AND WORLD DEVELOPMENT

From the same publishers for the Development Studies Association

DEVELOPMENT PERSPECTIVES FOR THE 1990s
Edited by Renee Prendergast and H. W. Singer

CONFLICT AND CHANGE IN THE 1990s:
Ethics, Laws and Institutions
Edited by Anthony Carty and H. W. Singer

Market Forces and World Development

Edited by

Renee Prendergast
Lecturer in Economics
The Queen's University of Belfast

and

Frances Stewart
Director, Queen Elizabeth House
University of Oxford

St. Martin's Press

First published in Great Britain 1994 by
THE MACMILLAN PRESS LTD
Houndmills, Basingstoke, Hampshire RG21 2XS
and London
Companies and representatives
throughout the world

A catalogue record for this book is available from the British Library.

ISBN 0–333–59484–3

Printed in Great Britain by
Antony Rowe Ltd
Chippenham, Wiltshire

First published in the United States of America 1994 by
Scholarly and Reference Division,
ST. MARTIN'S PRESS, INC.,
175 Fifth Avenue,
New York, N.Y. 10010

ISBN 0–312–10175–9

Library of Congress Cataloging-in-Publication Data
Market forces and world development / edited by Renee Prendergast and Frances Stewart.
p. cm.
Includes index.
ISBN 0–312–10175–9
1. Marketing. 2. Economic development. I. Prendergast, Renee, 1952– . II. Stewart, Frances, 1940–
HF5415.M284 1994
338.9—dc20 93–25823
CIP

Contents

List of Tables

List of Figures

Acknowledgements

This volume, the third in the Development Studies Association's conference series, contains a selection of papers presented at the Association's Annual Conference held at the University College of Swansea in September 1991. The editors wish to record their thanks to the Conference Organiser, David Marsden, without whose invaluable assistance this volume would not have been possible. They also wish to thank Mary Trainor and Eileen Maguire of Queen's University, Belfast, for editorial assistance and Carol Clarke for secretarial assistance.

Notes on the Contributors

Alexandre Rands Barros is Professor in the Department of Economics, Universidade Federal de Pernambuco, Recife, Brazil. His research interests include macroeconomics, growth and cycles theory and economic development.

Edward Clay is a Research Fellow at the Overseas Development Institute, London. His main research interests are in food aid.

Des Gasper is a Senior Lecturer at the Institute of Development Studies in The Hague. His main research interests are in policy analysis and evaluation, and Southern Africa.

Dharam Ghai is Director of the United Nations Research Institute for Social Development (UNRISD), Geneva. His research interests include the social dimensions of environment, structural adjustment and global integration.

Nigel Harris is Professor of Development Planning at the Development Planning Unit, University College London. His main research interests are in economics of urbanisation.

Renee Prendergast is a Lecturer in Economics at Queen's University, Belfast. Her research interests include development theory and technology and development.

Kunibert Raffer is Associate Professor at the Department of Economics, University of Vienna. His research interests include foreign trade and international debt.

H. W. Singer is Professor at the Institute of Development Studies, University of Sussex. His research interests include international trade, international economic relations, rich and poor countries, and food aid.

Peter Smith is Visiting Senior Economist at the International Centre for Agricultural Research in Dry Areas, Aleppo, Syria. His research interests include individual and institutional decision-making under uncertainty, and project identification.

Frances Stewart is Director, Queen Elizabeth House, at the University of Oxford. Her research interests include adjustment and poverty.

John Toye is Director, Institute of Development Studies, and Professorial Fellow, University of Sussex. His research interests include development theory, evaluation of aid, and public finance.

Introduction: Market Forces and World Development

RENEE PRENDERGAST AND FRANCES STEWART

During the 1980s there was a strong shift in balance from the state to the market, in the allocation of resources of every kind in almost every part of the globe. This change reflected an ideological shift, in which first Keynesian thought, and later, more dramatically, Marxism seemed discredited, to be replaced by neo-liberal ideas. The powerful ideological revolution was accompanied by technological changes – particularly in communications – which made a world-wide market an unavoidable, and to some extent uncontrollable, reality. In both developed and developing countries policy changes followed, enhancing the role of the market and reducing that of the state.

This book is concerned with some important implications of the shift to market forces. It opens with a bold thesis. The nation state, Nigel Harris claims, has had its day. It will remain around for a while yet but it can no longer be seen as exercising significant control over the economic activity that takes place within its territory. We are moving towards a single integrated world economy in which the forms of relatively autonomous national development practised by many, if not most, developing countries in the post-war period no longer make sense. In this more open world economy major changes can occur at extraordinary speed, with the result that, from the point of view of each individual competitor, the system seems very unpredictable. As a result there is a premium on organisational flexibility and markets come to appear as the sole means available to manage complexity.

Harris's claim is large and controversial – probably intentionally so. But it should not be dismissed lightly. The fact of increasing global integration, which is more fully documented in Dharam Ghai's paper (Chapter 2), is beyond question. It is also a fact that this increasing integration has been accompanied by widespread deregulation of economies as well as measures to reduce taxes and government expenditure. This liberalisation, taken together with the abandonment of communal ownership and central planning in the former Soviet Union and in several East European states, has created a widespread impression that the market system has triumphed over planning and that state intervention in the economy has been shown to be impotent. Part of the argument in this volume is that this impression is mistaken.

The first point to be noted is that what is usually described as a market system is by no means all market. Marx long ago pointed to the difference between the division of labour in the workshop and the division of labour in society. In our own century, Coase, in an article which like *Capital* is much cited but little read, pointed to the fact that, outside the firm, price movements directed production while, within the firm, resources were directed by the entrepreneur. These islands of conscious power within the international economy have become increasingly important in the post-war period. As Ghai notes, the driving force behind the increasing international division of labour is transnational corporations rather than the market. As these corporations have extended their operations nationally and internationally, they have become the most insistent advocates of market forces insofar as they have sought the progressive removal of all obstacles to the free deployment of their own resources. However, while the general thrust of this powerful interest group has been in favour of liberalisation and deregulation, this is by no means uniformly the case. In the United States and in Europe, particular firms and industries have successfully advocated state intervention (usually in the form of non-tariff protection) when faced with intense competition from competitor transnationals and developing country firms.

If the rule of market forces is to a substantial extent a matter of dominance by large firms, this greatly weakens the welfare-theoretic justification for unregulated markets, which rests on the assumption of competition between large numbers of small and independent firms. Instead what is at issue, to a considerable extent, is the replacement of government bureaucracies by those of massive international firms. Arguments to the effect that resource allocation is optimised by markets rather than states are then to some extent beside the point. The demand for the free play of market forces then turns out to be not so much a demand that allocation be left to the markets as that firms should be allowed to plan their activities with the minimum interference from states and locate those activities wherever the rate of return promises to be highest. While moves towards greater autonomy and freedom of movement for capital have increased aspects of competitiveness, they have also increased the bargaining power of capital *vis à vis* states and labour, resulting in an effective reduction in sovereignty and of the role and power of labour organisations.

To the extent that states have experienced real reductions in sovereignty in recent years, this is due more to the greater freedom achieved by capital than to changes in the international division of labour *per se*. The sets of production processes carried on within individual states are less self-contained than formerly, but this seems to have led not so much to a loss of sovereignty as to a change in its nature. A useful analogy is the change in an individual's autonomy as society moves from an economy based on subsistence agriculture to one based on a more advanced social division of labour. Provided the individual can acquire the wherewithal to participate in the new social division of labour and can share in the additional benefits which it generates, it seems reasonable to argue that individual autonomy has not so much been lost as changed in its nature. On the other hand, if individuals lack the resources (for example capital) to participate fully and on fair terms in the new social division of labour, we might regard them as having suffered a real loss of sovereignty. If this analogy is plausible, it would seem that whether or not there is a loss of national sovereignty hinges substantially on the state's relationship with domestic capital. Where this is strong and positive, as say in Korea, it has been possible to devise polices and instruments which improve the prospects of the state's domestic actors in the international arena. Such policies have by no means always involved increased freedom for the enterprises concerned. On the contrary, as Amsden (1988) has shown, the main difference between the policy regimes pursued by the Latin American countries and their more successful East Asian counterparts lay in the degree of discipline to which firms were subjected in the latter.

While the first section of the book is concerned with the interaction between changes in the international division of labour and changes in the nature of economic institutions, a second group of papers presents a broad-ranging critique of the market from a number of perspectives. In Chapter 3, Renee Prendergast considers some recent contributions to the literature on increasing returns and shows that models which make allowances for positive feedback or cumulative causation typically involve a multiplicity of equilibria. In such models, the outcome of competitive processes in terms of the precise equilibrium which is reached can depend on history and expectations. In general, history or the initial starting point of the economy will be more important the higher the discount rate and the weaker increasing returns. The lower the discount rate and the stronger increasing returns, the more important expectations are likely to be. If history rather than expectations are likely to be the main determinant of equilibrium, development traps are possible and active government intervention may be necessary to allow a better equilibrium to be reached. On the other hand, if expectations are likely to be the main determinant of the equilibrium reached by the economy, this points towards the importance of measures to create convergent expectations. As well as measures to promote social solidarity, these could include factors such as planning and political leadership.

In Chapter 4, Peter Smith provides a critique of the theoretical underpinnings of the market forces solution to development problems. He considers several criticisms of the market forces paradigm, among them the possibility that key markets in modern economies may in fact be chaotic, so that there is no equilibrium and the path followed may be erratic and unpredictable. Smith notes that regardless of their theoretical or empirical validity, paradigms or visions of how things are provide a useful support in managing everyday life. Most real life decision-making is done with an almost total lack of data and under pressure of time but at the same time there is often a premium on prompt, fluent and consistent actions. Such actions are made possible by systems of belief about how things are and what strategies are likely to work. Thus any paradigm is likely to have some use, to be true in some sense and to have a certain survival value. But the fact that it emphasises some problems and solutions and demotes others may sometimes have disastrous consequences. Smith shows that in the case of common property resources such as groundwater, strategies for management based on self-seeking individuals may rule out more effective solutions based on building long-term relationships among a stable set of actors.

In recent years increasing returns to scale have featured prominently in the international trade literature. Decreasing returns which may be a feature of certain primary commodities produced by developing countries have not received much attention. Kunibert Raffer (Chapter 5) redresses this imbalance by returning to a case first set out by Graham in 1923, in which trade according to static comparative costs can result in immiseration and decreased global output when one country specialises in a product subject to decreasing returns to scale. While Graham also assumed that the second country in his model specialised in a product subject to increasing returns to scale, Raffer shows that this is not strictly necessary for Graham's argument to hold. Raffer points out that it is possible for Graham-type losses to be outweighed by improvements in the net barter terms of trade. But he goes on to show that Graham himself had argued that there was no reason to suppose that falling unit costs in the country specialising in the increasing returns product and increasing unit costs in the other country would be reflected in a shift of net barter terms of trade in favour of the latter. In Raffer's view, Graham's case provides a theoretical underpinning for the Prebish-Singer thesis and shows why protection should be adopted as a rational policy by the country specialising in the decreasing returns commodity. Combined with recent non-Marxist approaches to unequal exchange, Raffer believes that this can also help explain the trade policies adopted by industrialised countries, especially protectionism in agrarian trade.

Alexandre Rands Barros's paper (Chapter 6) on development and the standard of living represents a radical departure from existing conventional wisdom according to which high wages are a result of economic development and not its cause. While Barros does not deny that increased wages and standard of living may result from increases in income, he emphasises the reverse causation as an important element in economic development. Barros adopts a classical notion of wage determination according to which the real wage is determined by historical, social and ideological factors. He then argues that rising real wages are helpful to development because they create pressure for technical progress and ever-increasing productivity. Barros is careful to note that there are limits to wage increases that have a positive effect on income and that if wages rise excessively, employment might fall to an extent that more than compensates for additional demand though higher wages. In this case, stagnation could be the consequence of wage increases. Barros's discussion of development in Sweden and in the various regions of Brazil seems to suggest that a strong cultural identification between workers and capitalists, which creates pressure for a reduction in any gap in the standard of living between them, could be beneficial for long-term development. The suggested positive relationship between real wages and productivity represents a severe challenge to current structural adjustment packages which emphasise the need to *decrease* real wages.

In the course of his overview of structural adjustment in the global economy, Ghai argues that, in the industrialised countries, the dynamics of the globalisation process tipped the balance in favour of adjustment policies as a result of the interplay of contending social groups. In African and Latin American economies, in contrast, the decisive element was pressure exerted by creditor countries, commercial banks and international financial institutions. This was especially true in Africa, with many countries having no domestic lobby for liberalisation and deregulation. Where there are strong domestic lobbies in favour of structural adjustment (SA), it seems reasonable to suppose that such policies are expected to generate long-run benefits for a powerful segment of the population whatever the short-run costs associated with them. Where adjustment has few or no domestic advocates, this seems to suggest that perceived long-run benefits are not regarded as substantial and/or that short-run costs are likely to be extremely high. In such circumstances, it seems incumbent on those imposing SA measures to demonstrate that benefits will arise from adherence to such measures. Some of the methodological problems which arise in the appraisal and evaluation of structural adjustment lending (SAL) programmes are discussed by John Toye in Chapter 7. While Toye looks at these problems from the perspective of the lender, many of the same problems arise when the issue is addressed from the point of view of the country undergoing the adjustment. What emerges from Toye's paper is that there is no entirely satisfactory method of evaluation, especially when account is taken of deficiencies in the available data. While the overall impact of SA programmes may be difficult to evaluate, their effects on income distribution, poverty incidence and various forms of social provision have been, as Ghai demonstrates, almost wholly negative, sometimes to the extent of seriously endangering the existing social fabric. Moreover, as Frances Stewart in her paper on adjustment and education in the 1980s (Chapter 8) shows, in some intensively adjusting countries, there seems to be a severe danger that the adverse effects of adjustment policies may seriously impair long-term development efforts through negative impacts on the quantity, quality and distribution of education. This is not only because of the direct contribution of improved education to the development of human capital, but also because improved education has a favourable impact on such things as household income, health, nutrition and fertility. In the majority of countries in Latin America and Africa, years of progress in extending education were ended and even reversed during the years of adjustment, with likely negative effects on future economic and social progress.

Issues relating to the ethics of conditionality are beginning to be discussed in the development literature and will probably become an important area of investigation for those interested in development ethics. Des Gasper's survey (Chapter 9) indicates that until now this problem has been formulated as one of what conditions should be attached to aid to increase the chance of achieving desirable effects. This is clearly a valuable starting point but much more is required to fully reflect the radical and far-reaching nature of conditionality imposed in more recent years. That said, Gasper's paper shows that important work has already been done in terms of thinking through the relationship between rich and poor countries, of justifying aspirations towards greater equality at national and international level and of defending the provision of aid to poorer countries. Concern with the effectiveness of aid is normally part of any such defence. As is clear from the papers on food aid by Edward Clay (Chapter 10) and Hans Singer (Chapter 11), such assessments are fraught with difficulty. As Singer notes, much of what is called food aid is in fact direct balance of payments support because by replacing commercial food imports, it sets foreign exchange free for other uses. At the same time, financial aid used to support food imports might well be considered as food aid. Moreover, because of their depressing effect on international prices, Western food surpluses may be regarded as food aid for food importing countries and a levy or tax on food exporters. In Singer's view, the effect of this last category may in fact be far more important that what is officially called food aid.

Taken together, the main argument of this volume can be summed up as follows. Interdependence in the global economy is greater now than at any time in the past but, contrary to what the market-forces paradigm would lead us to believe, increasing interdependence is not leading to a greater degree of convergence in terms of the various indicators of welfare and development. In diverse ways, the book helps to explain why this is the case and why competitive forces in any economy do not necessarily lead to a single optimal equilibrium. More important than this, it provides strong arguments in support of the view that a greater degree of social solidarity at many levels – small community, national, regional and world – would promote rather than hinder world development.

References

Amsden, A. (1988) 'Private Enterprise: The Issue of Business Government Control', *Columbia Journal of World Business* vol. 23, 37–42.

Coase, R. H. (1937) 'The Nature of the Firm', *Economica*, IV, 386–405.

1 Nationalism and Development

NIGEL HARRIS

INTRODUCTION

Much social science theory is made and remade relative to the great events of the moment. In August 1991, one such event was the rather astonishing climacteric in the Soviet Union, the implications of which for the national state and national economic development will take quite some time to absorb. Hitherto, the state system which directs the political administration of the world, has enforced a fair degree of unity on each of the constituent national parts, making it most difficult to divide old or create new territorial states. The instincts of the Great Powers have been to retain the forms and resist territorial change, even when governments are violently overthrown. But in the case of the Soviet Union, as also Yugoslavia, the disciplines have not worked. Indeed, the new states are scarcely formed before being threatened by further subdivisions, as in the case of the Russian Federation, Azerbaijan, Georgia and so on. If the disciplines have weakened, the system – for so long held in place by the rivalries of the Great Powers, particularly since 1945, in the competition between Moscow and Washington – may no longer be able to enforce territorial integrity.

If that is the case, is there a government that can afford to be complacent on the issue of national unity? The implications affect most directly the large powers – India, now with almost a continual civil war in one part of the country or another; China, with growing tensions between the economically advancing south, and to a lesser extent, the maritime provinces generally, and the more backward inland areas; Indonesia, Brazil, Nigeria. There is even talk of the Pacific and Atlantic economies pulling apart the United States somewhere in the Midwest.[1] Smaller powers are not immune, as the persistence of Quebecois, Catalan, Basque, Breton, Scottish and Welsh nationalisms or the rise of German secessionism in northern Italy suggest. A redistribution of power in unified Europe is encouraging the currently fashionable talk of a *Europe des régions*. Do these straws in the wind augur a new phase in the history of the territorial State, or are they no more than a passing impulse, the indulgence of a legion of fantasy Ruritanias?

Apart from the settlement of the two world wars, only decolonisation permitted a general reorganisation of the state system, and in all three cases, the process was one ordered and executed by the dominant powers. Now however, the disintegration of the Eastern Bloc, the disappearance of Soviet nationalism into fifteen Republican nationalisms – without revolution or a clear alternative programme – was accomplished in the face of the opposition of the Great Powers.

However, we should note that this political fragmentation has been accompanied by the openly expressed wish of the resulting new governments for greater economic integration, whether in the world at large or in the European Community. Indeed, some commentators have detected part of the impulse for national independence in the different degrees to which parts of countries have already been economically integrated in the European Community – for example, Slovenia and Croatia, as compared to Serbia.[2] In some sense, political nationalism seems to be the companion of an explicit economic internationalism (even when a new country's nearest neighbours are rejected for economic collaboration, as the Ukraine has rejected Russia). Thus, the programme for political national self-determination appears to have become entirely detached from any aim of economic self-determination: politics are national, economics global.

DEFINITIONS AND ASSUMPTIONS

There are some underlying assumptions in this account which should perhaps be specified at the outset. First, nationalism is seen not as primarily embodied in, or a product of, an affection for a locality, community, people, culture or language; on the contrary, these affections are the result of a nationalist commitment rather than its source. Nationalism is defined as loyalty to, or the aspiration to create, a modern national state. It is thus interwoven with the institutional structure by which the world is administered and subjected to the disciplines of a competitive state system. Nationalism is thus fundamental to the organisation of the world polity, so much so it is almost impossible for us to detach ourselves from its operation. A quiet and even resentful obedience to the State and its laws is rather more the norm of nationalism than the aggressive forms of national liberation.

Secondly, 'national economic development' is seen as a process designed to create, or leading to the creation of, a fully diversified modern national economy, in principle a microcosm of the world economy, with the full range of sectors of production of goods and services and only a marginal dependence on external trade, foreign capital and technology. In its early formulations, it is supposedly driven by domestic demand; the economy was fully self-reliant if not necessarily entirely self-sufficient. The process is marked, as is well known, by radical changes in the composition of a growing output – the expansion of heavy and capital goods industries, the capacity to 'make the machines which make machines'. The sectoral and geographical redistribution of the labour force, increased intensity of work and in the participation rate, sustained increases in the capital and skill level per worker, and in final productivity, supposedly followed on from the central drive to transform national output. In its economic formulation – and in historical practice – the process was compatible with many different forms of political order, social and income inequalities and moral codes. But it is decisively defined by its *national* form.

The alternative model made the centrepiece of national growth external markets. There was no question of creating a 'balanced' or fully diversified economy, only of participating in a much wider pattern of specialisations which were far beyond local control and even knowledge. Indeed, attempts to create a fully diversified economy, regardless of any comparative advantage, would, in this account, waste resources and so reduce the level of world output and welfare below the optimal. The nearest contemporary equivalent to such a model would be Hong Kong.

Thirdly, the chapter assumes – in highly simplified fashion – that there are two parallel and interacting systems, each with comparable but different attributes. The first is a world economy, consisting of competing companies that produce an output of goods and services, the main short-term determinant of which, 'other things being equal', is relative prices. The second is a system of competing states, defined territorially. Within each country, the State normally holds a monopoly of the legitimate use of physical force and 'moral domination' within its territory. States are driven to compete in order to secure, defend or extend the prerogatives of national independence, sovereignty over a share of the world's territory, people, production and capital.

STATES AND ECONOMIES

This last distinction – between a state system and a world economy – allows us to consider relationships between capital and the state which otherwise tend to become lost in 'the nation', as if loyalties were generally self-evident (as governments would like them to be).

In the early years of the growth of European capitalism, the political scene was dominated by the permanent rivalries of states in the form of princes and dynasties. War was of the essence of this competition, and its scale and duration were often limited only by the capacity of the rulers to raise funds and troops to fight. It would take this account too far afield to discuss the different phases of this history and the ways in which competitive rivalries shaped each state.[3] However, the issues concerned dominated the methods of rule, the modes and scale of state financing and the forms of public bureaucracy. The obsession with war was a powerful motive for governments to take an interest in the economy, the source of funds with which to fight (an interest which ultimately became rationalised in the creation of economics) and, much later, in the concept of national economic development. The state system imposed a particular form on economic development that was most commonly guided by or rationalised in mercantilism. Indeed, mercantilism – economics formulated almost exclusively in the interests of state power (disregarding whether it is presented as being governed by the interests of the 'nation') – seems everywhere to be the instinctive theory of a developing state, particularly where it is in competition with more powerful states. Import substitution industrialisation strategies are thus only the modern variant of an old tradition of mercantilist practice and theories.

The underlying governmental motive for national economic development is the pursuit of the means to enhance the capacity of the state to compete in the state system. An interest in the welfare by-products of development for the mass of the population would then be only an incidental spin off, albeit a useful one if this induced greater loyalty, greater willingness and capacity of the citizens to pay and to fight for the state.

The effect of the competition of states upon economic development can be illustrated from the history of many countries. In the British case, an extreme one since it is one of the earliest, industrialisation appears almost as an accidental by-product of state rivalries, as embodied in warmaking. During the most important period of the transition from mercantile to industrial capitalism, the maintenance of the armed forces was the main rationale of first the English, and then the British State. From 1695 to 1820, between 78 and 95 per cent of public spending was devoted either to military – particularly naval – matters, or to servicing debts incurred to finance past wars (in real terms, the volume of public spending increased five times over[4]). In the 127 years from 1688 to 1815, the country was engaged in major wars for roughly 70 years. In the last years, during the Napoleonic Wars, some 350 000 men were under arms (1801), a total that had risen to half a million – or nearly 10 per cent of the domestic labour force – by 1811. Many more civilians were engaged in supplying the armed forces. By 1801, gross public expenditure to cover this phenomenal operation may have been equal to over half national expenditure. Indeed, in the half century after 1780, government consumption was larger than the value of exports, suggesting the process of British economic development was led by government spending on war rather than the stimulus of production for export.[5]

In summary, the government's reaction to systemic rivalries produced a sustained rise in national output, transformed its composition (with disproportionate growth in the metallurgical, textile and coal industries), and flattened the output fluctuations which a market-led pattern of growth might have been expected to produce. The curtailment of imports from Europe during the Blockade period of the conflict with France not only did not precipitate the slump for which Napoleon had designed the policy of depriving English producers of continental markets, it accelerated growth by introducing an element of protection, increasing the intensity of the use of the factors of production and further diversifying national output. The burden of this process appears to have been borne by a familiar redistribution (implicit in most import substitution strategies) from popular consumption to public revenue and profits. To oversimplify, British industrialisation in this period appears to be a by-product of the ancient rivalries of states rather than the 'spontaneous' expansion of commercial markets.

One might usefully explore other cases of the sequence: state rivalries to increasing military spending to industrialisation. The case of Tsarist Russia in the 1890s or of Mehmet Ali in early nineteenth-century Egypt would be relevant. So also would be Japan, despite the very different industrial and military context. Between 1874 and 1945, Japan was engaged in ten major wars, two of them world wars. From 1886, military spending was on average equal to 10 per cent of gross national product, and 12 per cent in the three decades to 1945. Starting from a very low base point in terms of modern military capacity, by the 1920s, Japan had become the third largest naval and fifth largest military power. In the thirties, the demands of war were the source of both the giant *zaibatsu*, subcontractors to government demand, and the prodigious growth of key industries – heavy and chemicals, electrical and transport equipment and so on. From the experience of the thirties, Morishima draws the conclusion that:

> Economic growth was certainly not achieved through using the mechanism of the free operation of the economy; it was the result of the government or the military, with their loyal following of capitalists, manipulating and influencing the economy in order to realize national aims ... the price mechanism scarcely played an important role, and the questions of importance were how to raise capital and to meet the government's demand

and the nature of the demand generated from the enterprises at the receiving end of a government demand.[6]

Finally, in the post-war period, systemic rivalries were powerful forces motivating the drive of South Korea (scene of an extraordinarily destructive war) and Taiwan (the government of which was driven from the mainland by war to become an active participant in the Cold War) to industrialise in the sixties and seventies. One of the differences with the earlier cases was that the process of national economic development, driven by military insecurity, came to depend – through, on the one hand, a series of accidents affecting the States concerned, and on the other, a structural change in the world economy[7] – on exporting manufactured goods. However, the process still depended upon continuing State initiative and import substituting policies, now married to export promotion.

Of course, military rivalries do not invariably produce the same effects. Circumstances determine all. The world rivalries shaping the British government in the late nineteenth century may have led London to use India as, in Lord Salisbury's words (1882), 'a barracks on the Oriental seas from which we may draw any number of troops without paying for them',[8] and without the need for Parliamentary approval, but the resulting drive to national economic development was very weak. It might have been that nearly half Indian government revenues were spent directly on the maintenance of the army, and its interests lay behind most infrastructural development policies,[9] but the benefits in terms of industrialisation were to the Empire and to London.

We can see also that the peculiar form of national economic development in the Soviet Union was perhaps more the result of the state insecurities of the inter-war period than the imperatives of an inherited ideology. Born in world war and civil war, maturing in the Great Depression, and precipitated yet again into a second world war, the Soviet Union was created in a period of unprecedented state rivalries (and savageries). The USSR entered the system with two peculiar features. First, a post-revolutionary social structure where the normal patterns of established interests did not exist to constrain State action and the bureaucracy had almost unlimited power over society. Second, Moscow, governing a vast but poor society, chose to enter the system as a Great Power, competing in conditions of the most intense rivalry. The combination led, as is well known, to a no less unprecedented degree of social, economic and administrative centralisation, a semi-militarised society, governed by a continuing paranoia. National economic development, seeking to create a completely independent economy, reached its most extreme form in the Soviet case with little distinction tolerated between state and civil society, between systemic imperatives and domestic accumulation, between civilian and soldier. The extremity of the case was only heightened by the employment of the language of liberation to describe it.

STATES AND CAPITAL

The Soviet case highlights the historical specificity of the relationship of capital accumulation, (normally the activity of companies) and systemic state rivalries, particularly in relationship to what seems to be a rather different relationship between the two in our own times. Indeed, with a touch of heroic oversimplification we might identify a series of historical phases, exaggerating the differences to highlight this relativity.

(i) In the early phases of historical accumulation, capital was promiscuous – in the main, operating almost independently of the interests of states[10] although always with a minority of companies exploiting corrupt relationships to different aspects of state power, using state authority for private advantage (not unlike 'cronyism' in the Philippines), to eliminate rivals and so on. On the other hand, the state tolerated capital as a kind of necessary parasite in the pursuit of its main purposes, its justification being that it provided most superior and swift sources of funding, material and transport for warmaking.

(ii) Such a system led in the nineteenth century to the creation of what Charles Jones (1988) calls a 'cosmopolitan bourgeoisie'. Taking advantage of the areas of peace laid out by empires, but not at all constrained by the interests of the imperial power, businessmen seem to have interacted as rivals without, in general, close alignments to states.[11] Empires were useful areas of operation, but by no means defined the destinations of capital.[12] States were also increasingly concerned to draw sharp lines between their own interests and operations and those of private companies. Global markets provided the basis for a classical economics in which the state had strictly only a passive economic role if there was to be the optimal employment of the world's factors of production.

(iii) These earlier features stand out in striking contrast to the subsequent 'age of imperialism' (as opposed to the operation of empires), roughly after 1870. Now the interests of states increasingly began to divide a cosmopolitan bourgeoisie into constituent national (and racial) entities, even where the 'national' included empire. The state now came to take a much closer and continuing interest in the 'economy', that is, the affairs of companies, even to the point, in time of war, of partial fusion. State capitalism and corporatism were growing responses to a period of extraordinary systematic rivalries in the twentieth century's wars and slump, most extreme, as we have seen, in the case of the Soviet Union, but leaving no Great Power untouched. The patriotism of capital may never have been as great as it seemed, but the heyday of *national* capital involved a marriage between business and the state. Virtually all governments returned to strong traditions of mercantilism, now embodied rather misleadingly in something called 'Keynesianism' (and east of the Elbe, 'socialism').[13] As always, the perception of how peculiar the system was came only late in the day; even as Andrew Shonfield was completing *Modern Capitalism*[14] (an account of a set of national economies, each in principle fully controlled by state policy) the world economy was beginning to be transformed once again.

(iv) From the early 1960s, a single integrated world economy appears to be emerging, superseding the old form of a set of interacting but relatively autonomous national economies. Of course, the process still has far to go to be fully realised and still only covers part of the world. But it has already created a pool of global capital and patterns of integrated manufacture which make it most difficulty to identify what the economic interests of any particular state are (and therefore what a positive national economic policy ought to be). Even the most powerful state, that in the United States, is decreasingly able to manage its domestic economic affairs without global collaboration, On the other hand, global capital, embodied in transnational enterprises, appears to recreate, if not a single cosmopolitan bourgeoisie, at least a set of global baronies that operate with limited contingent relationships to many states. Indeed, governments appear now less as representing a people to the world at large and rather more as representing a world system to a people. Liberalisation, privatisation, structural adjustment, affecting all states and companies, establish consistency between domestic and external prices, and the predominant influence of world markets on domestic economies. Of course, the process assumes a dramatic transformation in technology, providing the technical basis for almost instantaneous global operations. Finally, the transition from Keynesianism to neoclassical economics offers a theoretical counterpoint to the re-emergence on a much grander scale (without the old scaffolding of empire) of an integrated world economy.

In an open world economy the system seems, for any individual competitor, to be much more unpredictable (a feature perhaps reflected in the present disatisfaction with macroeconomic forecasting). Major changes can occur with extraordinary speed – as when the United States moved within three years from being the world's largest creditor to the world's largest debtor. There is a resulting premium on organisational flexibility, affecting not only the old command economies but the old form of centralised transnational corporation. Enhanced risks lead to the increased spinning off of ancillary corporation activities and the rise of hosts of subcontractors and consultants who absorb the risk in their sheer multiplicity. Markets come to appear as the sole means available to manage such dynamic complexity. Without timely change, whole sections of the system are threatened with economic decline – forcing, for example, the implosion in the Soviet Union and Eastern Europe.

There is, as we noted earlier, still far to go in the process.[15] Stagnation and recession in the system conjure up the ghosts of the past, not necessarily in the form of the old territorial State (although there are also resistances to economic integration) but rather in the semi-internationalised form, not now of empire, but of regional federation: Europe, North America and the Asia Pacific Rim.[16] The concept of these regions concerns primarily trade since no one is yet raising the question of the reimposition of controls on capital movements and the free international movement of labour has in general never been liberalised, although Europe is now moving towards this aim within its boundaries. Yet even with trade, the prospects for regionalism are limited, since, to different degrees, the United States, Europe and Japan are pre-eminently global economic powers, not regional. For them to be restricted to their respective regions would be an economic catastrophe for them. Intra-regional trade provided just over a third of the trade total for the proposed East Asian Economic Group, and about 44 per cent if China and Australia were included. North American trade accounts for around 40 per cent of US trade. Europe's intra-regional trade supplies two thirds of its total. The situation can change but it would seem that the chances of political authorities being able to coax an increasingly large share of intra-regional trade from each region to the point where a significant degree of economic and thus political autonomy came to exist are very limited, When 55 per cent of US exports go to Europe and Asia, it seems hardly credible that Latin America – let alone Canada and Mexico – could take over that share. In economic terms, regions make little sense; but as part of the bargaining weaponry of the leading powers to combat each others' protectionism, particularly in the context of a floundering Uruguay Round and the possible threat of Europe's political integration, they may make much more sense.

On the other hand, the Great Powers are now, despite their disagreements about their particular positions, more united in their view of what should be the economic and political behaviour of governments than at any time since the First World War; the 'new world order' mimics the heyday of empire. The Great Powers now as then make and change the rules governing activity, and seek to do so in their own collective and individual interests. The orthodoxy of today, embodied in an explicit agenda making democratisation, privatisation, liberalisation, etc. mandatory, has become the condition for borrowing. In the past, such conditionality would have been denounced as political interference in the sovereignty of the borrowing power (as an example of the shift, compare the articles of the World Bank with those of the new European regional development bank). However, seeing the change of policy stance in developing countries as simply imposed – whether directly through bilateral aid programmes or through the loan conditions of the International Monetary Fund and the World Bank – is to underestimate the profundity of the change in the system. The Great Powers have been no less obliged to conform to the agenda, and the developing countries have, in many cases, embraced parts of the programme less because they were imposed conditions, more because they seemed 'to make sense', that is, they had become sensible as the result of radical changes in the world economy.

The consensus must be temporary. Too many conflicting interests are imprisoned in the orthodoxy to give it long-term viability. But whatever the new heterodoxies, they will be forced to start from a global economy. The structures now seem so well established, it is difficult to see how they could in general be reversed.

CONCLUSIONS

National economic development, as defined here, appears now as a historical phenomenon, part of the last period of imperialism and state capitalism, marked by two world wars and the Great Depression. Nationalism embodied a drive to create a fully diversified independent national economy. For developing countries, the programme of political national self-determination included as an intrinsic part the aim of economic self-determination, covering trade, technology, the ownership of capital. Each state strove to act as the exclusive agent or dominant partner in national capital accumulation.

That system is now in an advanced state of decay, robbing both the old political Right (the corporatists) and the Left of their inherited programmes. For the Left, the State – supposedly the neutral agency to transform the material conditions of the mass of the population – can apparently no longer be employed successfully for reform, except on conditions laid down externally. The old national economies become increasingly specialised contributors to a global output, drawing on a global stock of capital. Indeed, it becomes increasingly difficult to identify economically what is national and what foreign.[17] Only for those managing the national balance of payments does the distinction matter, and even then it is by no means self-evident what policies should be pursued in the interests of the state (in the British case, consider the slightly comic public disputes over who should be allowed to take over Westland helicopters, Cadbury's chocolate, etc.). The national economy becomes less a fixed location for the manufacture of a finished good, a starting or finishing point in manufacture, rather a junction in flows of goods, finance, people (although here mobility is still the most limited) and information. The source of domestic change lies beyond the power – and often, even the knowledge – of government.

In closing, we might indulge ourselves in some little fantasies. It seems that what has happened in the Soviet Union is affecting the most long-lasting expression of the state system, military power. For most of this century, disarmament talks have been a permanent career for those involved in them; one could be confident that there would never be serious disarmament. Now however, there is a significant trend to disarm which, if sustained, is powerful evidence of a fundamental change in the state system so far as the Great Powers are concerned. The new conditionalities of World Bank lending now include an insistence on shifting defence to social spending. Despite some aspiration to be the world's policeman, even the United Sates, driven by the destabilising effect of its budget deficit on the American and world economies, is obliged to undertake some radical trimming of its military might. Sadly, the trend among the leading powers is yet to affect the developing countries – the highest rates of increase in military spending are now in the Middle East and East and South East Asia. War will be with us for a long time yet, and at its worst, among some of the poorest people. But if the power of the state weakens, it is possible that nationalism then may cease to have its ferocious military-economic focus of the past period, dominated by the centralised and authoritarian state, and become more an innocent affection for localities and cultures. Political fission may become a permanent fashion, quite tolerable while accompanied by economic fusion.

If the state is relatively weakening, is power rising to a regional and global level (transnational corporations and international agencies), and sinking to a local level? The fashion for decentralising governments and initiating city economic strategies is another part of the new orthodoxy. It is too early and uncertain to hazard many guesses about the trend. The rivalries of the State system still remain a powerful element in corseting the old state form, and deterring any dispersal of power.

However, if that change is coming about, another utopian aim perhaps begins to enter the realm of practicality: world government. In one sense, it is already here, not as a single institution but as a complex of regulatory agencies located in many different parts of the world and subject to greater or lesser degrees to the influence of the dominant powers. With time, these institutions may grow into effective governance, but it will require the weakening of the states to achieve it.

If the old programme of national economic development is now past, the economic future of the developing countries depends upon the relationships they establish with the world economy, the patterns of changing specialisation that they can capture. Many governments in developing countries have, willingly or not, acknowledged the changed context; some at least have become champions of free trade, opposing the incipient protectionism of some of the developed.

The decline of war and the state is a daydream, far from reality at the moment. The horror of Sarajevo, the appalling slaughter of Iranians and Iraqis, the terrifying exhibition of United States military power in the Gulf, the growing numbers of those driven out of their countries, all indicate the samurai are far from being pensioned off to doze in Cheltenham. Famine, poverty in village and city slum, the exploitation of child labour, all the horrors remain. Yet amid the bleakness of a world still so dominated by poverty and the sacrifice of hopes, the trends may be a little more promising on at least one part of the programme of progress after August 1991. Charles Tilly (1990, p. 4) observes at the end of his analysis of states in Europe over a thousand years:

> States may be following the old routine by which an institution falls into ruin just as it becomes complete. In the meantime, nevertheless, States remain so dominant that anyone who dreams of a stateless world seems a heedless visionary.

Notes

1. Compare *The bi-coastal economy: regional patterns of economic growth during the Reagan administration*, a Staff Study by the Democratic Staff of the Joint Economic Committee of the Congress of the United States (mimeo), Washington DC, 9 July 1986.
2. In the spring of 1990, *The Economist* observed that 'Slovenia's economic survival depended on how quickly it cut itself free from the Yugoslav disaster' (14 April 1990).

3. The issues are discussed with great illumination in Tilly (1990).
4. The basic data are derived from Mitchell and Deane (1962) and Mitchell and Jones (1971). See also Mann (1980).
5. See Deane (1975).
6. See Morishima (1982, pp. 96–7).
7. These issues are explored in more detail in chapter 2 of my *The End of the Third World* (1986, pp. 30–69).
8. Cited by Johnson (1990, p. 238).
9. Washbrook (1990, p. 42).
10. In Braudel's world, the merchants operate apparently with only distant relationships to rulers, often little better than territorial tax collectors.
11. Compare a comment on the relationship between companies in eighteenth-century British India:

    in their [unorientalised] world categorical oppositions, [they] did not separate the "Indian"and "European". Alliances formed and opposed one another for reasons that made sense in that world; and they fought for the fruits of merchant capital (Ludden, 1990, p. 164).

12. Discussed with much illumination in O'Brien (1988).
13. The theoretical parallels are not chronologically exact. Classical economics and its neoclassical, marginalist descendants, did not cease with the onset of 'imperialism' from the 1870s, but continued to exercise predominant influence to the 1920s, at least in the country with the most persistent adherence to free trade, Britain.
14. 'The state controls so large a part of the economy that a planner can, by intelligent manipulation of the levers of public power, guide the remainder of the economy firmly towards any objective that the government chooses' (Shonfield, 1965, p. 231). Compare Galbraith (1967, p. 296) – 'In notable respects, the corporation is an arm of the state' and later on, 'the state, in important respects, (is) an instrument of the industrial system'.
15. Perceptions – if not behaviour – by the managers of international companies still lag behind what seems to be the structure of the global economy: see Kanter (1991, pp. 151–64).
16. With an appropriate reconsideration of free trade and industrial policy: cf. Thurow (1989); Dornbush et al. (1988) and Dornbush et al. (1989).
17. *The Economist* noted some examples recently: a $55 000 John Deere excavator purchased in the United States was assembled in Japan, and its 'Japanese' rival, a $40 000 Komatsu, was made in Illinois. Of seven US car models, made by Pontiac, Chevrolet, Mercury, Honda, Dodge and Plymouth – only one was built in the United States, the Honda.

References

Bose, S. (ed.) (1990) *South Asia and World Capitalism* (Delhi: Oxford University Press).

Braudel, F. B. (1981–4) *Civilization and Capitalism, Fifteenth to Eighteenth Centuries, 3 vols* (London: Fontana).

Deane, P. (1975) 'War and Industrialization' in J. M. Winter (ed.), *War and Economic Development: Essays in Memory of David Joslin* (Cambridge: Cambridge University Press).

Dornbusch, R. W., J. Poterba and L. Summers (1988) *The Case for Manufacturing in America's Future* (Rochester NY: Eastman Kodak).

Dornbusch, R. W., P. Krugman and Y. C. Park (1989) *Meeting World Challenges: US Manufacturing in the 1900s* (Rochester NY: Eastman Kodak).

Galbraith, J. K. (1967) *The New Industrial State* (London: Hamish Hamilton).

Harris, N. (1986) *The End of the Third World: Newly Industrialising Countries and the Decline of an Ideology* (London: Tauris; Harmondsworth: Penguin; New York: Viking, 1987).

Johnson, G. (1990) 'Government and Nationalism in India, 1880–1920' in S. Bose (ed.), op. cit.

Jones, C. A. (1988) *International Business in the Nineteenth Century: the Rise and Fall of a Cosmopolitan Bourgeoisie* (Brighton, UK: Wheatsheaf).

Kanter, R. M. (1991) 'Transcending Business Boundaries: 12 000 World Managers view Change', *Harvard Business Review*, May-June.

Ludden, D. (1990) 'World Economy and Village India, 1600–1900: Exploring the agrarian history of capitalism' in S. Bose (ed.), op. cit.

Mann, M. (1980) 'State and Society, 1130–1815: an Analysis of English State Finances' in M. Zeitlin (ed.), *Political Power and Social Theory* (Greenwich, Conn. and London: JAI Press).

Mitchell, B. R. and P. Deane (1962) *Abstract of British Historical Statistics* (Cambridge: Cambridge University Press).

Mitchell, B. R. and H. G. Jones (1971) *Second Abstract of British Historical Statistics* (Cambridge: Cambridge University Press).

Morishima, M. (1982) *Why has Japan 'Succeeded'? Western Technology and the Japanese Ethos* (Cambridge: Cambridge University Press).

O'Brien, P. K. (1988) 'The Costs and Benefits of British Imperialism, 1846–1914', *Past and Present*, no. 120 (Aug.), 163–200.

Shonfield, A. (1965) *Modern Capitalism: the Changing Balance of Public and Private Power* (London: Royal Institute of International Affairs/Oxford University Press).

Thurow, L. (1989) 'Must we manage trade?', *World Link*, World Economic Forum, MIT, June.

Tilly, C. (1990) *Coercion, Capital and European States, AD 990–1990*, Studies in Social Discontinuity (Oxford: Blackwell).

Washbrook, D. (1990) 'South Asia, the World System and World Capitalism' in S. Bose (ed.), op. cit.

2 Structural Adjustment, Global Integration and Social Democracy

DHARAM GHAI[1]

INTRODUCTION

Structural adjustment was one of the key themes of economic and social policy in the 1980s in countries around the world. It is likely to continue to be the focus of national and global concern in the 1990s. Much of the discussion on the subject has focused on adjustment experiences at country or regional levels. Likewise much of the literature has tended to compartmentalise the discussion into economic, social or political aspects of adjustment. This has resulted in an excessive emphasis being placed on national conditions and policies as determinants of the need for and success of adjustment measures and a consequent neglect of the role played by world economic forces. It has also impeded an analysis which takes into account the interaction between economic, social and political consequences of these measures.

This chapter attempts to provide a global and integrated perspective on the adjustment process which is defined simply as increased reliance on market forces and reduced role of the state in economic management. The essence of the argument advanced here is that structural adjustment is a world-wide phenomenon with an interdependent and mutually reinforcing relationship with the globalisation process. The latter refers to increasing integration of the world economies. The processes of adjustment and globalisation have generated wide-ranging socio-political consequences. They have contributed through a variety of mechanisms to intensification of poverty and inequalities within and among countries, and indirectly to a range of other social problems. They have also led to important shifts in balance of power nationally and internationally. These shifts have contributed to an increasing gap between power and accountability and resources and responsibility. The result is a growing paralysis in the handling of social problems at the national and international levels. Social problems need to be addressed not only in the interest of national cohesion and solidarity but as a necessary investment for future growth. It is therefore a task of the highest importance to explore the new configuration of social forces and institutional arrangements to meet the social challenges of the 1990s.

The structure of the chapter follows the argument set out above. The next section discusses the origin and underlying forces behind the thrust for structural adjustment in different parts of the world. Following this the diverse contexts and patterns of adjustment measures in different regions are examined. The relationship between structural adjustment and global integration is then analysed. This is followed by a discussion of some social consequences of the processes of adjustment and globalisation. Finally, the implications of these processes for power relationships and social democracy are explored.

Given the vast scope of the subject treated here, it has not been possible to provide detailed analytical and empirical support for the arguments advanced. Rather, the basic purpose is to set the theme of structural adjustment within the broad context of global economic integration and political and social democracy and to draw attention to some key relationships which have been either largely neglected or insufficiently recognised in the mainstream literature on the subject. In order to make the discussion manageable, it was decided to omit an analysis of the reform process in Eastern and Central Europe as well as in the communist countries in Asia. Their experience nevertheless is extremely pertinent to the issues treated here and raises many points of contrasts and similarities.

STRUCTURAL ADJUSTMENT: ORIGINS AND UNDERLYING FORCES

The process of structural adjustment was first initiated in the industrialised countries and then 'exported' to developing countries. It was the result in both groups of countries of a combination of conjunctural and secular forces. The former were represented by the economic crisis in the post-1973 period, first in the industrialised and then in the developing countries; the latter by upsurge of world economic integration in the post-war period. This section looks first at the forces which propelled a reorientation of economic policies in the advanced countries, before turning to an analysis of the dynamics of structural adjustment in the less developed regions of Africa, Latin America, South Asia and South-East and East Asia.

Industrialised Countries

The years immediately after the first petrol shock in 1973 were characterised in most OECD countries by falling growth rates, rising unemployment, increasing inflation and declining investment and profit rates (see Table 2.1). This constituted a sharp reversal of the experience on the preceding two decades. For instance, annual output growth fell from 4.9 per cent over the period 1960–73 to 2.7 per cent in 1974–9. Inflation more than doubled from 4.1 to 9.7 per cent per annum over the two periods. Productivity growth declined from 3.8 to 1.6 per cent and investment expansion tumbled from 7.6 to 2.3 per cent per annum. The rate of unemployment rose from 3.3 to 5.1 per cent and the expansion in trade fell from 9.1 to 4.3 per cent.

This adverse performance generated wide-ranging enquiries into the state of the economy and analyses of previous policies. The result was a gradual emergence of a new consensus on the diagnosis of economic ills and a way out of stagflation.[2] The dominant view was that the economic problems of the 1970s were directly due to the past pursuit of policies of high aggregate demand, full employment, high rates of taxation, generous social welfare benefits and growing state intervention (OECD, 1987; Britton, 1991). It was argued that these policies had led to inflationary pressures through excessive wage demands, introduced rigidities in factor and product markets, and thus blunted the incentives to save, work, invest and take risks. The first priority was to bring inflation under control. This was done with tight monetary policies and high interest rates. To restore

Table 2.1 OECD economy: summary indicators of performance (average annual percentage change)

	1960–73	*1974–79*	*1980–82*	*1983–86*	*1987–89*
Output (a)	4.9	2.7	1.0	3.4	3.8
Investment (b)	7.6(c)	2.3(c)	0.3	5.0	8.7
Trade (d)	9.1	4.3	0.0	6.0	7.0
Productivity (e)	3.8	1.6	0.7	2.1	2.0
Prices (f)	4.1	9.7	9.3	4.5	3.7
Unemployment	3.3	5.1	6.9	8.1	6.9

Notes:

(a) Real GNP.

(b) Real gross private non-residential fixed investment.

(c) Seven largest OECD countries only (accounting for some 85 per cent of OECD GNP).

(d) Average of merchandise imports and exports, in volume terms.

(e) Real GNP per person employed.

(f) Consumer price deflator.

Sources: Llewellyn and Potter (1991); OECD (1991).

economic growth in the medium term required more radical measures to promote market forces and curb the role of the state.

A somewhat different view on the crisis of the 1970s emphasises changes in national and global political economy, such as the shift in the balance of power in favour of labour, the end of American hegemony and disorder in the international financial and trade systems (Marglin, 1988; Glyn et al., 1988; Kolko, 1988). While arguing that declines in productivity improvements and in profit shares had set in before 1973, these authors nevertheless concur with the neoclassical argument concerning the role played by full employment policies and union militancy in putting pressure on profit rates.

A more complete analysis of the slowdown in growth in the 1970s would no doubt include a discussion of the exhaustion of some other special factors in the early post-war decades such as reconstruction of infrastructure, farms and factories; the catching up in Japan and Europe with advanced technology and management techniques in America; the liberalisation of trade and payments; creation of free trade areas; and the spurt of technological progress in products and services with mass demand (Britton, 1991).

While the crisis provided the immediate justification for the shift in policies, the deeper causes behind the upsurge of market forces and the retreat of the state must be sought in the increasing global integration facilitated by developments in the post-war period. These included the elimination of government controls on allocation of resources in the domestic economy, the progressive removal of restrictions on external trade and payments, expansion of foreign investment, loans and aid, and rapid technological progress. It was above all the expansion of transnational enterprises (TNEs), facilitated by market liberalisation and technological progress, that made a powerful contribution to internationalisation of the world economy. At the same time, all these factors created strong pressures for and powerful vested interests in the continuance and intensification of free-market policies.

The opportunity provided by a favourable combination of conjunctural and secular factors was seized upon by conservative forces to press their own agenda of balanced budget, reduction in progressive taxation, social security and welfare, and a diminished role of the state in economic management. The promise of tax reductions widened the constituency for reform. A combination of monetary, neoclassical and supply side theorists furnished the intellectual support for the position that the material prosperity of the industrial countries and the rapid economic progress of the East Asian countries was the result of their reliance on market forces. In contrast, they held, the poorer economic performance of the communist countries and much of the Third World resulted primarily from extensive state intervention in the management of the economy.

Developing Countries

A combination of the conjunctural crisis and pressure from creditor countries and institutions was responsible for the shift in the policies of most developing countries towards structural adjustment. The contractionary policies pursued by the industrialised countries resulted in a sharp increase in world interest rates (thereby adding to the debt burden), massive deterioration in the commodity terms of trade and virtual cessation of private capital flows in the wake of the debt crisis and capital flight, thereby creating the conditions for a prolonged crisis in the majority of developing countries, especially in Latin America and Africa.

For instance, short-term real interest rates in the United States rose from an annual average of -0.7 per cent in 1972–5 to 5.0 per cent in 1980–2 (OECD, 1983). The index of the terms of trade of non-petroleum exporting developing countries fell from 110 in 1973–5 (1980 = 100) to 94 in 1981–3 and further to 84 in 1989–90 (UNCTAD, 1990). The net flows of private capital declined from over US$ 70 billion in 1979–81 to barely US$ 28 billion in 1985–6, while capital flight from 13 highly indebted countries rose from US$ 47 billion at the end of 1978 to US$ 184 billion at the end of 1988 (OECD, 1991; Rojas-Suárez, 1991).

In sub-Saharan Africa excluding Nigeria, the net deterioration in the external financial situation from these three factors amounted to US$ 6.5 billion per annum over the period 1979–81 to 1985–7. These amounts, which take into account debt rescheduling but ignore capital flight, attained roughly one third of the total annual imports of goods and services of these countries in the early 1980s and about 45 per cent of average annual export earnings (United Nations, 1988). In Latin America, the net external resources turned around from an inflow of US$ 15.8 billion in 1978–79 to an outflow of US$ 22.8 billion in 1987–8, equivalent to 22.5 and 20.5 per cent of exports of goods and services in the two periods (Ghai and Hewitt de Alcántara, 1991).

While the emergence of the acute crisis in the late 1970s and early 1980s provided the immediate justification for the adoption of adjustment policies, some major weaknesses in development policies constituted structural barriers to efficiency and sustained rapid growth. These included excessive taxation of agriculture, indiscriminate protection of industry, overvalued exchange rates, extensive state intervention in resource allocation by administrative means, inefficiencies in state enterprises and widespread corruption and mismanagement (World Bank, 1981; Griffith-Jones and Sunkel, 1986). The overwhelming importance of the external environment is, however, indicated by the fact that these weaknesses in economic policy and management did not prevent most of these countries from achieving substantial rates of economic expansion in the preceding two to three decades.

The favourable growth experience of many Asian countries during the 1980s does not constitute a rebuttal of the above argument. Several of these countries continued to follow the type of policies described above. Their relatively favourable performance in an adverse international economic environment would appear to be due at least in some measure to special features of their economies and their relationship with the world economy. For instance, some of the large countries such as Bangladesh, China, India and Pakistan are much less dependent on world trade than most Latin American and African countries.[3] The weight of manufactures in the exports of Asian countries is much greater than in African and Latin American countries. Manufactured goods as a percentage of South and East Asian exporters were already 44 per cent in 1970, compared to 4 per cent in West Asia, 7 per cent in Africa and 11 per cent in Latin America. By 1988, manufactured goods comprised 76 per cent of South and East Asian exports, compared with 16, 16 and 34 per cent in West Asia, Africa and Latin America respectively (UNCTAD, 1990).

Three other factors must be mentioned. The debt burden in the early 1980s was considerably greater in Latin America and Africa than in Asia: in 1983, the debt service ratios in the three regions were 25, 37 and 18 respectively (OECD, 1991). Asian countries also benefited disproportionately from remittances from their migrants in the booming Middle Eastern oil-exporting countries in the 1970s and early 1980s. In 1975, 1.6 million migrants were employed in these countries, of which over 20 per cent came from South and South-East Asia. The number increased to three million by 1980, 25 per cent of which were from South and South-East Asia, the majority of the remaining coming from the neighbouring Arab countries (Burki, 1984; Talal, 1984). Workers' remittances accounted for more than 28 per cent of the exports of goods and non-factor services in Pakistan in 1975 and 80 per cent in 1982. For India the remittances increased from 5 per cent of exports in 1972 to 25 in 1982. The corresponding figures for Sri Lanka are 1.4 per cent in 1974 and 22 in 1982 and for Thailand 1 per cent in 1976 to over 10 per cent in 1983 (World Bank, 1990).

Proximity to the most dynamic industrialised economy in the world greatly boosted the economies of neighbouring countries in East and South-East Asia. Indonesia, Malaysia, the Philippines, South Korea and Thailand have exported significant shares of their exports to Japan since at least 1970: South Korea 28 per cent in 1970; Malaysia 24 per cent in 1985; and Indonesia 49 per cent in 1980. However, some of these shares declined in subsequent years (UNCTAD, 1990). Japan has also greatly increased its investment in South-East Asia. For instance, between 1980 and 1987, the annual flow of Japanese foreign direct investment increased fivefold in Thailand, fourfold in Singapore and almost sixfold in Taiwan (Lim and Fong, 1991).

It would be pointless to deny the importance of national policies in adapting to the changing world conditions. Countries in South-East Asia have put in place a number of policies to attract foreign investment. And East Asian and more recently the South-East Asian countries have given export promotion a high priority. But these policies have often involved active state intervention in a number of areas.

The preceding discussion brings out some contrasts in the origins of and underlying forces in the adoption of structural adjustment policies in different regions of the developing world. As in the industrialised countries, the crisis triggered off changes in economic policy in African and Latin American countries. The weaknesses in previous policies and economic management intensified the need for adjustment. But whereas in the industrialised countries, it was the dynamics of the globalisation process which tipped the balance in favour of adjustment policies through the interplay of contending social groups, in African and Latin American countries, it was the pressure exerted by creditor countries, commercial banks, international financial agencies and TNEs which proved the decisive element. This was especially the case in Africa where there was practically no organised lobby for deregulation and liberalisation. It was less true in some Latin American countries where free market policies had been associated with military and conservative regimes and were also espoused by some technocrats and large businesses in mining, agriculture, manufactured exports, finance and trade.

In Asia, experiences have been more diverse. While some of the countries in the region such as Taiwan, and South Korea were among the first to adopt some elements of reform, especially those relating to trade, foreign exchange liberalisation and promotion of manufactured exports, others such as India and Pakistan were converted to the cause only in the 1990s. Most of the South-East Asian countries began to introduce reform measures in the 1980s (Lim and Fong, 1991).

Similarly diversity characterised the underlying forces behind the drive for liberalisation. The economic crisis and foreign pressure played some part in India and Pakistan but there was also an increasingly powerful domestic lobby, constituted by big business and the bureaucratic and technological élite, which felt that liberalisation of the domestic and foreign economy was essential for the modernisation and rapid growth of the economy. The reforms in the South-East Asian countries were greatly influenced by the experience of the four tigers and had much less to do with economic crisis or pressure from creditors.

STRUCTURAL ADJUSTMENT: CONTEXT AND PATTERNS

While liberalisation has become a truly global phenomenon, the contexts in which it has been carried out and the patterns it has assumed have tended to vary by regions and countries. As a broad generalisation, it may be stated that, whereas liberalisation represents in many respects a continuation of the trends in the post-war period in the industrialised countries, it constitutes a sharp reversal of the past policies in most developing countries. Furthermore, there are significant variations in the pace and patterns of the reform effort in different parts of the world. This section first reviews the broad features of liberalisation in the industrialised countries before turning to the contrasts and similarities in the major regions of the developing world.

Industrialised Countries

In the first two to three decades after the Second World War, the industrialised countries pursued policies which reduced the role of the state in some areas and expanded it in others. The liberalisation thrust was exemplified by the dismantling of a plethora of controls on domestic economic activity and on international trade and payments. For instance, allocation of resources by administrative means, price controls and rationing were gradually phased out in the early post-war years. By the mid-1950s, the process of trade liberalisation was well under way with quantitative restrictions largely removed. By the early 1960s, most non-tariff barriers had been removed or eased.[4] Members of the two trading blocs – the European Free Trade Area and the European Economic Community – achieved practically free trade in manufactures among member states. Currency convertibility was restored for payments and restrictions eased on capital mobility and foreign direct investment. Likewise, considerable progress was made in dismantling the domestic and international cartels that had proliferated in the inter-war period (OECD, 1987).

Some of the post-war policies went in the opposite direction and strengthened the role of the state in the economy. Several countries nationalised a wide range of enterprises in utilities, transport, communications, mining, steel and banking. Furthermore, the welfare state, whose foundations were laid in the late 1930s, was greatly expanded in the post-war period. Improved provisions were made for health, education and housing as well as for children's allowances, old age pensions and unemployment, and sickness and accident benefits. Public expenditure and tax revenues showed a sustained rise as a share of GDP. For the 11 largest OECD countries, public expenditure rose from 28 per cent in 1960 to 32.9 per cent in 1973 and further to 40.2 per cent in 1988. Tax revenues as a percentage of GDP rose form 28.1 in 1965 to 34.6 in 1979 and further to 39 in 1988 (Boltho, 1992).

The policies pursued in the 1980s represent elements of both continuity and reversal. Removal or reduction of state regulations in a wide range of economic sectors such as banking, foreign exchange, stock markets, transport, communications and utilities constitute elements of continuity with the earlier reforms. On the other hand, restraint or curtailment of public expenditure, cuts in social security and welfare programmes, reduction in progressive taxation, abandonment of full employment policies, curbs on trade unions, creation of more flexible labour markets and privatisation of state enterprises constitute reversals of earlier policies.

The liberal reforms were not undertaken with the same zeal in all domains. In three respects at least, developments over the past decade and a half represent violations of the liberal creed of the age of reform. This period, which was characterised by sweeping deregulations, also saw an intensification of agricultural protection, growing restrictions on some categories of international trade and increasing barriers on immigration of unskilled persons. Agricultural protection increased in the 1970s and 1980s in most industrial countries. Average producer subsidy equivalent in OECD countries rose from 32 per cent in 1979–81 to 50 per cent in 1986–7 before declining to 45 per cent in 1988. The transfer to agriculture from consumers and tax payers rose from US$ 61 billion in 1979–81 to US$ 270 billion in 1988 (World Bank, 1992).

In recent years, there has also been a reversal of the liberalisation trend in trade in manufactures. Quantitative restrictions, voluntary agreements to limit exports, managed trade, subsidies and cases of dumping have multiplied. These barriers have affected not only labour-intensive products such as textiles and clothing, toys and leather goods but also automobiles, electronics and steel. The share of OECD manufactured imports from developing countries subject to non-tariff barriers rose from 26.5 per cent in 1981 to 28 per cent in 1990. If protectionist barriers in the European Community, Japan and the United States were to be reduced by 50 per cent, exports from developing countries could increase by 15 per cent or US$ 50 billion in 1988 prices or US$ 54 billion in 1991 prices. This is equivalent to the aggregate net resource flows from official sources to developing countries in 1991 (World Bank, 1992).

The third area in which the liberal creed has been violated is emigration from developing countries. Restrictions on movements of unskilled labour are increasing. Between 1950 and 1973, net immigration into Western Europe reached nearly 10 million people. Several millions found new employment opportunities and higher living standards in the United States (OECD, 1987). With the sharp reversal of policies since 1973, new immigration has virtually disappeared. The numbers of foreign workers either stabilised or decreased in most European countries in the 1980s, with the exception of Switzerland and the United Kingdom (Appleyard, 1991). Net immigration has continued in Australia, Canada and the United States but is increasingly biased in favour of better-off persons with professional and technical skills and considerable financial resources. The loss of potential income to developing countries (direct and indirect) from immigration controls has been estimated at US$ 250 billion (UNDP, 1992).

Although these departures from the liberal trends of the 1980s have negatively affected the interests of a few industrialised countries, on the whole these measures have been most harmful to the developing countries. Even apart from these exceptions, there have been considerable differences among the industrial countries regarding the pace and pattern of liberalisation. Members of the European Economic Community and the European Free Trade Area achieved greater liberalisation in transactions with partner states than in transactions with outside countries. The Anglo-Saxon countries that provided the ideological and political leadership in the drive for liberalisation have implemented reforms in a more thoroughgoing fashion than other industrialised countries.

It is worth noting the difference between the pattern of reform in Anglo-Saxon countries and some others such as Austria, Germany, Japan, the Netherlands, the Nordic group and Switzerland. This difference relates to whether the measures taken represent a continuation or reversal of earlier reforms. On the whole, while most industrialised countries have followed policies to deregulate finance, transport, communications and utilities, the Anglo-Saxon countries have pursued with equal vigour measures to reduce taxes and government expenditure on social security and welfare, create flexible labour markets and promote privatisation. The others have proceeded much more cautiously in these areas (Cox, 1991). This divergence has a bearing on social cohesion and economic performance, a theme which is taken up later.

Developing Countries

In contrast to the industrialised countries, the adoption of structural adjustment measures represents a sharp reversal of the previous policies of state-directed modernisation and industrialisation in most developing countries. Although there was variation in the extent and depth of state intervention, in many countries it was pervasive and affected such areas as protection and location of industry; marketing of agricultural products; allocation of credit and foreign exchange; regulation of imports and exports, foreign investment, technology, labour markets and collective bargaining. The role of the state extended further to the ownership and management of a wide range of industrial, agricultural, marketing and financial enterprises.

Reforms started earlier and have gone further in Latin America than in other regions of the Third World. With Chile leading, the reform process has now spread to most countries in the region, the latest converts being Argentina and Brazil. In the first phase, the reforms have focused on stabilisation of the economy through control of public expenditure and increase in tax revenues, liberalisation of prices, foreign trade and payments and currency devaluation. Privatisation of state enterprises has come later but now forms an important part of the reform package in a number of countries. The extent and depth of reforms in Latin America reflect the severity of the crisis, the intensity of foreign pressure, the existence of influential domestic lobbies in favour of liberalisation and the interplay of ideological conflicts.

In sub-Saharan Africa, on the other hand, the reform process started later and has been less consistent and thoroughgoing. The emphasis has been on price liberalisation, reduction or removal of subsidies, control of state expenditure, currency devaluation and a limited amount of trade liberalisation. In general, progress in removing quantitative restrictions on foreign trade and payments has been patchier and few countries have made significant headway with privatisation. In the absence of strong pro-reform domestic lobbies, the pattern and pace of reform have reflected in varying degrees the timing and balance of foreign pressure and popular domestic opposition (Helleiner, 1992). The progress in implementing adjustment measures has been slower than in other regions, in part because the ruling political, bureaucratic and military elites have a greater vested interest in maintaining state controls and ownership as sources of political patronage and personal enrichment.

In South Asia, with the exception of Sri Lanka where liberalisation policies were initiated earlier, limited effort was made to reduce state controls in domestic economic activity and foreign transactions in the 1980s.

More recently, however, significant steps have been taken to decontrol investment and prices and liberalise foreign trade, payments and investment. It is only in Pakistan that a serious effort is under way to privatise state enterprises. In South-East and East Asian countries, there has been less detailed state regulation of the economy. In South-East Asia, the reform efforts in the 1980s were on trade and foreign exchange liberalisation, provision of incentives to foreign investment and exports of manufactured goods. Under pressure from the industrial countries, the reform process in the East Asian countries has been directed at further liberalisation of trade and foreign exchange, currency appreciation, opening up to foreign investment stock exchange markets, banks and other financial and service sectors.

STRUCTURAL ADJUSTMENT AND GLOBAL INTEGRATION

Structural adjustment and global integration are interdependent and mutually reinforcing. While the processes of globalisation gave birth to structural adjustment as a response to world economic crisis, the adoption of reform measures have in turn widened and deepened the thrust towards global integration. Driven by technological progress and spearheaded by transnational enterprises, the globalisation process has been fuelled in the 1980s by measures of internal deregulation and falling barriers on foreign investment and on flows of capital and technology. The accelerating pace of global integration in the economic domain is reflected in the rapid expansion of world trade in commodities and services, of foreign investment, technology transfers, foreign exchange transactions and telecommunications. In the social and cultural sphere it is reflected in sharp growth in travel and tourism; in the establishment and meetings of world associations of professional, business, labour and other interest groups; and in the rapid spread of Western consumption patterns, and of ideas, news, fashion and music through television, radio, press and films.

A few examples may serve to highlight the rapidity of change in international exchanges. In every decade in the post-war period, trade has grown noticeably faster than output. While the volume of trade grew by 8.5, 5.0 and 4.0 per cent per annum in the 1960s, 1970s and 1980s respectively, the corresponding figures for the expansion of world output were 6.0, 4.0 and 2.5 per cent (GATT, 1990). The share of exports of goods and services as a proportion of GDP for the Group of Seven rose from 10.1 per cent in 1960–7 to 15.4 per cent in 1980–9 (OECD, 1991). Trade in services has expanded even more rapidly than in commodities: between 1970 and 1990, it grew by 12 per cent per annum (UNDP, 1992).

Foreign direct investment (FDI) has played a key role in shaping patterns of trade, in the international division of labour and in the transfer of technology. It grew rapidly in the 1950s and 1960s. After a slowdown in the 1970s, FDI spurted ahead vigorously in the 1980s. Between 1983 and 1989 the value of world FDI flows expanded at an annual average rate of 34 per cent, nearly four times the annual rate of growth of 9 per cent in the value of world merchandise exports (Blackhurst, 1991).

Technology transfers have become important components of international consultancy service transactions. Their value, as represented by royalty payments and outright sales of technology, research and development and advisory and consultancy services, has grown exponentially in the 1980s. The share of high technology in the exports of the OECD countries has increased from over 20 to nearly 26 per cent between 1962 and 1982 (Marcum, 1984). The corresponding shares for Japan and the United States have increased from 28 to 40 per cent and from 17 to 30 per cent respectively. The global share of technology-intensive exports jumped from 21.5 per cent in 1978 to 28.6 per cent by 1988 (World Bank, 1992).

Deregulation and technological progress have also transformed foreign exchange and financial markets. The 1980s have seen a virtual explosion in foreign exchange trading. In New York, for example, trading has grown at about 40 per cent annually since 1986. By 1989, US$ 650 billion a day were being traded in foreign exchange markets around the world (Blackhurst, 1991). There has also been a sharp increase in international transactions in bond and equity markets, especially with the possibility of non-stop trading now that all major markets are linked electronically. Foreign investment in equity markets grew 20-fold in the decade from 1979 to 1989. The result was a more than doubling, from 6.2 to 14.2 per cent, in the share of cross-border trade in equities in total world stock turnover. At year-end 1989, trading by non-residents in United States government securities reached US$ 3 trillion, or roughly US$ 12 billion per day. In Germany, bond transactions involving non-residents increased on average by 43 per cent a year from 1985 to 1989 and now account for over one-third of the value of all transactions in German bond markets (Blackhurst, 1991).

Telecommunications and information processing technologies have played a critical role in the globalisation process in recent years. Outgoing international telecommunications traffic expanded annually by 20 per cent in the 1980s. This growth has been greatly facilitated by rapid technological progress resulting in sharp declines in charges. For instance, the cost of leasing the American half of a private transatlantic voice channel fell from US$ 12 000–14 000 a month in 1983 to between US$ 4000 and US$ 5000 in 1990 (Pipe, 1990). The cost of information processing dropped by about 65 per cent between 1975 and 1985 (OECD, 1988). The average cost of a three-minute call between New York and London fell drastically from US$ 54.86 in 1950 to US$ 31.58 in 1970 and to a mere US$ 3.32 in 1990 (World Bank, 1992).

Likewise, technological progress in transportation has greatly facilitated the growth of trade and tourism. The average ocean freight and port charges per short ton of import and export cargo fell from US$ 34 in 1950 to US$ 27 in 1970 and US$ 24 in 1980 before rising to US$ 25 in 1990. The average air transport revenue per person/mile fell from US$ 0.30 in 1950 to 0.16 in 1970 and 0.10 in 1990 in constant dollars (World Bank, 1992).

The relative importance of different aspects of the internationalisation of the economy has changed over time. For instance, in the 1950s and 1960s, the rapid expansion of international trade was the driving force behind globalisation. In the 1970s, the lead role was played by flows of capital financed by the commercial banks. The 1980s were marked especially by an explosive growth in foreign direct investment and technology flows.

Transnational enterprises (TNEs) have been at the heart of global economic integration. They have spearheaded technological progress and foreign direct investment and played a central role in international transactions in goods and services, foreign exchange and stocks and bonds (Julius, 1990). The total number of parent corporations and foreign affiliates was estimated at 35 000 and 147 200 respectively in 1990. Global sales of foreign affiliates in host countries were estimated at US$ 4.4 trillion in 1989 compared to world exports of US$ 2.5 trillion, and have grown at an annual average rate of 15 per cent since the mid-1980s (United Nations, 1992). By the early 1980s, trade between the 350 largest TNEs contributed about 40 per cent of global trade (Oman, 1991). TNEs are the main vehicles for FDI, access to foreign markets, and transfer of technology and management skills.

The role of developing countries in global exchanges has tended to shrink in recent years. The notable exceptions to this trend are a few countries in East and South-East Asia. In trade, the developing country share has declined from 31 per cent in 1950 to 21 per cent in 1989 (UNCTAD, 1990). In 1968, they accounted for over 30 per cent of the stock of world foreign direct investment. This had fallen to just over 21 per cent by 1988 (Griffin and Khan, 1992), much of it concentrated in a handful of countries. Five countries – China, Indonesia, Malaysia, South Korea and Thailand – accounted for about a quarter of all foreign direct investment. There are likely to be even greater imbalances in the transactions in technology and finance.

From the evidence presented earlier, it is clear that the world is now moving strongly towards a single market for goods, services, technology, capital and skills. It is only with respect to unskilled workers and some categories of agricultural and manufactured products that national boundaries continue to constitute effective barriers to mobility and free trade.[5] The accelerating integration of the world economy and continuing technological progress are likely to have far-reaching effects on patterns and location of production and distribution of resources within and across countries. They can also be expected to exert influence on national and international distribution of power and hence on social structures and political processes. Some of the social and political consequences of adjustment and globalisation processes are taken up in the following sections.

SOCIAL CONSEQUENCES OF ADJUSTMENT AND GLOBALISATION

The implementation of structural adjustment policies and developments in the world economy over the past decade or so have had wide-ranging impacts on poverty, income and wealth distribution within and across countries. The policies have contributed indirectly to a range of other social problems as well. Discussions on adjustment often tend to focus exclusively on issues of efficiency in resource allocation. But markets are also a mechanism for determining returns to labour, land, capital and enterprise through their effect on prices of products and factors of production. A good deal of the analysis of markets continues to be influenced by the textbook model of perfect competition. In reality, a substantial proportion of transactions is carried out in situations characterised by monopolistic, oligopolistic or embryonic markets. Individuals, enterprises and associations often have recourse to a variety of means to influence product and factor prices in their favour.

Developments in the international economy and processes of adjustment and globalisation have influenced patterns of income and wealth distribution through changes in the level of economic activity and in relative product and factor prices. It was noted earlier that the anti-inflationary policies pursued by the industrialised countries were primarily responsible for a marked slowdown in the growth of the world economy over the past decade and a half. This has affected the level and distribution of income world-wide both directly and indirectly through its impact on product and factor prices. At the same time, processes of adjustment and liberalisation have profoundly affected relative prices. Policies such as removal of trade barriers, foreign exchange controls and state subsidies, and price fixing; promotion of interest rate and labour market flexibility; and deregulation and privatisation illustrate this. In addition, changes in the level and pattern of state expenditure and revenues have had a powerful impact on income distribution.

These policies have resulted in an intensification of competition nationally and internationally. The increase in the international mobility of capital and enterprise in particular has put great pressure on businesses to cut costs to maintain or enhance their competitive position. This in turn has been reflected in attempts to cut labour costs through mechanisation, reduced wages, greater flexibility in labour markets, curbs on trade union power and improved managerial efficiency.

Despite problems of data and interpretation, there appears to be sufficient evidence to warrant the generalisation that these processes and policies have contributed to a significant redistribution of income and wealth from the poor to the rich both nationally and internationally. At the international level, the inequality in income distribution worsened between 1970 and 1989: the countries with the richest 20 per cent of world population increased their share of global GNP from 73.9 to 82.7 per cent. The countries with the poorest 20 per cent of world population saw their share fall from 2.3 to 1.4 per cent (see Table 2.2). The ratio between the average incomes of the two groups of countries rose from 32 to 1 to 59 to 1 over the period. The Gini coefficient, a measure of overall inequality, rose from 0.71 in 1970 to 0.87 in 1989 – a figure far in excess of anything seen in individual countries (UNDP, 1992).

The redistribution of income in favour of the rich countries has not prevented a worsening of income distribution there nor even an increase in the incidence of poverty in many cases. Between the late 1970s and the mid-

Table 2.2 Global income disparity, 1960–89

	Poorest 20 per cent (%)	*Richest 20 per cent (%)*	*Richest to poorest*	*Gini coefficient*
1960	2.3	70.2	30 to 1	0.69
1970	2.3	73.9	32 to 1	0.71
1980	1.7	76.3	45 to 1	0.79
1989	1.4	82.7	59 to 1	0.87

Source: UNDP (1992, Table 3.1)

Table 2.3 Trends in income distribution in selected OECD countries (in percentages, mid-1970s to mid-1980s)

	Quintile	*Mid 1970s*	*Late 1970s*	*Mid 1980s*
France	Highest	43.6	42.4	43.0
	Lowest	5.3	6.1	5.9
	Ratio	8.2	7.0	7.3
Germany (FRG)	Highest	44.8	39.5	38.7
	Lowest	6.9	7.9	6.8
	Ratio	6.5	5.0	5.2
Italy	Highest	46.4	40.4	42.2
	Lowest	5.2	7.4	6.9
	Ratio	8.9	5.5	6.1
Japan	Highest	37.8	38.0	38.6
	Lowest	8.3	8.8	8.0
	Ratio	4.6	4.3	4.8
Netherlands	Highest	37.1	37.0	38.3
	Lowest	8.5	8.1	6.9
	Ratio	4.4	4.6	5.6
Sweden	Highest	31.4	30.2	30.9
	Lowest	10.7	11.2	11.1
	Ratio	2.9	2.7	2.8
United Kingdom	Highest	38.0	39.0	42.0
	Lowest	6.6	6.5	6.1
	Ratio	5.8	6.0	6.9
United States	Highest	42.8	39.9	41.9
	Lowest	4.5	5.3	4.7
	Ratio	9.5	7.5	8.9

Source: Boltho (1992, Table 12).

1980s, income distribution worsened in the eight major industrial countries, including Japan, the Netherlands and Sweden (see Table 2.3).

More recent data capturing trends in the late 1980s show the continuation or even accentuation of these trends. Between 1984 and 1987, the proportion of income going to the top quintile of taxpayers in France rose from 44 per cent to 46 per cent (Davidson, 1989). The proportion of households living below the poverty line (defined as less than average income) in the United Kingdom rose from 9.4 per cent in 1974 to 11.9 per cent in 1983 and to 20 per cent in 1988, with their numbers jumping from 5 to 12 million between 1974 and 1988. The number of children living in poor households rose from about 1.6 million in 1979 to 3 million by 1988, or a quarter of all children in Britain (Millar, 1991). In the United States, the income share of the lowest quintile fell from 5.4 per cent in the early 1970s to 4.6 per cent in the late 1980s, while that of the highest quintile rose from 41.5 per cent to 44.5 per cent. Likewise, the poverty rate, after declining substantially between 1959 and the early 1970s, rose by 4 per cent in the 1980s (Cutler and Katz, 1991).

Although comprehensive and reliable data on poverty and income distribution are scarce or non-existent for most developing countries, the available evidence points to similar trends. In most of Latin America, the incidence of poverty increased and income distribution worsened in the 1980s. A recent survey of data on Latin America concluded that 'studies of Latin American countries demonstrate increasing inequality in income distribution as measured by Gini coefficients in Argentina, Brazil, El Salvador, Mexico, Panama, Peru and Puerto Rico' (Cardoso and Helwege, 1992). After surveying data from various sources, another writer stated that 'average per capita incomes fell, while income distribution worsened in the 1980s, for almost every country for which data are available' (Stewart, 1992). Data also show that, while the 1970s saw a reduction in the incidence of poverty in Latin America as a whole from 40 to 35 per cent, this was reversed in the 1980s when the incidence of poverty rose to 37 per cent by 1989 (Stewart, 1991).

Comparable data are not available for the African region but trends in per capita income, employment, real wages and government expenditure all point to increasing incidence of poverty in the late 1970s and 1980s (Cornia and Stewart, 1990; Ghai, 1989; Jamal and Weeks, 1988; JASPA, 1988; Stewart, 1992). In its report on poverty, the World Bank noted that 'with few exceptions, the evidence supports the conclusion that poverty in sub-Saharan Africa is severe and has been getting worse' (World Bank, 1990).

In several Asian countries the proportion of people living in poverty has declined. For instance, the incidence of poverty declined from 50 to 43 per cent in India (1977–83), from 28 to 17 per cent in Indonesia (1984–7), from 15 to 14 per cent in Malaysia (1984–7) and from 21 to 20 per cent in Pakistan (1979–84), though it rose in Thailand from 20 to 26 between 1981 and 1986 (World Bank, 1990). However, income distribution seems to have worsened in recent years in many countries, including the South-East and East Asian countries.

The above changes in the pattern of income distribution and incidence of poverty in different parts of the world have resulted from developments in the world economy and policies of stabilisation and adjustment. In the industrialised countries, the marked slowdown in growth in the post-1973 period has been an important factor. In combination with changes in the international division of labour and rapid technological change, it has contributed to a substantial increase in unemployment (Standing, 1989). At the same time policies to promote greater labour flexibility, such as easing or removing regulations protecting worker security and remuneration and curbing union power, have interacted with increased international competition and technological change to enhance the importance of casual, part-time and informal sector employment (Kolko, 1988). These trends in income distribution have been reinforced by regressive changes in public expenditure and taxation which, in turn, were brought about by cuts in the level and coverage of welfare programmes and increased reliance on indirect taxes and social security contributions. Summarising surveys of income distribution and household welfare in the industrialised countries since the first oil shock, Boltho (1992) states:

> despite continual increase in public expenditure, the combined effects of shifts in spending away from major social programmes and in tax policy toward a broadly regressive position meant that in the 1980s most OECD countries spurned or severely moderated the concept of the generous welfare state that had been current during the 1960s. This was most evident in the United Kingdom and the United States, but even Germany, the Netherlands and Sweden were affected. Elsewhere, the impact may not have been as intense, but no economy went against the tide.

In developing countries, especially in Latin America and Africa, stagnation or decline in economic activity was a major factor contributing to increased impoverishment. Its effects on incomes and welfare were magnified, as discussed earlier, by resource transfers to industrialised countries through increased debt burden, deteriorating terms of trade, declining flows of private capital and accelerating capital flight. Stabilisation and adjustment efforts further reinforced poverty and inequalities through such policies and mechanisms as restraint or decline of public expenditure, especially on social services and welfare; reduction in progressive taxation; removal of subsidies on goods and services of mass consumption; the increase or imposition of user charges; increase in real interest rates; decline in employment and real wages; and rise in casual, part-time employment and in informal sector activities (Cornia and Stewart, 1990; Jamal and Weeks, 1988; Rodgers, 1989; Standing and Tokman, 1991).

These changes have had differential effects on social groups. The burden of adjustment in most developing and industrialised countries has fallen largely on the low and middle income strata of society. Urban workers have been hit especially hard, while certain categories of highly skilled persons have been more successful in preserving their incomes. There has been a shift of income in favour of capital, especially in services and manufacturing engaged in international transactions. In the industrialised countries, the groups most seriously affected include the unemployed, new entrants to the labour force, pensioners, state officials and professional employees. On the other hand, those engaged in foreign trade and owners of property (at least until the recent slump in prices), of financial assets and of enterprises successful in exports have gained relative to other groups.

In African and Latin American countries, the fall in income is not confined to unskilled and semi-skilled persons but extends much further up the skill hierarchy. In particular, middle and senior level public officials have suffered sharp declines in living standards. In most countries, peasant incomes have held up better or have declined by less than those of urban workers. Among those deriving their income from capital, the groups affected relatively favourably include persons with access to foreign exchange and owners of foreign assets; those engaged in banking, finance, property transactions; commercial, agricultural and industrial enterprises in the export business and those dealing in scarce commodities, smuggling and drugs. The losers include those producing for the shrinking domestic markets previously protected from foreign competition, pensioners, holders of fixed interest bonds and other assets which failed to keep up with accelerating inflation.

The growth of poverty and glaring inequalities in consumption have severely strained the social fabrics of these countries. Many countries have experienced a marked increase in crime, violence, smuggling and trading in illicit goods. There is also growing reliance, as part of the survival strategy, on child labour, prostitution and intensification of female labour. An increasing number of people have taken to migration in their search for employment opportunities. Social tensions have increased and these frustrations often find expression in social explosions, ethnic conflicts and growth of fundamentalist and extremist movements.

The global distribution of income and wealth will be increasingly affected by flows of capital and technology primarily through transnational enterprises. These in turn will be determined largely by the cost effectiveness of different countries as centres of production. The social, political and physical environment will also assume increasing importance in the investment decisions of global enterprises. The preferred choice will be countries that succeed in creating a hospitable climate for capital, invest in physical infrastructure, upgrade human capabilities, encourage entrepreneurial talents and foster social harmony and political stability. The next section looks at how adjustment and globalisation have affected power relationships and social cohesion and solidarity.

ADJUSTMENT, GLOBALISATION AND SOCIAL DEMOCRACY

Processes of globalisation and adjustment have been associated with important shifts of power at the national and international levels. Internationally, the balance of power has shifted further away from the developing countries to the benefit of foreign creditors and investors, international financial organisations and industrialised countries. Among the industrialised countries, there has been a concentration of power in the Group of Seven, principally Germany, Japan and the United States. Yet everywhere the power and the reach of the state have declined. Internally, there has been a significant shift of power in favour of capital, especially that linked with the international economy, and away from the organised working class and to some extent the middle class.

The decline in the power wielded by developing countries has been mediated by the slump in commodity prices and the growth in the burden of foreign debt. Their bargaining power has been further eroded by the collapse of the communist regimes in the Soviet Union and Eastern Europe. The weakened state of the Third World is reflected in an effective transfer of decision-making in vital areas of economic and social policy to an alliance of international financial organisations, corporate capital and industrialised countries. This weakness finds a concrete expression in an ever increasing list of conditionalities attached to economic policy, social priorities, military expenditures, political systems and human rights.

Among the industrialised countries, the economic pre-eminence of the United States has declined even though its military supremacy has attained new heights. The European Community, Japan and, to a lesser extent, the East and South-East Asian countries, have emerged as rival economic powers. The smaller and medium-sized industrialised countries have become more dependent upon larger countries, especially in the context of various trading arrangements and forms of economic union. Increasingly, there is a tendency for economic and political policy to be co-ordinated by the Group of Seven.

A number of processes have contributed to the erosion of the power of the nation state. All countries have been affected, but the loss of sovereignty varies with their size and military and economic strength. The growing integration of the world economy has steadily diminished the scope and effectiveness of public policies in areas such as taxation, public expenditure, money supply and interest rates, social protection and wage policies. National autonomy has eroded even more severely for countries in regional economic and political groupings.

This limitation on sovereignty in national policy is reinforced by the international mobility of capital, enterprises, and professional and managerial staff. A corollary of this is the trend towards convergence of social and economic policy in a number of key areas of public concern. Two recent examples illustrate these points. Sweden, the pioneer of a model of social democracy widely acclaimed world-wide for economic efficiency, social justice and political participation, was forced to abandon these policies by the pressures exerted by the flight of capital and increased international competition. The sweeping reduction of taxes on corporations and wealthy individuals initiated by the Thatcher and Reagan administrations was followed by tax changes in countries around the world.

In many countries, national sovereignty is also being challenged from below by growing separatist movements based on ties of ethnicity, language, religion and culture. The three extreme examples of this phenomenon are Ethiopia, the former Soviet Union and Yugoslavia, where the process has carried through to its logical conclusion in the disintegration of the country into a number of more or less independent entities.

The countries affected by economic crisis and therefore forced to seek assistance from international financial agencies, creditor countries and commercial banks, have experienced further weakening of the power of the state. A vital part of decision-making in the social and economic domain has been transferred to foreign creditors. The squeeze on state finances has compelled governments to reduce public services, investment in infrastructure, and employment and wage levels in the public sector. The growing privatisation, marketisation, informalisation and internationalisation of the economy mean that an increasing proportion of economic activity is slipping beyond the direct control of the state. The power of the state has been further weakened by the loss of qualified officials, decline in the morale of the civil service and increase in crime, violence and lawlessness.

The above changes have also been accompanied by important shifts in the balance of power among different social groups at the national level. As noted above, the foreign investors and creditors, sometimes working in partnership with certain segments of domestic capital, have increased their power and influence in national policy-making. Likewise, the influence of domestic business groups, especially those with links or access to foreign capital, technology and markets, has greatly increased. The working class and parts of the middle classes have seen a dwindling of their power to shape national policies.

These changes are also reflected in social institutions and social movements. Some established social organisations such as the trade unions and co-operatives have declined in power and influence in many countries. In developing countries especially, there has been a significant expansion of private development associations and grassroots rural and urban initiatives to assist the basic needs provisioning and empowerment of marginalised groups. There is also a mushrooming of new movements championing a diversity of causes such as ecology, feminism, ethnic recognition, religious fundamentalism and xenophobia (Ghai and Hewitt de Alcántara, 1991).

In sum, the processes associated with adjustment and globalisation have undermined the social alliance and national consensus on economic and social goals and policies established in the post-war period in both the industrialised and developing countries (Ghai, 1991; Singh, 1991; Tironi and Lagos, 1991). A new coalition of social forces underpining and legitimising new economic regimes has not yet fully emerged and consolidated itself in most countries. The transitional period is characterised by fluidity and uncertainty. The adverse social consequences generated by the new economic regime have diluted the social and economic content of democracy in the industrialised countries. These consequences are no doubt partly responsible for the widespread malaise and disenchantment with the political processes in these countries, as reflected, for instance, in low electoral participation and distrust of political parties and politicians.

The past decade and a half were marked by the resurgence of democracy, first in Latin America and Asia, then in Eastern and Central Europe and now increasingly in Africa and the Middle East. The temporal coincidence of economic reform with liberal democracy has led many observers to postulate an organic relationship between the two phenomena. There is, however, little theoretical or empirical justification for such a relationship. Capitalism preceded political democracy by centuries in some cases, and by decades in others. In recent history, economic regimes based on market forces such as in East and South-East Asia were characterised until a few years ago by authoritarian political systems. On the other hand, until their fairly recent economic reforms, several of the democratic regimes, such as in India and Sri Lanka, have long been considered examples of highly regulated economies.

The recent upsurge of democracy has resulted from varied and complex factors in different regions of the world. Both rapid and broad-based growth as in South Korea and Taiwan, as well as acute and prolonged crisis as in Africa and Latin America, have been contributory factors. The internal struggles for democracy in many of these countries have been reinforced by external pressures and assisted by the end of the Cold War era. Nor can one underestimate the influence of dominant ideologies propagated world-wide through a powerful media or the attraction of the Western model of liberal democracy and material prosperity.

In the short to medium term at least, there are some obvious conflicts between the processes associated with adjustment and globalisation and the consolidation of new democracies (Gibbon, Bangura and Ofstad, 1992; Nelson et al., 1989). The adverse social consequences described above are occurring precisely at a time when the democratic process is generating demands for additional services and resources. As it becomes increasingly difficult to meet these demands, the democratic reform is robbed of its social and economic content. Furthermore, through the weakening of popular organisations, the erosion of the middle class and the dilution of institutions of civil society, the economic crisis and adjustment measures may undermine the very foundations of a democratic society. With the discrediting of socialist and radical ideologies, the frustration of popular aspirations for improved living standards may be exploited by demagogic and reactionary forces to fan the flames of ethnic conflicts and religious and cultural fundamentalism.

Some of these developments pose a threat to social solidarity and capacity for durable growth. Social solidarity is built around a widely shared vision of national objectives; due recognition of the legitimate interests of different groups; a perception that both the fruits of growth and the burdens of austerity are distributed fairly; equality of opportunities in access to social and economic services, employment and productive resources; and prospects for promotion and upward mobility. The importance of social cohesion and solidarity as a determinant of the rate and sustainability of economic growth is largely neglected in the development literature (Banuri, 1991). Yet it can be argued that the existence or creation of solidarity has made a substantial contribution to the social and economic progress achieved by countries as diverse as Austria, Germany, the Netherlands, the Nordic group and Switzerland in Europe, and Japan, Singapore, South Korea and Taiwan in Asia.

The advent of democratic regimes provides an opportunity to create social solidarity and a national consensus to face the challenges of crisis, adjustment and growth. Ironically, just at a time when they are called upon to play this creative role, states everywhere have watched not only the steady diminution of the resources they control but also their sovereignty in social and economic matters through internationalisation of their economies and societies. Power in these spheres has shifted towards transnational enterprises, international financial agencies and a handful of industrialised countries. The concentration of economic power, however, has not been accompanied by a corresponding shift in their political and social responsibilities for global welfare or in their accountability to the peoples of the world.

This imbalance is one of the greatest challenges facing the world community in the 1990s and into the next century. It appears likely that over the long haul the processes of economic and social globalisation are irreversible and accelerating and that nation states are condemned to a steady and progressive erosion of their sovereignty.[6] The incapacity of the states to cope with pressing problems extends also to areas such as the environment, traffic in illegal drugs, spread of infectious diseases, organised crime and violence. The gravity of the social and economic problems confronting the world requires a redefinition of the role and responsibilities of the major forces shaping the international economy and society. It calls for a better balance between power and accountability and resources and responsibility.

This can only come about through a strengthening and coalition of social groups committed to a better balance between collective needs and individual incentives and between economic advance and social progress. There are many groups and organisations, including workers' unions, environment movements, women's associations, human rights activists and popular development agencies, as well as concerned individuals in influential strata in both developing and industrialised countries who are aware of the potentially serious consequences of the continuation of the present social and economic trends and would thus be prepared to support efforts to achieve consensus and solidarity around broad-based programmes of human development. Such efforts would need to extend beyond national frontiers to regional and global levels.

It is a task of the highest importance to explore the political, social and economic configurations of new arrangements to articulate and implement an agenda of reform addressing the critical social problems of the world. Some of the needs can only be met through action at the international level. Some will require initiatives at the regional level. Many problems can be handled appropriately by states at the national level. There are also likely be more opportunities for social programmes conceived and implemented at sub-national and grassroots levels. There will need to be corresponding diversity in the institutions vested with the responsibility for different programmes ranging all the way from international organisations to extended families. Religious bodies, business corporations, charitable societies, neighbourhood associations, village committees and popular development agencies can all be appropriate vehicles for initiating social programmes. The resources for implementing these programmes will also need to be tapped in novel ways from many sources. Only a reform effort of these multiple dimensions can provide the basis for a renewal of social consensus and solidarity necessary for political stability and sustainable growth on a global scale.

CONCLUSION

This chapter has attempted to provide an integrated and global perspective on adjustment and globalisation. These two processes are seen as interdependent and mutually reinforcing. The dynamics of global integration in the post-war period interacted with the economic crisis in the post-1973 period to strengthen the forces and pressures for adjustment policies. The latter, reflected in liberalisation, deregulation and privatisation, in turn reinforced the thrust of global economic integration in the 1980s. Structural adjustment policies originated in the industrial countries and then spread to other regions of the world. In the former, they represent elements of both continuity and break with the economic and social policies pursued in the post-war period. In the developing countries, they constitute a sharp break with the earlier policies of state-directed modernisation and growing reliance on administrative methods for resource allocation. The pace and pattern of liberalisation show considerable country and regional variation in the Third World, reflecting socioeconomic structures, the severity of the crisis, the intensity of foreign pressure and the interplay of contending social groups.

The 1980s witnessed a marked acceleration of the globalisation process which extended beyond economics to embrace science, technology, culture and lifestyles. In the economic domain, it was reflected in rapid growth of trade in goods and services, of foreign investment, technology transfers, foreign exchange transactions and telecommunications. With some notable exceptions, the role of the developing countries in the global exchanges has tended to shrink in recent years. This is due in part to discrimination in the pattern of liberalisation. In an era of extensive deregulation, the protection accorded to agriculture was enhanced, non-tariff barriers multiplied on some manufactured goods of export interest to developing countries and controls on immigration of unskilled persons were tightened. Nevertheless, the world moved strongly in the direction of an integrated market for goods, capital, technology and skills. The process was fuelled by technological progress and mediated by transnational enterprises that increasingly became the vehicle for trade and investment and access to technology, skills and markets.

The processes of adjustment and globalisation have been associated with wide-ranging social and political changes. They contributed to intensification of inequalities nationally and internationally and an increase in the incidence of poverty in most countries. The slowdown in economic growth in the post-1973 period played a major role in this. However, changes in relative product and factor prices and in patterns of taxation and expenditure exacerbated poverty and inequalities. The groups which suffered most include the unemployed, new entrants to the labour force, urban workers and sections of the middle class. The chief beneficiaries include those deriving their income from capital, especially those engaged in financial, manufacturing and commercial enterprises in the export business. The intensification of poverty and inequalities has severely strained social fabrics and accentuated social conflicts world-wide.

These changes reflect important shifts in power at the national and international levels. Internationally the balance of power has shifted further away from developing countries in favour of foreign creditors and investors, international financial organisations and industrialised countries. Everywhere the power and the reach of the state have declined. Internally, there has been a shift of power in favour of capital, especially that linked with the international economy, and away from the organised working class and to some extent the middle class.

These developments have undermined the social alliance and national consensus on economic and social goals and policies established in the post-war period in both the industrialised and the developing countries. Together with intensification of poverty, they have generated a wide array of social problems. They pose serious threats to political stability and sustainable growth. Social problems need to be addressed not only in the interest of national cohesion and solidarity but also as a necessary investment for future growth. Unfortunately, nation states are increasingly both unwilling and unable to cope with the social crisis. At the same time, the economic power wielded by the new dominant forces nationally and internationally has not been matched by a corresponding shift in their political and social responsibilities for global welfare or in their accountability to the peoples of the world. It is a task of the highest importance to explore the political, social and economic configurations of new arrangements to articulate and implement an agenda of reform addressing the major social problems of the era.

Notes

1. This paper is based on my presentations at the 1991 meeting of the UK Development Studies Association and the faculty seminars at the Witwatersrand University and the University of South Africa. I am grateful to participants at these meetings for their comments and suggestions. The paper has also greatly benefited from comments made by Yusuf Bangura, Cynthia Hewitt de Alcántara, Frances Stewart, Peter Utting and David Westendorff. I am grateful to Veena Jha, Jane Parpart, Tim Shaw and Harsha Singh for stimulating discussions on this subject. I would like to thank Akpan Etukudo, Frédéric Grare and Rose-

mary Max for assistance with documentation, Jenifer Freedman for editing the paper and Rhonda Gibbes for proof-reading and formatting it.

2. An OECD publication, *Structural Adjustment and Economic Performance* (OECD, 1987), contains a good discussion of the rationale as well as the contents of the emerging consensus on economic policy.
3. Singh has argued that China and India outperformed Brazil and Mexico after the second oil crisis, not because they had more open and export-oriented trading regimes and followed appropriate exchange rate policies, but because they were less integrated in the world economy (Singh, 1985).
4. Tariffs on dutiable manufactured goods had come down from 18 to 13 per cent. The Kennedy Round reduced them to an average of 8–11 per cent and the Tokyo Round to 6 per cent or less (OECD, 1987).
5. The growth of regional trading blocs could slow or even reverse the process of global economic integration by raising commercial barriers against non-members. In recent decades, such blocs do not appear to have caused significant trade diversion.
6. There is, however, always the possibility that national crises and pressures exerted by the globalisation process could provoke reactions resulting in rolling back the advances in economic integration for limited periods.

References

Appleyard, R. T. (1991) *International Migration: Challenge for the Nineties*, IOM (Geneva).

Banuri, T. (ed.) (1991) *Economic Liberalization: No Panacea* (Oxford: Clarendon Press).

Blackhurst, R. (1991) Notes from a lecture – revised 5 June.

Boltho, A. (1992) *Growth, Income Distribution and Household Welfare in the Industrialised Countries Since the First Oil Shock*, Innocenti Occasional Papers (Florence: UNICEF).

Britton, A. (1991) *Economic Growth in the Market Economies, 1950–2000* Economic Commission for Europe Discussion Paper No. 1 (New York: United Nations).

Burki, S. J. (1984) 'International Migration: Implications for Developing Countries', *The Middle East Journal*, vol. 38, no. 4, Autumn.

Cardoso, E. and A. Helwege (1992) 'Below the Line: Poverty in Latin America', *World Development*, vol. 20, no. 1, January.

Cornia. G. A. and F. Stewart (1990) *The Fiscal System, Adjustment and the Poor*, Innocenti Occasional Papers (Florence: UNICEF).

Cox, R. W. (1991) *Structural Issues of Global Governance: Implications for Europe*, mimeo.

Cutler, D. and L. Katz (1991) 'Macroeconomic Performance and the Disadvantaged' in W. C. Brainard and G. L. Perry (eds), *Brookings Papers on Economic Activity* (Washington DC: Brookings Institution).

Davidson, I. (1989) 'Inequality grows in "socialist" France', *Financial Times*, 24 November.

GATT (General Agreement on Tariffs and Trade) (1990) *General Agreement on Tariffs and Trade: What It Is, What It Does* (Geneva: Information and Media Relations Division).

Ghai, D. (1989) 'Economic Growth, Structural Change and Labour Absorption in Africa' in B. Salomé (ed.), *Fighting Urban Unemployment in Developing Countries* (Paris: OECD).

—— (ed.) (1991) *The IMF and the South: The Social Impact of Crisis and Adjustment* (London: Zed Books).

—— and C. Hewitt de Alcántara (1991) 'The Crisis of the 1980s in Africa, Latin America and the Caribbean: An Overview' in D. Ghai (ed.), op. cit.

Gibbon, P., Y. Bangura, and A. Ofstad (eds) (1992) *Authoritarianism, Democracy and Adjustment* (Uppsala: Scandinavian Institute of African Studies).

Glyn, A. et al. (1988) *The Rise and Fall of the Golden Age* UNU/WIDER Working Papers (Helsinki).

Griffin, K. and A. R. Khan (1992) *Globalization and the Developing World: An Essay on the International Dimensions of Development in the Post-Cold War Era* (Geneva: UNRISD).

Griffith-Jones, S. and O. Sunkel (1986) *Debt and Development Crises in Latin America: The End of an Illusion* (Oxford: Clarendon Press).

Helleiner, G. K. (1992) 'The IMF, the World Bank and Africa's Adjustment and Structural Debt Problem: An Unofficial View', *World Development*, vol. 20, no. 6, June.

Jamal, V. and J. Weeks (1988) 'The Vanishing Rural-Urban Gap in Sub-Saharan Africa', *International Labour Review*, vol. 127, no. 3, 1988.

JASPA (Jobs and Skills Programme for Africa) (1988) *African Employment Report* (Addis Ababa: ILO).

Julius, DeAnne (1990) *Global Companies and Public Policy: The Growing Challenge of Foreign Direct Investment* (London: Pinter Publishers).

Kolko, J. (1988) *Restructuring the World Economy* (New York: Pantheon Books).

Lim, L. Y. C. and P. E. Fong (1991) *Foreign Direct Investment and Industrialisation in Malaysia, Singapore, Taiwan and Thailand* (Paris: OECD Development Centre).

Llewellyn, J. and S. J. Potter (eds) (1991), *Economic Policies for the 1990s* (Oxford: Blackwell).

Marcum, J. (1984) 'Trade in High Technology – Results of work in the OECD', *New Technologies and World Trade, Ministry of Foreign Affairs* (Stockholm).

Marglin, S. A. (1988) *Lessons of the Golden Age of Capitalism* (Helsinki: WIDER).

Millar, J. (1991) 'Bearing the Cost' in S. Becker (ed.), *Windows of Opportunity: Public Policy and the Poor* (London: CPAG).

Nelson, J. et al. (1989) *Fragile Coalitions: The Politics of Economic Adjustment* (New Brunswick: Transactions Books).

OECD (Organisation for Economic Co-operation and Development) (1983) *Historical Statistics 1960–1981* (Paris).

—— (1987) *Structural Adjustment and Economic Performance* (Paris).

—— (1988) 'The Telecommunications Industry: The Challenge of Structural Change', *Information Computer Communications* no. 14 (Paris).

—— (1991) *Historical Statistics 1960-1989* (Paris).

Oman, C. (1991) *Trends in Global FDI and Latin America*, Paper presented at thc InterAmerican Dialogue Meeting.

Pipe, G. R. (1990) 'Telecommunications', *The Uruguay Round: Services in the World Economy* (Washington DC: World Bank).

Rodgers, G. (ed.) (1989) *Urban Poverty and the Labour Market* (Geneva: ILO).

Rojas-Suárez, L. (1991) 'Risk and Capital Flight in Developing Countries', *Determinants and Systemic Consequences of International Capital Flows*, Occasional Paper (Washington DC: IMF).

Singh, A. (1985) *The World Economy and the Comparative Economic Performance of Large Semi-Industrial Countries* (Bangkok: ARTEP/ILO).

—— (1991) 'Labour Markets and Structural Adjustment: A Global View' in Standing and Tokman, op. cit.

Standing, G. (1989) *European Unemployment, Insecurity and Flexibility: A Social Dividend Solution*, Working Paper (Geneva: ILO).

—— and V. Tokman (eds) (1991) *Towards Social Adjustment: Labour Market Issues in Structural Adjustment* (Geneva: ILO).

Stewart, F. (1991) 'Many Faces of Adjustment', *World Development*, vol. 19, no. 12, December.

—— (1992) *Protecting the Poor during Adjustment in Latin America and the Caribbean in the 1980s: How Adequate was the World Bank Response?*, Development Studies Working Papers (Oxford: Centro Studi Luca d'Agliano/ Queen Elizabeth House).

Talal, H. B. (1984) 'Manpower Migration in the Middle East: An Overview', *The Middle East Journal*, vol. 38, no. 4, Autumn.

Tironi, E. and R. Lagos (1991) 'The Social Actors and Structural Adjustment', *CEPAL Review*, no. 44, August.

UNCTAD (United Nations Conference on Trade and Development) (1990) *Handbook of International Trade and Development Statistics* (New York: United Nations).

UNDP (United Nations Development Programme) (1992) *Human Development Report 1992* (New York: Oxford University Press).

United Nations (1988) *Financing Africa's Recovery* (New York: United Nations).

—— (1992) *World Investment Report: Transnational Corporations as Engines of Growth* (New York).

World Bank (1981) *Accelerated Development in Sub-Saharan Africa: An Agenda for Action* (Washington DC).

—— (1990) *World Development Report 1990* (New York: Oxford University Press).

—— (1991) *World Bank Support for Trade Policy Reform*, vol. I: Main Report (Washington, DC).

—— (1992) *Global Economic Prospects and the Developing Countries* (Washington DC).

3 Increasing Returns and Economic Development

RENEE PRENDERGAST

INTRODUCTION

Not so long ago, Deepak Lal claimed that the demise of development economics was likely to be conducive to the health of both the economics and economies of developing countries (Lal, 1983, p. 109). Lal attributed the analytical failures of development economics to a neglect of welfare economics and, in particular, to a misinterpretation of the theorem of the second best. Most development economists interpreted the theorem to imply that that there was a case against the introduction of piecemeal market reforms since there was no guarantee that they would lead to increased welfare. In Lal's view, this emphasis was wrong. What the theorem really implied was that there should be a reduction in government intervention in the economy since there was no guarantee that any particular intervention would be welfare increasing. As Toye (1987) has shown, the function of the discussion of the second-best theorem in Lal's argument seems to have been largely rhetorical. Ultimately his welfare economics argument involves little more than an assertion that the optimality results of competitive equilibrium hold, albeit approximately, in the real world. Some of the presumptions underlying this kind of argument have been addressed elsewhere, for example Toye (1987) and Killick (1989). This chapter seeks to supplement their critique by focusing on the question of the suitability of the neoclassical general equilibrium (GE) model for the analysis of developmental problems in the third world or elsewhere.

In his 1990 Presidential Address to the Development Studies Association, Hans Singer reminded us that Adam Smith regarded increasing returns as a normal feature of a competitive economic system. This position was taken for granted by all the classical economists and the conventional wisdom was not disturbed when in 1834 Cournot, the pioneer of marginalist economics, demonstrated the incompatibility of increasing returns and equilibrium for a competitive industry. Around 1870, Marshall took up Cournot's marginalist method and began to develop it in diagrammatic form. Initially, Marshall seems to have presumed that increasing returns could be represented simply by postulating a downward sloping industry supply curve. However, it quickly became clear to him that with such a supply curve and a downward sloping demand curve neither the uniqueness nor the stability of equilibrium could be guaranteed. Furthermore, he realised that, as Cournot had shown, a downward sloping industry supply curve could not be explained by increasing returns to individual firms. Marshall was loath to abandon either increasing returns or competition or, for that matter, his newly adopted marginalist framework. His search for a solution began twenty years before the publication of the first edition of the *Principles* and continued to receive attention for a long time thereafter. By the time he published his *Principles of Economics* in 1890, Marshall had arrived at a very ingenious solution. This was to make external economies the sole cause of increasing returns in a regime of competition. As a theoretical device, the concept of external economies was original and ingenious. However, it is difficult to conceive of sources of external economies which have operational content and are consistent with competitive equilibrium.[1] The point here is not to deny the possibility or importance of external economies of scale but to suggest that they may be best considered in some other framework.

Having produced a theoretically consistent, if empirically vacuous solution to the problem of reconciling increasing returns and competition within the marginalist framework, Marshall did not rest satisfied. In succeeding editions of the *Principles*, there was increasing emphasis on an evolutionary conception of economics. 'Fragmentary statistical hypotheses' were, he argued, useful as 'temporary auxiliaries to dynamical – or rather biological – conceptions: but the central idea of economics, even when its Foundations alone are under discussion, must be that of living force and movement' (Marshall, 1961, I, p. xv). Marshall thus bequeathed on posterity two rather different visions of the economic process – one evolutionary, the other mechanistic. Of these, only the latter was consistent with the marginalist approach and the evolutionary model was not seriously developed.

As is well known, the neoclassical general equilibrium model which triumphed in the post-war period requires the assumption that returns are diminishing or non-increasing. While genuine efforts were made by some theorists to relax the assumptions of the model so as to accommodate realistic sources of increasing returns, these attempts have not generally been successful (Scarf, 1981). Perhaps as a result of the failure to accommodate them within the dominant theory, increasing returns tended to disappear from view or at best to be handled in an unsatisfactory manner (Gold, 1981). Amongst the economists who failed to be seduced by the elegance and generality of the GE model and who continued to insist on the importance of increasing returns and cumulative causation were those concerned with Third World and regional development problems. This is hardly surprising.

As Arthur (1990) has pointed out, the standard neoclassical model is based on negative feedbacks. These in turn imply that any major changes will be offset by the very reactions they generate and that development will tend to spread rather than concentrate. If the starting point for analysis is the fact that wide disparities exist between countries or between regions, then it is reasonable to take the view that the model does not reflect all the pertinent features of the existing reality.

While 'big push' and other models taking account of positive feedbacks were influential in the post-war/post-colonial period, they fell out of favour from about the early 1970s onwards. It was claimed that the policies based on these theories, in particular the large scale government intervention which they sanctioned, were responsible for stagnation and inefficiency in the developing world. Increasingly, it was asserted that one form of economics, namely that of the free market, was appropriate for both the developed and the developing world. It is ironic that at the very time when the development fraternity seemed poised to cave in under the weight of the neoclassical assault, the neoclassical theory should find itself under attack precisely because of its failures with regard to increasing returns and cumulative causation mechanisms.

THE NEW LITERATURE ON INCREASING RETURNS

The new literature on increasing returns emerged in the 1980s principally in the United States. It has now become quite voluminous, so our examination of it at this point will necessarily be patchy. Two accessible starting points are Arthur's 1990 article in *Scientific American* and David's 1985 article on the economics of QWERTY. The role of increasing returns in the emergence of a dominant technology is considered in both papers while Arthur's paper also examines a number of other issues including the development of regional specialisation.[2]

The emergence of a dominant technology can be illustrated with reference to the history of the video-cassette recorder (VCR). The market started out with two competing formats, VHS and Beta, each selling at approximately the same price. Both systems were introduced at roughly the same time and both initially had access to roughly the same market shares. It was not clear at the outset which of these standards would eventually dominate the market. Other things being equal, it might have been expected that the Beta technology would win, since it was reputed to be technically superior. This, however, did not happen. To understand how the VHS format came to predominate, consider what would happen if for some reason the VHS format increased its share of the market at the expense of Beta. Software dealers would now be encouraged to stock more tapes in VHS format thereby enhancing the value of owing a VHS recorder and leading more people to choose VHS rather than Beta. We know from experience that in this particular case the cumulative causation process resulted in an equilibrium in which the VHS format dominated the market. We can also accept that, at the outset, the possibility that Beta would end up as the dominant format was at least as likely.

Problems of the type we have described can be represented using a non-linear probability schema. Imagine an urn to which balls are added one at a time. The balls are either blue or violet. The colour of the ball to be added next is unknown but the probability of a particular colour being added depends on the proportion of balls of that colour already in the urn. The system can demonstrate positive feedback provided an increasing proportion of balls of a given colour increases the probability of adding another ball of the same colour.[3] Arthur, Ermoliev and Kaniovski (1983, 1986 and 1987) have shown that as balls continue to be added, the proportions of each colour must settle down to a 'fixed point' such that the probability of adding each colour is equal to the proportion of that colour already in the urn. Where the process is characterised by unbounded increasing returns, it can be predicted that the proportional share of one of the colours will, with probability one, converge to unity. This case has two fixed points: one in which nearly all the balls are blue and one in which nearly all the balls are violet. Alternatively, if the degree of increasing returns levels off as the number of balls added increases, the fixed points of the system will be a mixture of blue balls and violet balls in some proportion. The latter corresponds to the case where, for example, two different technologies end up sharing the market between them.

Where two or more fixed points are possible, history can be important in determining which of the possible equilibria is eventually selected. In the VCR case, external circumstances, luck and corporate manoeuvring seem to have tipped the balance in favour of VHS at an early stage. David (1985) made a detailed study of the history behind the ascendancy of the QWERTY typewriter keyboard. He shows that the vital factor in the ultimate dominance of QWERTY was the fact that, from its inception in the 1880s, touch typing was adapted to this keyboard. This became a source of system scale economies which enabled QWERTY to win out over its rivals. Despite the subsequent emergence of superior systems, society remained locked into QWERTY because the balance of costs was such that it was privately profitable in the short run to adapt machines to the habits of typists rather than the other way round.

Having argued that technical interrelatedness, scale economies and irreversibility were the key features of the evolving production system which gave rise to the ultimate dominance of the QWERTY standard, David noted that if choices were made in a forward looking way rather than myopically on the basis of the currently prevailing costs of different systems, the final outcome could have been influenced by expectations. In particular, he suggested that provided network externalities were important and depended on the size of the network, a particular system could triumph because purchasers of hardware or software expected that it would do so (David, 1985, p. 335). The relative importance of history and expectations has been examined in recent papers by Matsuyama (1991) and Krugman (1991). The main results of their investigations are summarised briefly below.

HISTORY VERSUS EXPECTATIONS

The possibility of multiple equilibria in the presence of external economies was discussed by Marshall in his *Pure Theory of Domestic Values* and in Appendix H of his *Principles*. Referring to the market for a single product, Marshall observed that if demand and supply happened to be in unstable equilibrium, a small passing disturbance would be sufficient to move the industry to one of its positions of stable equilibrium (Marshall, 1961, I, pp. 806–7). Furthermore, he noted that if the first point of intersection of demand and supply were an unstable equilibrium, this would indicate that the commodity in question could not be produced remuneratively on a small scale. Consequently, some passing accident such as a temporary increase in demand would be necessary for production to commence at all. Alternatively, Marshall suggested, some enterprising firm might be prepared to sink much capital in overcoming the initial difficulties of production, and in bringing out the commodity at a price which would ensure large sales (ibid., p. 807).

It is evident from the above that Marshall thought that history might have a role in equilibrium selection or even in allowing production to begin. At the same time his reference to the possibility of initial difficulties being overcome by an enterprising firm indicates that he had an inkling that history was not the sole arbiter of events. While Marshall's formulation of this matter leaves much to be desired, recent research in the area indicates that his basic intuition was indubitably correct.

The issues raised by Marshall have been given a clear formulation in recent papers by Matsuyama (1991) and Krugman (1991). Matsuyama represents the industrialisation process as a shift of resources from agriculture to industry and he explores the relative importance of history and expectations using two-sector static and dynamic models of the economy. Matsuyama assumes a small open economy in which agriculture operates under conditions of constant returns to scale. Manufacturing is subject to economies of scale which are external to the firm and internal to the industry. Manufacturing labour supply is taken to increase with the relative wage in manufacturing giving an upward sloping supply curve. The labour demand curve can be taken to represent the relative wage manufacturing firms can offer, given the level of employment in manufacturing. Because manufacturing is subject to increasing returns, the marginal product of labour and hence the wage that can be offered increases with the size of the sector. Hence, the demand curve will also be upward sloping, so multiple equilibria are possible. Three equilibria are depicted in Figure 3.1. Of these, two, S_0 and S_h are stable equilibria and one, S_1, is unstable. If the initial employment in manufacturing is somewhere between S_0 and S_1, the economy converges to S_0 and thus can be trapped in a state of pre-industrialisation. If, on the other hand, the initial employment level exceeds S_1, the economy will converge to S_h and exhibit a high level of manufacturing employment. Finally, if the initial position of the economy is the unstable equilibrium S_1, then a passing disturbance could tip the balance and send the economy in the direction of S_0 or S_h.[4]

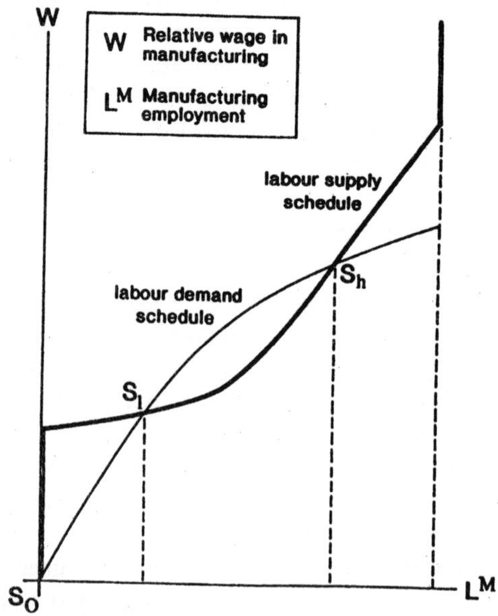

Figure 3.1 Manufacturing employment in the static economy

Source: Based on Matsuyama, 1991.

As we have depicted it so far, the equilibrium selected seems to depend entirely on the past history of this economy. But like Marshall, we are entitled to suspect that there might be some way of jumping to S_h from some initial level of employment between S_0 and S_1. Both Matsuyama (1991, p. 625) and Krugman (1991, pp. 653–4) note that the usual objection to a pure self-fulfilling expectations story is that inertia and adjustment costs make instantaneous movement of resources difficult. They then suggest that, if this is the case, the choice of sector by an agent should be regarded as an investment decision which will depend not only on current returns but also on expected future returns. Since, in the presence of external economies, future returns will depend also on the decisions of other agents, there is room in this model for self-fulfilling prophesy. To the extent that the discount rate is high, investments are irreversible and economies of scale are weak, history also can play a role.

Krugman explores the relative importance of history and expectations within a two-sector dynamic model in which the cost of shifting labour is a function of the rate at which labour is moved between sectors. The model has two equilibria. With some sets of initial conditions, it is only possible to reach one of the equilibria (in Krugman's terminology, there is no overlap) so that the outcome is history-determined. With other sets of initial conditions, either of the long-run equilibria can be reached (that is, there is overlap) and which one is reached depends on expectations. More than one set of expectations may be consistent with each equilibrium.

In Krugman's model the factors influencing the relative importance of history and expectations are: the size of the discount rate, the degree of external economies and the speed of adjustment. A high discount rate favours history over expectations because if people discount the future heavily their expectations about the future actions of other individuals will have little influence on their present choice of action. Small external economies reduce the interdependence among decisions and as a result eliminate the possibility of self-fulfilling expectations. Finally, if the economy adjusts slowly history will always be decisive. This is because, with slow adjustment, factor rewards will be near current levels for a long time regardless of people's expectations about the future.

Matsuyama (1991) examined the relative importance of history versus expectations by constructing a dynamic model in such a way that its stationary states coincided with the equilibria of the static economy analysed earlier. Overlapping agents were assumed to make irreversible career decisions at the start of their lives. They were also assumed to be endowed with perfect foresight and to choose their careers so as to maximise wealth. Because of irreversibility, an agent's career decision depends not only on present wages but on future wages and because of externalities, these future wages depend on the decisions of other agents. Matsuyama first analysed the global dynamics of his model assuming a zero rate of time preference. By perturbing this model, he then examined the dynamics of an economy with a small positive rate of time preference. The consequences of a large positive rate of time preference were derived from a separate model. The main results of Matsuyama's analysis are summarised briefly below.

Matsuyama defines an underdevelopment trap as a state with a low level of industrialisation from which the economy cannot escape under a system of *laissez faire* (p. 620, n.). With a zero rate of time preference, such underdevelopment traps exist when increasing returns are weak but not when they are strong (pp. 634–5). Since the threshold level of employment from which S_h (the equilibrium with a high level of manufacturing employment) can be reached is lower than that corresponding to S_1, not all initial levels of employment below S_1 should be regarded as unemployment traps. With weak increasing returns, it was also the case that self-fulfilling pessimism might cause the economy to deindustrialise regardless of the level of initial manufacturing employment (ibid.). With strong increasing returns, deindustrialisation due to self-fulfilling pessimism was possible for some initial levels of manufacturing employment but not for others. The threshold, from above which deindustrialisation was not possible, was greater than the employment level corresponding to S_1 (pp. 635–6). With a small positive rate of time preference, the implications for history versus expectations in Matsuyama's model remain the same as in the zero time preference case for both weak and strong scale economies (pp. 637–8). For a large positive rate of time preference, there exists a unique perfect foresight equilibrium for any initial condition. In this case self-fulfilling expectations have no role and history alone determines the long-run outcome (p. 644).

HISTORY VERSUS EXPECTATIONS – IMPLICATIONS

As Krugman (1991, p. 654) notes, a world in which history matters and a world of self-fulfilling expectations are different both from each other and from the standard competitive view. If expectations are likely to be the main determinant of equilibrium choice, then the main task of development policy is to create convergent expectations which will enable the most favourable equilibrium to be reached. The *locus classicus* of this kind of argument is considered to be Rosenstein-Rodan's 1943 article on problems of industrialisation in eastern and south-eastern Europe. The argument has been recently formalised by Murphy, Shleifer and Vishny (1989). If history rather than expectations is likely to be the main determinant of equilibrium choice and if underdevelopment traps are possible, more active government intervention may be appropriate. In the models under consideration this might take the form of a subsidy or a tariff on the manufactured good (Matsuyama, 1991, pp. 640–2). Matsuyama, however, notes that while such a subsidy may make sustained industrialisation possible, a take-off could fail to materialise if excessive intervention choked off private-sector initiative.

As both Krugman and Matsuyama note, their models ignore many important aspects of the actual development process such as capital accumulation, technology transfers, education, etc. Nevertheless, the models represent a step in the direction of realism inasmuch as they provide a rationale not only for government intervention in the usual economic sense but also for factors influencing expectations about the future, for example, planning, political leadership and general sociological factors. At a practical level, there is some evidence to suggest that forms of government intervention and expectations about the future may be quite closely linked. For example, referring to the Korean case, Westphal (1990, pp. 42–3) notes that, in the later 1950s, the Korean economy was considered something of a basket case and was expected to remain that way for the forseeable future. 'Policy makers,' he adds, 'behaved in ways that were consistent with this view and helped to reinforce it.' According to Westphal, Korea's economic take-off occurred at the end of a period of major economic policy reforms which were motivated by the view that 'the only way to negate Korea's dependent status was by fundamentally changing the economy's trajectory away from industrialisation focused on the domestic market'.

Dynamic models exhibiting positive feedback may provide useful insights into development processes in late-industrialising countries. The industrialisation process in such countries has been described by Amsden (1988, 1989). Amsden argues that industrialisation in the twentieth century has occurred on the basis of learning how to use foreign technology rather than on the basis of new innovations. In these circumstances, productivity increases depend (i) on the efficiency with which foreign technology is used, (ii) on the realisation of scale economies and (iii) on how extensively borrowed technology is introduced. These three variables depend in turn on the growth rate of output so that the growth–productivity dynamic exhibits positive feedback. Consequently, Amsden argues, once growth is under way, there is a greater chance than otherwise for government to sustain the growth momentum. In addition to emphasising positive feedback, Amsden also stresses the need for government intervention because of the existence of underdevelopment traps from which the economy will not escape if left to its own devices. Such traps can exist because the initial level of industrialisation is low, because infant industries need time to learn and because the minimum efficient scales of production are often quite large.

A mixture of support and discipline was characteristic of the industrialisation strategies of Japan, Korea and Taiwan. In the case of Korea, infant industries were often granted absolute protection in the domestic market as well as access to cheap credit and various forms of export subsidy (Westphal, 1990, pp. 47–8). In return for this, they were required to meet various targets including rapid productivity growth and the sale of a rising proportion of their output on the export markets. Such enforcement of performance targets helped to ensure that intervention aimed at facilitating escape from underdevelopment traps did not stifle private-sector initiative or divert economic effort towards various forms of rent-seeking activity. Late industrialisers in Latin America also provided government support for industrialisation in the form of protection and subsidies but while they were sometimes subject to performance targets, the degree of discipline was much less than in the case of the East-Asian economies. In Amsden's view this, and not excessive government intervention, is what accounts for the relatively poorer growth performance of the Latin American economies.

In the case of Korea, a comprehensive planning framework as well as the stringent enforcement of performance targets may both have encouraged the expectation of high growth rates and helped to ensure their fulfilment. While expectations of high growth rates can be self-fulfilling in the presence of strong external economies, it is unlikely that such expectations were decisive in the Korean case. This is because the organisational framework of the Korean industrialisation strategy was such that the principal economies of scale were internal to the large oligopolistic firms (*chaebol*) which dominated the Korean manufacturing sector. In part, the success of Korean government intervention was due to the fact that, as a follower, it was industrialising on the basis of well known but up-to-date foreign technologies. It was possible to plan because the consequences of making various investments were known. The fact that technologies were known entities might also be regarded as favourable to a rather different strategy involving smaller-scale firms and decentralised decision-making since it would facilitate the formation of convergent expectations about the future and hence allow the realisation of positive feedback through specialisation and external economies. There is some evidence that such a strategy involving decentralised decision-making and greater reliance on the market mechanism has emerged in Taiwan (Amsden, 1985; Mody, 1990; Levy and Kuo, 1991). Since a certain volume and depth of economic activity is necessary to support the emergence of specialised firms, the pursuance of such a strategy by Taiwan may have something to do with the fact that its GDP in the early sixties was approximately twice that of Korea.

This contrast between the two ways in which positive feedbacks can be realised emerges very clearly in a recent study by Levy and Kuo (1991) of the strategic orientation of keyboard and personal computer assemblers in Korea and Taiwan. Levy and Kuo note that Korean firms tended to adopt what they call an assembly strategy while Taiwanese firms adopt what they call a bootstrap strategy. The central ingredient of the former they describe as a readiness to start up at a high volume. This permits the new entrant to move rapidly down the learning curve thereby reducing costs. Once assembly has been mastered, the firm can undertake in-house the tasks of product design and component fabrication (ibid., p. 366). The bootstrap strategy on the other hand allows small size at entry but expansion can be rapid. Investment tends to be low even when expansion is taking place, due to heavy reliance on sub-contracting networks. The low costs of entry are regarded by the authors as being favourable to risk-taking activity and to innovation as opposed to learning. The point to be stressed here is that the two forms of organisation described, complete vertical integration and specialisation within a network, are alternative ways of achieving economies of scale. Since Marshall's time they have been called respectively internal economies and external economies of scale. Theoreticians desirous of using the competitive models have tended to emphasise the external economies. It is important for practitioners to realise that strategies based on the internalisation of economies of scale combined with tough performance standards may also be a viable route for countries starting with a low industrial base.

CONCLUSIONS

Positive feedbacks in the economy have become an important area of theoretical investigation in the last decade. The new literature emphasises the possibility of multiple equilibria and shows that both history and expectations may influence which of the possible equilibria is eventually selected. The models developed provide a justification for forms of government intervention such as protection and subsidisation which facilitate escape from development traps. They also point to the importance of factors such as political leadership and planning which influence expectations' formation and convergence. Recent research on the development experience of late-industrialising countries seems to indicate that the economics of positive feedbacks is of considerable practical relevance. It seems, therefore, that Lal's pronouncements on the demise of development economics were unfortunately timed and that they might better have been directed at the general equilibrium framework.

Notes

1. On this point see Prendergast 1992 and 1993.
2. More detailed discussions of these topics can be found respectively in Arthur 1989 and 1988.
3. If the relationship between the probability of adding a ball of a particular colour and the proportion of balls of that colour is a decreasing one, we have the case of diminishing returns and there will be a single equilibrium point.
4. The economic interpretation is as follows: With initial employment in manufacturing somewhere between S_l and S_h, the relative wage W in manufacturing is higher than that required to keep employment in manufacturing constant. Thus, more agents switch sectors. Labour supply in manufacturing increases and the economy gradually converges to S_h.

References

Amsden, A. (1985) 'The Division of Labour is Limited by the Rate of Growth of the Market', *Cambridge Journal of Economics*, vol. 9, 271–84.

Amsden, A. (1988) 'Private Enterprise: The Issue of Business Government Control, *The Colombia Journal of World Business*, vol. 23, 37–42.

Amsden, A. (1989) *Asia's Next Giant* (New York: Oxford University Press).

Arthur, W. B. (1988) 'Urban Systems and Historical Path Dependence' in J. H. Ausebel and R. Herman (eds) *Cities and Their Vital Systems* (Washington: National Academy Press).

Arthur, W. B. (1989) 'Competing Technologies, Increasing Returns and Lock-in by Historical Events', *Economic Journal*, vol. 99, 116–31.

Arthur, W. B. (1990) 'Positive feedbacks in the Economy' *Scientific American*, February, 80–5.

Arthur, W. B., Y. M. Ermoliev and Y. M. Kaniovski (1983) 'A Generalised Urn Problem and its Applications', *Cybernetics*, vol. 19, 61–71.

Arthur, W. B., Y. M. Ermoliev and Y. M. Kaniovski (1986) 'Strong Laws for a Class of Path-dependent Urn Processes', in V. Arkin, A. Shiryayev and R. Wets (eds), *Lecture Notes in Control and Information Sciences 81* (New York: Springer).

Arthur, W. B., Y. M. Ermoliev and Y. M. Kaniovski (1987) 'Path-dependent Processes and the Emergence of Macro-structure', *European Journal of Operational Research*, vol. 30, 294–303.

Cournot, A. (1960) *Researches into the Mathematical Principles of the Theory of Wealth*, trans. by N. T. Bacon (London: Hafner).

David, P. A. (1985) 'Clio and the Economics of QWERTY', *American Economic Review*, Papers and Proceedings, vol. 75, 332–7.

Gold, B. (1981) 'On Size, Scale and Returns', *Journal of Economic Literature*, vol. 199, 5–33.

Killick, T. (1989) *A Reaction too Far* (London: Overseas Development Institute).

Krugman, P. (1981) 'Trade, Accumulation and Uneven Development', *Journal of Development Economics*, vol. 8, 149–61.

Krugman, P. (1991) 'History Versus Expectations', *Quarterly Journal of Economics*, vol. 105, 651–67.

Lal, D., (1983), *The Poverty of Development Economics* (London: Institute of Economic Affairs).

Levy, B. and W. J. Kuo, (1991), 'The Strategic Orientation of Firms and the Performance of Korea and Taiwan in Frontier Industries...', *World Development*, vol. 19, 363–74.

Marshall, A. (1961) *Principles of Economics*, 2 vols, ed. C. W. Guillebaud (London, Macmillan).

Matsuyama, K. (1991) 'Increasing Returns, Industrialization, and Indeterminacy of Equilibrium', *Quarterly Journal of Economics*, vol. 105, 616–50.

Mody, A. (1990) 'Institutions and Dynamic Comparative Advantage: The Electronics Industry in South Korea and Taiwan', *Cambridge Journal of Economics*, vol. 14, 291–314.

Murphy, K. M., A. Shleifer and R. Vishny (1989) 'Industrialization and the Big Push', *Journal of Political Economy*, vol. 97, 1003–26.

Packard, N. H. (1988) 'Dynamics of Development: A Simple Model for Dynamics away from Attractors' in P. W. Anderson, K. J. Arrow and D. Pines (eds), *The Economy as an Evolving Complex System*, vol. V, Santa Fe Institute, Studies in the Sciences of Complexity, (California: Addison-Wesley).

Prendergast, R. (1992) 'Increasing Returns and Competitive Equilibrium – the Content and Development of Marshall's Theory', *Cambridge Journal of Economics*, vol. 16, 447–62.

Prendergast, R. (1993) 'Marshallian External Economies', *Economic Journal*, vol. 103, forthcoming.

Rosenstein-Rodan, P. N. (1943) Problems of Industrialization of Eastern and South-Eastern Europe, *Economic Journal*, vol. 53, 202–11.

Scarf, H. E. (1981) 'Production Sets with Indivisibilities, Part II. The Case of Two Activities', *Econometrica*, vol. 49, 395–423.

Toye, J. (1987) *Dilemmas of Development* (Oxford: Basil Blackwell).

Westphal, L. E. (1990) 'Industrial Policy in an Export Propelled Economy: Lessons from South Korea's Experience', *Journal of Economic Perspectives*, vol. 4, 41–59.

4 Market Forces and Development

PETER SMITH

INTRODUCTION

The importance of market forces solutions (MFS) to the problem of promoting development scarcely needs illustrating; yet, despite the confidence with which such solutions are still being advocated, there is growing disquiet with both their practical effects and their theoretical underpinnings (Campbell, 1991; Smith, 1991a). Unfortunately, this opposition of confidence and disquiet has failed to generate effective dialogue, and this raises major questions – with serious implications for the way in which policy, explanation and action interrelate – about the failure of the two sides to enter into dialogue and resolve it 'scientifically'.

There are really two sets of questions here:

(i) Given that the theoretical basis for opting for MFS (that is, that they optimise the use of society's resources) rests on a monumental and apparently rigorous body of reasoning, do valid criticisms of that basis really exist? If so, what are they?

(ii) If there are valid criticisms, how does the widespread preference for MFS survive the (apparently) inevitable clashes with reality? (Presumably, if we uncover a mechanism that gives dominant models a degree of protection against empirical attack, that will have considerable implications for managing development.)

The case presented below is that there *are* valid criticisms of that theoretical basis and that the survival of MFS is only a particular case of a more general phenomenon: the conditioning of rigorous, objective study and criticism by the currently dominant imagery of 'how the world really is', that imagery being neither rigorously logical nor objectively well-founded; it is important to realise how radically this consideration changes the agenda of debate about *any* dominant school of thought and its alternatives.

The imagery supporting MFS is analysed and the constraints it has imposed in an important area of development practice are discussed. That area, common property resource management, is central to both development work with pastoral communities and to developing strategies to deal with the problems of water resources in the arid and semi-arid regions of the world; the latter issue is pregnant with conflict and the imagery underlying (not generated by) MFS makes the chances of an unhappy delivery even greater.

BASIC CRITICISMS OF MFS

The proposition advanced by proponents of MFS is that there is a rigorous case for the belief that market forces, if allowed free play, would optimise the allocation of society's resources; that even if, for various misguided and political reasons (and the two are often implicitly defined as being the same thing), life cannot be surrendered to the market, commonsensical approximations to free-market conditions can still be arranged and these will capture the majority of the benefits attributed to the ideal competitive situation; that interference with the ability of individuals to contract freely for the supply of goods and services is inevitably a depressor of total production; and that the allocation of resources achieved by the market is optimal in a technical and value-free sense.

The Problem of the Equilibrium Price

The basic argument on the ability of the market to optimise the allocation of resources internally or in international trade (see Eckert and Leftwich, 1988, and Kenen, 1989 respectively, for excellent and up-to-date presentations of these) revolves around the concept of the equilibrium price. A starting point for models of both the domestic and international markets is a model of how a competitive market equilibrates: the (increasing) amounts of a good that a supplier will voluntarily put on the market can be represented by an upward-sloping graph of quantity against price; correspondingly, the tendency of consumers to take more off the market at lower prices voluntarily is represented by a downward-sloping graph of quantity against price. The two graphs intersect at the equilibrium price, where the quantities offered and sold balance, and the market clears itself without intervention. That price (P_E) is reached by suppliers price-cutting to dispose of unsold stocks (starting above P_E, with surpluses) or the offering of premiums by buyers to secure their wants (starting below P_E, with shortages); the process is seen as having essentially stable dynamics either homing in steadily or entering a state of stable oscillation (such as that which characterised pig, potato and jute markets in the absence of intervention). The latter is probably fairly unimportant in practice, as it is readily broken down by entrepreneurs with capital, storage and the wit to take advantage of the situation.

The vogue for chaos studies has revealed the error in this: there is a third mode of *chaotic* behaviour, that is, permanent, patternless oscillation, and it can arise from the *way* in which suppliers revise their price expectations and the quantities they offer. If this revision is non-linear (i.e. changes in price are disproportionate to the market gap initiating them), very complex behaviour can develop in what are essentially permanent patterns of over-correction. Such nonlinearity is rather likely in real commercial markets (Smith, 1991a). Models of chaotic markets are given by Chiarella (1988), by Urban and Jensen (1989) and by Smith (1991b). Cagan (quoted by Sheffrin, 1983, p. 3) developed a non-equilibrating model of foreign exchange markets in the 1950s, although he appears not to have realised the significance of this; Peters (1991) analyses instability in the capital markets using a chaotic model, and there is evidence that commodity markets also show chaotic behaviour, from the particular 'fractal' character of their movements over time and from the known relationships between fractality and chaotic dynamics (Sandefur, 1990, p. 409ff; Feder, 1989).

Chaotic behaviour *is* a real feature of markets, with commodities, foreign exchange and capital high on the list of likely venues – although the same could be said of any market in which price adjustments are likely to be nonlinear; and, of course, chaotic behaviour in any of these will unsettle markets linked to them by relationships of competition, complementarity or substitution. That we have failed to see this possibility until recently is an interesting aspect of a wider problem concerning the way we screen out phenomena that offend against our theoretical preconceptions and the imagery that supports them, both in the fields of systems dynamics (see for example Gleick, 1987; Stewart, 1989) and more generally (Kuhn, 1970; Laudan, 1977). Indeed, most neoclassical economists still refuse to acknowledge or deal with the implications of chaotic behaviour – the most significant feature of which is that the mere possibility of the phenomenon removes the most critical single component of the standard argument supporting the optimality of the market.

Building that case depends upon using the equilibrium price, which, for the generalised *nonlinear* market, is effectively nonexistent in the dynamic case. Let us call the graph of price against time for such a market its 'price trajectory'. Even if the market is characterised by well-defined supply and demand curves, intersecting nicely (i.e. there is a *static* equilibrium price), there is no *dynamic* equilibrium: for the system to come to rest, its price trajectory must arrive *exactly* at the equilibrium price; at the same time, there must be exactly zero unsold stocks and exactly zero unsatisfied demand.

Unlike the situation in the traditional model of system dynamics, there is no 'zone of capture' around the equilibrium, such that when the price trajectory enters it, it is guaranteed to home in subsequently on the equilibrium price itself: to put it slightly more technically, it is infinitely unlikely that the market will come to rest at PE ('infinitely' means you pick a small probability, say 0.000000001 – and it is even more unlikely than that – however small your starting figure). Minute deviations – between reality and model, or between successive runs of a model – grow exponentially into major divergences, and forecasting and planning become useless exercises, although qualitative knowledge of the family of behaviours open to the system can still be useful. Worse, chaotic systems show periods of quiescence, cycles of very small amplitude, followed by bursts of oscillation, resettlings into something near quiescence at a different level, etc. (the mathematical conditions under which these occur are now well known: see for example Sandefur, 1990); if the behaviour of such a model were shown to someone brought up in neoclassical economics it is virtually certain that he/she would see familiar phenomena such as 'shifts in the market', when, in fact, the system is merely working out the consequences of its own rules.

Pseudo-equilibria, pseudo-signals (apparent shifts in demand and price resulting merely from the internal dynamics of the market, in the absence of 'real' changes) and the exponential divergence of price trajectories that initially differ by minute amounts all mean that the rational expectations doctrine (Sheffrin, 1983) fails to save MFS. (The doctrine is that the expectations of the inhabitants of an economic system will converge onto its true behaviour in response to evolutionary pressures.)

In a chaotic market, price is generally not an indicator of the 'real value' of a good or service; the equilibrium price is nonexistent; and the core neoclassical arguments collapse from the absence of a key component. There is evidence that key markets in modern economies are chaotic, and the theoretical conditions required to produce such behaviour are neither strict nor implausible.

The Problem of Second Best

Even if freely competitive markets could be relied upon to develop into stable equilibrium there remains the problem of translating the ideal into reality; recent practice seems to suggest a belief, and a reasonable one at first sight, that if free competition is the ideal, then removing any one piece of regulatory machinery, any one subsidy or tariff, will put us on the road to capturing more of the benefits of the ideal situation. Unfortunately, this simple idea does not work, as a celebrated (but largely ignored!) study by

Lancaster and Lipsey (1956) clearly showed. The optimum that free competition develops is a Pareto optimum, that is, a situation where no one can be made better off without making at least one other person worse off. What Lipsey and Lancaster showed is that a Pareto optimum is special in the sense that approximations to it will differ from it in total economic welfare by an indeterminately large amount, so that there is no guarantee at all that getting rid of a single obstacle (or a set of obstacles) to free competition and exchange, but leaving some in place, will get us nearer to the competitive Nirvana. Indeed, the reverse is true: the presence of an obstacle to free competition and exchange may require the introduction of taxes, regulations and so on elsewhere, to restore Pareto optimality.

Readers may notice a family resemblance between this criticism and the preceding one: our expectations about the behaviour of both the real world and mathematical abstractions of it have proved wrong. In this case, the rule that seems to fail is: part way from A (current situation) to B (the competitive Nirvana) is nearer B than A is.

Practical solutions to this problem are lacking, Hartley (1977) points out that it is possible, under fairly restrictive conditions, and with an unlikely quantity of high-quality data, to calculate what other interventions are needed to accompany a 'liberalisation' to restore Pareto optimality; he also points out that the commonest reaction of policymakers is to ignore the problem. (See also Toye (1987) for an interesting discussion of attempts to neutralise the second best as a problematic issue in the context of development economics.)

Regulation as a Depressor of Productivity

The proposition that regulation inevitably depresses productivity seems to rest on an analogy with constrained optimisation problems: if you are using one of the available mathematical tools to optimise your plan of action (say, to make a profit from a farm), given the limitations on resources and so on, then every additional restriction is likely to depress the total amount of product (and can never increase it). The analogy is false because those problems are essentially games against nature; competition is a game against opponents who see your moves and react (changing your own choice of best strategy). As Schwartz (1978) shows, in that sort of formulation, it is entirely possible that regulation of totally free competition can *increase* production – and conversely, that competition can depress it. The conditions required to produce this effect are not particularly restrictive (or unlikely). The implication of the standard model is precisely that the market is a game against 'nature' – or at least against a non-adversary.

The Ethical Foundations

Some time ago, a World Bank staff member achieved short-lived fame by suggesting that it was justified – indeed, even 'rational' – to arrange things so that industrial operations carrying high risks to life and health should be sited in low-producing developing countries.

In effect, he was arguing that the true value of suffering – measured the only way that neoclassical economics knows how, in terms of the value of lost production – is less in those countries. It is only possible to produce a claim of such egregious stupidity with such aplomb if you start it with a major flaw in your system of reasoning. In this case, the flaw arises from simultaneously embracing two incompatible systems of ethics: one, utilitarianism, which assumes that all human delights and pains can be compared on a unique scale so that cost/benefit analysis is possible; the other, ethical egoism, which denies the possibility of such comparison. The latter underlies the concept of the Pareto optimum and you have to be an ethical egoist to support its use, which is based on the notion that:

> in general, we have no objective means of ... comparing the gains of ... one person with the loss suffered by another when the same event causes both.

In making such a claim, Eckert and Leftwich (1988, p. 12) are assuming that 'objective' means 'measurable on a numerical scale' (or, more precisely, on an interval scale). This is fairly unreasonable – a lot of things which cannot be measured can be ranked in a way that different observers will agree on, that is, objectively. Moreover, ethically egoistic positions are incompatible with any theory of ethics which proposes the existence of basic and inalienable rights: if such rights exist there is at least some level of interpersonal and objective (but not measurable) comparison possible via the knowledge of whether any one of us has too little or enough of that right. Feeding in, unconsciously, an ethically egoistic position at the beginning of the MFS argument all but guarantees that argument will conclude with strictures against regulation and control. However, this is merely regurgitation: what went in has simply come back out and no new justification of non-interference has been created. Hoffman and Moore (1990) give an excellent survey of the ethical dimensions of the arguments for and against unfettered competition.

Other Considerations

The foregoing are by no means all the radical criticisms of MFS and its associated body of theory. Here are a few:

— the problem of increasing returns to scale (see Prendergast, this volume);
— the omission of the consideration of inventories of physical plant, stocks of materials and so on from the basic model of price equilibration under competition strongly biases the whole argument towards a conclusion in which equilibrium states show up very favourably (the costs of attaining equilibrium are effectively set at zero by ignoring inventories, etc);
— the alleged benefits of market incentives in promoting innovation (based on appeals to the work of Schumpeter) ignore the fact that this archetypal innovator is explicitly not motivated by such incentives (see Schumpeter, 1961).
— the problem that many real markets are characterised by very uncertain information, going far beyond mere probabilistic risks attached to the known outcomes of a finite list of options (see, for example Littlechild, 1986).

At a less rigorous level, there is also a considerable body of material that questions the belief that market-style solutions to the problems of organising, motivating and suppressing corruption are either efficient or effective (see Smith, 1991a for a survey).

However, enough has been said to show that there *are* real and valid criticisms, and it is time to progress to the second issue: if the theory underpinning MFS is flawed, why hasn't it been refuted by the results of collisions with reality?

AN EXPLANATION OF THE PROCESS OF POLICY SURVIVAL AND SUCCESSION

Any theory sufficiently broad in scope to generate policy prescriptions will almost inevitably be based on a worldview, a largely inarticulate system of beliefs and images about 'how the world really is', physically, socially and logically – the sort of imageries that have been identified in various places above, in fact. Thomas Kuhn, in 'The Structure of Scientific Revolutions' (1970), adopted the word paradigm for these imageries. His ideas have subsequently gone through considerable criticism and development (and some relabelling), notably at the hands of Imre Lakatos (1970) and Larry Laudan (1977), and the current state of paradigm theory can be summarised as follows:

(i) Paradigms are the images that give the axioms and formal models their appearance of 'obviousness' or 'simplicity' and control what are valid – and promising – methods of explanation. The *formal* assumptions of market theory are the idealised competitive market, the axioms of consumer choice and so on; but they are only credible as unavoidably necessary axioms if you share the paradigm. That includes notions about the nature of the mathematical entities and processes which are to be used in sound thinking, including constructing the theory. This paradigm is explored in more detail below, but some of its elements have already been revealed, in the discussions of chaotic markets and the second best.

(ii) Paradigms seem to have been imported into formal sciences from everyday life. An essentially similar concept – as 'thought worlds' (Douglas, 1986), or 'cultural theories' (Spradley, 1972), or 'cosmologies' (Douglas, 1982) – has emerged in a variety of disciplines, as a (postulated) support to managing everyday life. Most real-life decision is done with an almost total lack of data and under impossible pressure of time (compared, that is, to what operations-research based schemes of the decision process present as desirable). On the other hand, there is a premium in many cases, on prompt, fluent and consistent action (especially in the social sphere, where others' ability to build stable interpretations of one's intentions and sound anticipations of one's behaviour are valuable). Conviction-carrying systems of belief about how things are, what strategies work, do have a survival value. One of the reasons why people resent so bitterly attacks on their paradigm is that these attacks threaten a very valuable life-asset: destroy it and large areas of life have to be re-thought, slowly and expensively.

(iii) Paradigms tend to disqualify counter-evidence against themselves. As an example from a formal science, contrast two views of how to get people to change their behaviour: Skinnerian behaviourism (which claims that people are merely very complex sets of conditioned reflexes) with Kellyian psychology which focuses on the (usually highly idiosyncratic) interpretations that people place on the world around them. There is very little possibility of crucial experimentation to settle which is the 'truer' of these because their worldviews differ so much. Kellyians disqualify all behaviourist materials as dealing with an irrelevant issue: everyone knows that meaning and intention is the real matter of psychology and this defines behaviourism as being as remote from their field of enquiry as is geology. Also Skinnerians disqualify all material on meanings and intentions as unscientific, because their image of what is 'good science' implies that if you can't *physically* demonstrate an entity, you can't use it as an explanatory device (Smith, 1991c).

As a result, people who inhabit the different thought-worlds of different paradigms spend most of their time shouting past their opponents at their own supporters. The relevance of this to the non-debate that occurs between monetarists and Keynesians, between marketeers and the rest, and between Marxists and the rest, is obvious.

(iv) There is a sense in which paradigms (within a particular arena, for example development) are all of equal validity. Naive realism (part of the paradigm underpinning MFS) suggests that there is a hard reality: if you have anything deviating from the one true theory, it will bring you into painful collision with that reality. This, and the pre-Kuhnian storybook view of science as a process by which truth is gathered in a cumulative, accretionary process, suggests that later theories will always be better theories. Actually, the dependent theories of a paradigm are *always* seen to work, provided they are viewed from within it. There are various mechanisms which ensure this, one of which was discussed above: the counter-evidence is either irrelevant or illegal. The second is the tendency to invoke external interference or special circumstances as agents preventing the full expression of our theory. The third is our (basically reasonable) willingness to accept the presence of 'random variation' and the need for remedial action in a cussed world when even the best of theories is applied. Smith (1991c) discusses cases in which theories seen as sound by some respected group, are seen as bizarre by another (at a different place and time); these range from ballistics to statistical hydrology; the material in Evans-Pritchard's (1976) classic studies of witchcraft on the failure of that art to collapse from empirical disproof is interesting (and entertaining) in this context, as is Robin Horton's (1970) study of African science and medicine. Paradigms distort the criteria of empirical success in their own favour.

(v) Paradigms promote some problems and demote others. Thus, the employment level becomes *defined* as a result of imbalances in the market for skills, labour and knowledge: there is no need to confirm this, it must be so, it is obvious to all reasonable people (that is, those who share the paradigm). Similarly, by focusing attention on some problems and techniques, others become relegated (or even defined as trivial); the emphasis on equilibrium analysis has relegated the problem of what engineers would call 'transients'. Firms – in reality, just as in the standard model – have no privileged knowledge of equilibrium price and production levels; given any big change (e.g. deregulation, but a genuine market shift would have the same effect), a spate of unfortunate decisions will always result, some ending in bankruptcy/insolvency, with at least some destruction of resources. In principle, it should be possible to anticipate and thereby alleviate this; in practice, the tools are not developed to do the job (or even transferred from disciplines in which they have been developed), because everyone focuses on the issues the paradigm lights up as important. Boldness in implementing 'liberalisation' policies – despite the opinion of enthusiasts such as Letwin (1988) – is not necessarily a good thing, as events in the finance, airline and property markets of the West is demonstrating and as at least some involved in Eastern Europe are beginning to realise.

(vi) Paradigms change via two mechanisms: Kuhn identified revolution, a sudden and catastrophic shattering of the old worldview as a result of the build-up of anomalies resulting from the denial of counter-evidence. Laudan (1977) identified another: conceptual pressure. It is difficult to hold one image of 'how the world really is' in your professional field of, say psychology or economics, when the political, literary or theological worlds you are also embedded in rely on a different view of reality. (Skinnerian psychology is on the wane not because it was refuted – which, *for its adherents* is all but impossible – but because of powerful changes in the intellectual and political climate that emphasised self-determination undermined it: 'self-determination' would be a nonsensical concept in a world of conditioned reflex machines). Tides in other areas of life influence the relative appeal of particular paradigms, partly by changing the perceived salience of problems.

(vii) As Laudan originally suggested, paradigms have two types of justification: for a new one, promise of handling newly-elevated problems; for an existing one, its proven explanatory and control successes. However, as we have also seen, paradigms distort the criteria of empirical success in their own favour and there is thus created a ratchet mechanism: new paradigms come in on cheap promises, but may only be abandoned after exceptionally costly empirical failure – if they are not superseded through conceptual pressure sooner. MFS came in on the promise of stimulating development when other approaches had failed.

THE ELEMENTS OF THE MFS PARADIGM

A number of elements of the MFS paradigm are readily identifiable and are discussed below.

First, the paradigm visualises problem space for thinking about the performance of economics as being very like everyday (Euclidean) space: all objects (for example policies) can be surely evaluated on all attributes (such as equity, productiveness) just as all physical objects can be evaluated on weight, latitude, longitude and so on, and because they can be evaluated they can be compared. (Euclidean problem space is the basis of the very characteristic style of graphical reasoning found in most standard economics texts.) As we have seen, the problem space that many complex entities (such as Pareto optima) inhabit has some non-Euclidean and therefore counter-intuitive properties.

Second, it visualises rational choice as necessarily a matter of ranking all available options along a single scale and opting for the best. This interacts with a third element, the vision of the world as a regular and knowable place (provided you are prepared to pay the price for the knowledge, of course) and the result is a search for the optimum choice in many cases where the optimum is undefinable. For example, it ought to be possible to decide which of the available options for dealing with the possibility of climatic change is best, but in fact, there is no best: the classic approach to evaluating options relies on their probability-weighted costs (the PWC of an event costing $100, that might occur with a probability of 3 per cent is $3, etc.), but this breaks down if you know neither the list of consequences nor their costs and probabilities accurately enough to prevent different neutral observers drawing different conclusions from the same set of vague data. Rational strategies for such ill-structured choices centre on carving out potentially effective coalitions and building commitment to managing the partly-unforseeable consequences of choice (see Smith (1990) and Appendix 4.1); yet this option is hidden somewhere in the void if you share the paradigm. The regularity-and-stability element is also responsible for the invisibility of chaos and it has implications for the durability of the planning model of development (see Appendix 4.2).

Third, there is a complex of interacting elements – perhaps some of the most interesting ones – including the images of human nature (that people are 'really' or 'essentially' individualistic competitive actors) and of the rigid, objective external world that the paradigm embodies; the latter results in a posture of naive realism (the perception that the world exists independently of our preconceptions and theoretical frameworks). Together, this group of elements has a variety of odd manifestations (the idea that 'there is no society' for example), but their biggest practical impact has undoubtedly been in the area of common property resources (CPR – open rangeland, aquifers, etc). Hardin (1968) built his thesis of the 'tragedy of the commons' on ideas of the essential nature of man derived from Hobbes. Hobbes

– in arguing that man invented certain social institutions to curb his own 'natural' myopic individualism – inferred that 'nature' from observing the behaviour of outcasts *from* society and assumed that it would also be the 'nature' of (very) hypothetical people existing *before* society. Hardin's thesis is that CPRs will always be wrecked by the competitive interaction of acquisitive individuals; in his view, people will always pursue their short-term advantage, to the detriment of the long-term advantage of all. (He does not explain why he ignores the possibility of a further invention of social institutions, following Hobbes's pattern.) There has recently been a substantial volume of criticism of this thesis from a variety of sources. These include: institutional economics (challenges to the idea that real people do or should indulge in the sort of one-shot, short-term optimisation proposed in the model of 'economic man', which are based on the theories of repeated and co-operative games, see for example Schotter (1981)); operations research (challenges to the alleged fragility of co-operation in the face of individualistic behaviour, derived also from game-theoretic modelling of situations of temptation to defect from coalitions, see for example Axelrod (1984)); from sociology and the sociology of science (material identifying Hardin's thesis as an element of a particular set of cultures at a particular time and place rather than a permanent unavoidably logical necessity, see for example Elster (1983)); and from socio-legal sources, especially within World Bank, that are suggesting innovative alternatives to the current institutional frameworks for property rights in range production (Bromley and Cernea, 1989). If these newer perspectives are correct, they will centre remedies to the problems of CPR management on building long-term relationships among a stable set of actors concerned with the particular CPR, within which they can evolve collaborative strategies; supporting the creation/emergence of such strategies; ensuring that the actors have not constructed counter-productive theories about the nature of the resource, what will degrade it, what will enhance it and so forth; working on their theories of the social consequences of adopting particular strategies; and developing a system of prompt, unmistakable but non-persistent sanctions against defectors from common strategies (Axelrod, 1984).

Similar considerations arise in the water resources arena; this is particularly true of groundwater, which is much more nearly a 'typical' CPR than is riverflow. Throughout the arid and semi-arid parts of the tropics and sub-tropics, there is growing tension over the management of these resources, both within and between states. While all of the ideas in the preceding paragraph apply here, the author's current research suggests that a major limiting factor in developing management strategies which deal in a fair and acceptable way with this issue is precisely that the prevailing imagery denies the possibility of any strategy other than coercion (or the threat of coercion), and excludes all alternatives other than a decline into rabid destructive competition. (And, of course, the super-incumbent formal model of MFS prescribes exactly that, not as a desperate last expedient, but as first choice.) The whole situation is aggravated by the fact that the naive realism inherent in the paradigm thrusts the parties involved into the objectivist view of conflict (Mitchell, 1980), which makes a creative and peaceable resolution even more unlikely.

There are two interesting and significant implications in all this. The first by now should be obvious: you are trapped inside the world of limited Hobbesian/Hardinesque opportunities if and only if you see a world of atomistic individuals with extremely short time-horizons ('see', not 'see the world as' – Kuhn's distinction between these processes is important). Second, having seen such a world, we have gone on to act out our vision: we have actually made some parts of the world more like our image of it, by selectively attacking the mechanisms which build the long-term relationships central to collaboration. An excellent example is the way that successive administrations in the countries of the Middle East have attempted to deal with the perceived problems of 'degradation' of the dry rangelands: while attempting to install regulatory and formal remedies, they have generally promoted unrestricted access to those areas, so that the most critical component of any stable and persistent collaboration – a stable set of actors who share a long-term interest in the resource – is destroyed (Chatty, 1986). Society – despite naive realism – is not a given thing, existing independently of the way transactions within it are carried out: in a real sense, how you do it is what you get.

GENERAL IMPLICATIONS

Perhaps (although the precedents are not encouraging) the next time we face a situation of dissatisfaction with a dominant paradigm, we will consider the issue of the guarantor: those features of a specialised discipline that give the laity confidence in the validity and relevance of its prescriptions (Churchman, 1971). In the case of neoclassical economics, the guarantor seems to be a belief that the problems of creating policy (including development policy) can be solved by pure reason, operating from a set of universally acceptable axioms; and that high quality reason is assured by handing the whole issue over to academia, where a system of rewards for intellectual brilliance in construction and criticism will result in the mere survival of a theory being a guarantee of its truth. As we have seen, the flaw in this is that reason alone does not determine the content of the prescriptions of any discipline; always, there is some pre-existing imagery that makes the basic suppositions (and even some of the tools of reasoning) seem credible and obvious. When managing the flow of ideas that underpins all practical action, we need to be aware of this; often dissent aims itself at cases and consequences of the dominant viewpoint when it would be more productive to aim at the imagery behind it.

Practical action is not a question of sending for the one true theory and using that to create blueprint policies and programmes. All policy and action takes place within some paradigm, and the trick seems to be to explore the limitations of our own and the possibilities of others and to use the skills of coalition-building and management to cope with the inevitable flexibility and uncertainty of the resultant nexus of theory/paradigm/practice interactions. In essence, although some structured techniques and a lot of insights are available for these purposes, this is a plea to restore policy to the sphere of public administration and politics, and the *unfettered* market to its proper place, the pricing and exchange of goods which are either marginal to society's survival, or whose supply and demand has approached Schumpeter's 'circular state', that is, a situation of small, linear corrections to deviations around an existing well-established equilibrium. Outside this, the signals of the market do have some function – but they also need to be interpreted with caution. Many 'restrictive practices' may have a beneficial function in restraining wild transient responses; and it is surely no coincidence that the successes of the NICs (Newly Industrialising Countries) in South-East Asia have been built on a combination of reading the market and carefully crafted intervention (Amsden, 1989).

APPENDIX 4.1: MANAGING UNCERTAINTY: AN EXAMPLE

Because the strategies referred to may be unfamiliar a concrete example is provided from the eminently uncertain area of research management. In recent years there has been considerable interest in how research funds should be allocated between different agencies/activities, particularly in the major international centres supported by the CGIAR (Consultative Group on International Agricultural Research). One widely canvassed possibility is the use of a probability-weighted cost scheme of the type briefly described in the text; this is unsatisfactory for the reasons given – the outcome is sensitively dependent on the assumptions used to convert vague information (and even mere opinion) into something that looks like 'data'.

With this degree of uncertainty, the optimal choice is undefined; forcing people to re-express genuinely uncertain problems in the format of probabilistic risk drives them towards certain recognisable patterns of behaviour. The most obvious – and reasonable – of these is simply to cheat: to generate the 'data' in a way that supports favoured causes, preconceived ideas and personally-rewarding positions. Where efficient audit prevents this, the choice becomes biased towards safe activities, that is, those whose outcomes are predictable.

Another common route out of the dilemma is for would-be scientific entrepreneurs to convert the problem to a bridge-style bidding game: more ambitious forecasts to funding agencies of the return on investing in the entrepreneur's activities are more likely to secure money, but carry the risks of not making the required number of tricks and of breaching some ill-defined credibility barrier. If the bid succeeds, the entrepreneur and his/her associates *have* to make it good by managing the flow of opportunity and disaster that ensues; and there is no objectively optimal choice, because this latter process depends on the actors' perceptions of their personal skills and resources. This is not choosing the optimal course of action: it is making the chosen course optimal. Like most strategies for handling uncertainty, it centres on a group which has found (or been brought together by) some issue on which they are prepared to commit themselves, to act and to deal with the largely unforeseeable consequences of action – including in the extreme case, managing damage limitation, salvage and escape.

It is, of course, possible to envisage a more structured version of this in which members of an institution are encouraged to explore their paradigms, with a view to finding a concensus (or concensi) around which such commitment could be built.

APPENDIX 4.2: THE MFS PARADIGM AND THE SURVIVAL OF PLANNING

There can be little doubt that blueprint approaches – despite the mass of evidence on their weaknesses – persist precisely because of the image of a stable and predictable world; planning *looks* as though it must be a necessary and sufficient condition for successful action, and the effort and loss of control implicit in learning-process approaches seem correspondingly pointless. This re-emphasises one of the central messages of paradigm studies: if you wish to change a paradigm-controlled situation, you have to realise that it is imagery – not logic – that you are operating with; for interesting histories of the strategies people use in such situations see Mandelbrot (1982) and Feyerbend (1978).

References

Amsden, A. H. (1989) *Asia's Next Giant: South Korea and Late Industrialisation* (Oxford: Oxford University Press).

Axelrod, R. (1984) *The Evolution of Cooperation* (Harmondsworth: Penguin).

Bromley, D. W. and M. M. Cernea (1989) *The Management of Common Property Natural Resources*, World Bank Discussion Paper 57 (Washington DC: World Bank).

Campbell, M., M. Hardy and N. Healy (1991) *Controversy in Applied Economics* (Brighton: Harvester-Wheatsheaf).

Chatty, D. (1986) *From Camel to Truck: Bedouin in the Modern World* (New York: Vantage Press).

Chiarella, C. (1988) 'The Cobweb Model: Its Instability and the Onset of Chaos', *Economic Modelling*, vol. 8, 377–84.

Churchman, C. W. (1971) *The Design of Inquiring Systems* (New York: Basic Books).

Douglas, M. (ed.) (1982) *Essays in the Sociology of Perception* (London: Routledge & Kegan Paul).

Douglas, M. (1986) *How Institutions Think* (Syracuse, NY: University of Syracuse Press).

Eckert, R. D. and R. H. Leftwich (1988) *The Price System and Resource Allocation* (Chicago: Dryden).

Elster, J. (1983) *Explaining Technical Change* (Cambridge: Cambridge University Press).

Evans-Pritchard, E. E. (1976) *Witchcraft, Oracles and Magic Among the Azande* (Oxford: Clarendon Press).

Feder, J. (1989) *Fractals* (New York: Plenum).

Feyerbend, P. (1978) *Against Method* (London: Verso).

Gleick, J. (1987) *Chaos* (London: Sphere Books).

Hardin, G. (1968) 'The Tragedy of the Commons', *Science*, vol. 162, 1243–8.

Hartley, K. (1977) *Problems of Economic Policy* (London: George Allen & Unwin).

Hoffman, W. M. and J. M. Moore (1990) *Business Ethics* (New York: McGraw-Hill).

Horton, R. (1970) 'African Traditional Thought and Medicine' in B. Wilson (ed.), *Rationality* (Oxford: Basil Blackwell).

Kenen, P. B. (1989) *The International Economy* (Englewood Cliffs, NJ: Prentice Hall).

Kuhn, T. (1970) *The Structure of Scientific Revolutions* (Chicago: University of Chicago Press).

Lakatos, I. and A. Musgrave (1970) *Criticism and the Growth of Knowledge* (Cambridge and New York: Cambridge University Press).

Lancaster, R. K. and R. G. Lipsey (1956) 'The General Theory of the Second Best', *Review of Economic Studies*, vol. 24, no. 63, 11–32.

Laudan, L. (1977) *Progress and its Problems* (Berkeley: University of California Press).

Letwin, O. (1988) *Privatising the World* (London: Cassell).

Littlechild, S. C. (1986) 'Three Types of Market Process' in R. N. Langlois (ed.) (1986) *Economics as a Process* (Cambridge: Cambridge University Press).

Mandelbrot, B. (1982) *The Fractal Geometry of Nature* (San Francisco: Freeman).

Mitchell, C. (1980) *Conflict and the Consultants Role* (Aldershot: Gower).
Peters, E. E. (1991) *Chaos and Growth in the Capital Markets* (New York: Wiley).
Sandefur, J. (1990) *Discrete Dynamical Systems* (Oxford: Clarendon Press).
Schotter, A. (1981) *The Economic Theory of Social Institutions* (Cambridge: Cambridge University Press).
Schumpter, J. A. (1961) *The Theory of Economic Development* (trans. R. Opie) (Oxford: Oxford University Press).
Schwartz, J. T. (1978) 'Mathematics as a Tool of Economic Understanding' In L. A. Steen, *Mathematics Today* (New York: Springer-Verlag).
Sheffrin, M. (1983) *Rational Expectations* (Cambridge: Cambridge University Press).
Smith, P. J. (1990) 'Redefining Decision: Implications for Managing Risk and Uncertainity', *Disasters*, vol. 14, 230–40.
—— (1991a) *Deregulation and Market Forces in Policy Formulation*, Discussion Paper 25 (IDPM, Manchester University).
—— (1991b) *A Chaotic Market Price Model*, Discussion Paper 30 (IDPM, Manchester University).
—— (1991c) *Managers and their Theories*, Discussion Paper 24 (IDPM, Manchester University).
Spradley, J. P. (ed.) (1972) *Culture and Cognition* (San Francisco: Chandler).
Stewart, I. (1989) *Does God Play Dice?* (Harmondsworth: Penguin).
Toye, J. (1987) *Dilemmas of Development* (Oxford: Basil Blackwell).
Urban, R. and R. V. Jensen (1989) 'Chaotic Behaviour in a Nonlinear Cobweb Model', *Economics Letters*, vol. 15, 235-40.
Wildavsky, A. (1980) *Budgeting* (New York: Academic Press).

5 Disadvantaging Comparative Advantages: The Problem of Decreasing Returns*

KUNIBERT RAFFER

The effects of increasing returns to scale have been discussed for quite some time by economists focusing on trade theory. By contrast, the case of decreasing returns has not received much attention so far. Even though this latter case was classified as posing little analytical difficulty by Jones and Neary (1984, p. 48), it is of particular interest because absolutely rational specialisation according to (static) comparative costs may finally result in immiserisation and decreased (global) output.

These negative effects of trade were analysed by Graham (1923). They are the result of one country specialising in a product subject to decreasing returns to scale. Graham's case, once hotly discussed, soon faded from public attention. In recent literature Helpman (1984, p. 332ff) touched on Graham's debate with Knight again, describing Graham's case briefly and correctly. After establishing sufficient conditions for a country to gain from trade Helpman showed how losses from free trade may occur in models with internationally and with nationally increasing returns to scale. In both cases he assumed a two-product world with one sector subject to increasing and the other to constant returns. The latter case of nationally increasing returns is specifically quoted as a confirmation of 'Graham's argument that a country may lose from trade' (ibid. 1984, p. 346). Helpman's model, though, goes even beyond Graham's case, which rests on the more restrictive assumption of a combination of increasing and decreasing returns.

Based on Viner's (1937) numerical presentation of Graham, this chapter will elaborate Graham's point more fully and show how it relates logically to two other approaches developed independently from Graham. In an admittedly less elegant way than Helpman's presentation it will be shown how a Graham constellation results in immiserising specialisation or, more

*For useful comment on an earlier version I am indebted to H. W. Singer and Adrian Wood.

pointedly expressed, disadvantaging comparative advantages. Graham's case, where one country specialises in raw materials, will then be combined with the findings of Raúl Prebisch (1949) and H. W. Singer (1950) for raw material exporting countries, and the new non-Marxist theory of Unequal Exchange (Raffer, 1987a).

In 1923 Frank Graham demonstrated the unpleasant sensitivity of the theorem of comparative advantages to changes in the not very realistic assumptions of constant costs. If it is dropped, specialisation, according to the theorem, may result in decreases in global and national production, and a diminished global GDP. Free trade may make people worse off.

Graham showed that if one partner specialises in a product with increasing returns to scale, such as watches, while the other produces a good subject to decreasing returns, for example, corn, while all other assumptions of the Ricardian case hold, global output might *decrease*. The country specialising in the product with diminishing returns will find itself in a less favourable position than before. In Graham's case country B, specialising in corn, a product with increasing unit costs, loses by trade. Graham showed convincingly that it can be disadvantageous for a country to specialise in goods with increasing unit costs even though specialisation is according to the theorem of comparative advantages, if unit costs depend on output. This result was apparently surprising enough to make his contemporaries label his case Graham's Paradox.

The last textbook discussing Graham in an attempt to disprove his logic seems to have been Viner's (1937). But instead of destroying the case Viner elaborated it even better than its author. Using Viner's figures, Table 5.1 presents the effects of Graham's assumptions, comparing Graham's case with the usual textbook (Ricardo/Torrens) outcome. Viner apparently chose his figures to illustrate Graham's point clearly.

Following both Graham and Viner the elements of the matrices in Table 5.1 are average productivities. In contrast to the traditional Torrens/Ricardo presentation, however, average and marginal costs (or productivities) are no longer identical in Graham's case. Marginal costs are decisive for specialisation since they determine prices in competitive markets. This poses no problem at all, because the theorem of comparative costs applies at the margin as well (see Graham, 1923; Viner, 1937, p. 471). Logical accuracy demands the addition of an assumption neither Graham nor Viner mention. The relations of productivities at the margin are identical to the relations of the averages at all stages in Table 5.1. This assumption simplifies the presentation of their numerical example conveniently, but it is not a necessary condition for Graham's case. As long as the two vectors of marginal productivities are linearly independent a limbo allowing gains for

Table 5.1 Graham's case (as presented by Viner)

Basic Assumptions: Countries A and B both have 400 Units of (nationally standardised, or homogeneous) Labour (LU); both produce Corn and Watches initially, then specialising according to Comparative Advantages; the international price (≡ net barter terms of trade) remains at 4C = 3.5W (or: $P_{intl} = 0.875$)

(1) Constant returns (Ricardian) case:
production per LU (≡ productivity)

	A	B
C	4	4
W	4	3

$$P_b = 0.75\ (4C = 3W) \leq P_{intl} = 0.875 \leq P_a = 1$$

Ricardian limbo = difference between domestic prices P_a and P_b
Changes in total production:
(LUs used to produce C and W respectively)

	Specialisation I			*Specialisation II*			*Total specialisation*		
	A	B	Σ(A+B)	A	B	Diff.*	A	B	Diff.*
C	800	800	1600	400	1200	0	0	1600	0
(LU)	(200)	(200)		(100)	(300)			(400)	
W	800	600	1400	1200	300	*+100*	1600	0	*+200*
(LU)	(200)	(200)		(300)	(100)		(400)		

(2) Graham's case:

	Specialisation II			*Specialisation III*		
		A	B		A	B
Productivity:	C	4.5	3.5	C	5	0.5
	W	4.5	2	W	5	0.25

$0.571 < P_{intl} = 0.875 < 1$ $0.5 < P_{intl} = 0.875 < 1$

Changes in total production:

	Specialisation II			*Specialisation III*			*Total specialisation*		
	A	B	Diff.†	A	B	Diff.†	A	B	Diff.†
C	450	1050	−100	5	199,5	−1395,5	0	200	−1400
(LU)	(100)	(300)		(1)	(399)			(400)	
W	1350	200	+150	1995	0,25	+595,25	2000	0	+600
(LU)	(300)	(100)		(399)	(1)		(400)		

* Difference in comparison with Specialisation I
† Difference to production in Specialisation I

both sides exists at the margin. Countries A and B will go on specialising in watches and corn respectively as long as $a_w/a_c > b_w/bc$, where a and b are A's and B's marginal productivities in w(atches) and c(orn).

The stage 'Specialisation I' may be interpreted as autarky, as is usually done in the traditional Ricardo/Torrens model, or as a stage where trade is restricted by, for example, quotas. It can be seen at once that Specialisation I is clearly better for B than strong specialisation. B's real income plummets from (800C + 600W) to only 200W because of specialisation on B's comparative advantage.

Changes of the GDPs of A, B, and the 'world' at different stages of specialisation resulting from Graham/Viner example are shown in Table 5.2. By specialising entirely in watches Country A increases its GDP dramatically by one-third or one-quarter respectively, depending on whether one measures in international or domestic prices. B's GDP, on the other hand, is reduced to less than one-seventh of its Specialisation I GDP at Viner's constant P_{intl}. Measuring it in B's domestic prices the loss is naturally more pronounced because of the deterioration of corn's domestic terms of trade.

In cases where more of W and less of C are produced, increases might or might not offset the values of decreases, as Pareto (1927, pp. 507ff) already observed, arguing that Ricardo's example was a possible, but not at all a necessary result of trade. Thus, clear statements on B's real income will not always be possible. Graham's case, however, has convincingly shown that specialisation according to comparative advantages *need not* have the beneficial effects often ascribed to it by economic policy advisers.

Global GDP at the stage Specialisation II deserves particular attention. It is higher than in Specialisation I due to A's gains, which more than compensate B's losses. In other words: an increase of global production through trade as well as a dramatic decrease of one trading country's production may result from Graham/Viner assumptions. The value of B's GDP depends, of course, on prices used to calculate it, which prompts the question: could B's loss in productivity be compensated by increases in the price of its corn?

Let us assume that B could trade at the upper limit of the Ricardian limbo, viz. at an international price of 1 or A's domestic terms of trade. This is the best deal B can get according to orthodoxy as A would refuse to trade at a price above the Ricardian limbo. Measured in international prices B's GDP at Specialisation II would then be 1250 W or 1250 C. Comparison with B's GDP measured at domestic prices (see Table 5.2) gives ambiguous results, as 1250 W is 50 W more than B's Specialisation I GDP (at domestic prices) expressed in W, but at the same time 350 C less than the same GDP expressed in corn. Also, 1250 W (or C) is clearly less than B's

Table 5.2 GDPs of A, B, and the 'world' under Graham/Viner assumptions

(1) GDPs at P_{intl} (4C = 3.5W)	*Specialisation I*	*Specialisation II*	*Total specialisation*
Country A			
in Corn units	1 714.3 C	1 992.86 C	2 285.7 C
in Watches	1 500.0 W	1 743.75 W	2 000.0 W
Country B			
in Corn units	1 485.7 C	1 278.57 C	200.0 C
in Watches	1 300.0 W	1 118.75 W	175.0 W
World (Σ A + B)			
in Corn units	3 200.0 C	3 271.43 C	2 485.7 C
in Watches	2 800.0 W	2 862.90 W	2 175.0 W
(2) GDPs at Domestic Prices			
Country A			
Corn/Watches	1 600 C or W	1 800 C or W	2 000 C or W
Country B			
in Corn units	1 600 C	1 400.00 C	200 C
in Watches	1 200 W	799.55 W	100 W

Specialisation I GDP measured by Viner's international price, which one might use, arguing that B could immediately trade its goods produced under Specialisation I at these prices when trade opens. Within the restrictions of the Ricardian limbo there exists no price in Viner's example at which B's GDP increases unequivocally.

The problem of prices is even more important if we drop the rather drastic changes in productivity Viner used to present Graham's argument so clearly, as lower productivity can be more easily compensated by higher prices of the good becoming scarcer because of specialisation. As supply curve shifts to the left create excess demand and result in higher prices, one could argue that compensation is built into the market mechanism unless changes are extraordinarily large.

According to standard neoclassical assumptions increased productivity would finally benefit the consumer (importer) as reduced production costs must result in lower prices. In the perfectly competitive equilibrium prices equal marginal costs, and – in the long run – average costs. Increasing returns to scale in watchmaking, as well as increasing costs in corn production due to the necessity of using less suitable land, more fertilisers and so on, must move NBToTs (Net Barter Terms of Trade) against A.

This productivity-induced fall in international watch prices does not, of course, not lead to A's immiseration. The effect on factor incomes can be shown with Double Factoral Terms of Trade (DFToTs), which are defined as

$$NBToTs(F_x/F_m) \equiv P_xF_x/P_mF_m \quad (1)$$

where F are productivity indices for exports (subscript x) and imports (m) respectively. If F_x doubles, halving P_x, DFToTs remain unchanged. The fall in prices is compensated by productivity increases. Constant DFToTs mean simply that productivity gains are not appropriated by one group but evenly distributed by the market mechanism among all those buying the product. In this case it actually would not matter what a country specialises in. Obviously, the essential neoclassical postulate that homogenous factors of production must command the same price in a perfectly competitive market, or factors of production are paid equally according to their contributions to production but irrespective of location, gender or race demands DFToTs = 1.

The distribution of gains does not follow from the comparative advantages model. Thus it has become usual to say that if a country did not gain by trading it would not do it. International prices must therefore remain within the limbo – no country will sell below its own domestic price. John Stuart Mill, by the way, did not fully share this view, stating once that goods might often be obtained from foreigners 'at a smaller expense of labour and capital than they *cost* to the foreigners themselves'(1976, p. 576, emphasis mine). Unfortunately he did not analyse this problem more fully.

In Viner's example the Ricardian limbo widens substantially from [1, 0.75] to [1, 0.5] putting B, the country specialising on the product with decreasing returns to scale, more and more at a disadvantage. Or, while the industrial country enjoys increased productivity, the raw material-exporting country gets less and less productive – underdevelopment starts growing. It should be noted that Portugal, which was made to specialise in wine by the Methuen Treaty rather than the market, produces both goods more efficiently in Ricardo's example, a fact which puzzled many economists both on the 'right' and on the 'left' later on. Samir Amin (1976, p. 134) inverts the example 'so as to bring it closer to reality'. Samuelson (1976, p. 100) speaks of the 'bizarre assumption of Ricardo that England is poor and Portugal rich'. Historical facts, however, show that Portugal was indeed rich, and Ricardo did apparently chose the right figures (compare, for example, List, 1920, p. 141).

The minimum international price at which B still 'gains' from trade (in the sense of static comparative advantages) falls below the initial limbo interval. This loss in productivity derives from higher production of a good, where higher quantities can only be produced at increasing costs per unit, while cutting back on the manufacture of the product (watches) where increasing output decreases unit costs. Conversely A shifting out of the decreasing returns activity and specialising on watches enjoys ever increasing productivity. By specialising *against* its comparative advantage, reducing its corn production and increasing its watch production, B would have become more productive in both industries.

The widening of the Ricardian limbo means, to put it plainly, that international prices initially unacceptable to B, for example, 0.6, become 'advantageous'. NBToTs can fall below the initial lower threshold of the limbo, which allows the industrial country to depress the NBToTs of its trading partner more easily without providing A any incentive to pass its own productivity gains onto B via lower prices. At the stage of Specialisation III, B would still have an incentive to specialise according its comparative advantage and to exchange internationally at $P_{intl} = 0.501 > P_b = 0.5$. At this stage into which B manoeuvred itself by specialising, any price above 0.5 offers apparent gains by exchange. The decision rule of comparative advantages would demand further specialisation, which would actually bring about a relative (and small) gain. In comparison with the starting point, which we called Specialisation I, however, B has lost enormously. Its real income has crumbled to 80C + 60.12W.

Two different effects emerge clearly: a positive effect of gains by exchange, shown by the gap between international and domestic prices, and a second effect of productivity changes triggered by increased output, which is extremely negative in Viner's presentation of Graham. Transfixed by his own didactic success in elaborating Graham's case, Viner did not explore the implications of Graham's case further but retreated to defending free trade with less than brilliantly convincing arguments. He failed, moreover, to show that both countries may still gain by trade under Graham's assumption if productivity decreases are sufficiently low.

It is important to note that the existence of decreasing returns in at least one product is a necessary but not a sufficient condition for Graham's case. Trade disadvantages only if specialisation losses outweigh specialisation gains – which, depending on production functions, may, but need not, be the case.

If B's productivity losses are smaller than its gains by exchange, both countries could gain by trade. If, for example, B's productivity vector changed to (3.9, 2.8) instead of (3.5, 2.0) in Specialisation II (A's productivity remaining constant) global output would increase, as in the textbook case, to (1620 C + 1630 W), namely (20 C + 230 W) more than under Specialisation I. The limbo would widen much less dramatically to [1, 0.7179487].

If B's productivities changed at the same rate – for example, to (3.9, 2.925) – P_b and thus the limbo would not change at all. At Viner's constant international price B's GDP would have increased slightly to 1,303.75 W or 1,490 C. If lower production costs in A and greater supply of watches drove their international price down, NBToTs would change in B's favour, or – in other words – the fruits of progress would be distributed to all consumers globally. B's GDP expressed in watches would increase. As long as DFToTs remained constant the whole 'world' would equally benefit from specialisation and it would, indeed, not matter what a country specialises in.

Graham's effect is not restricted to the combination of increasing and decreasing returns to scale, the case discussed by both Graham and Viner. If country A had constant unit costs while B was subject to decreasing returns, Graham's case might develop as well. If both countries specialised in products subject to decreasing returns to scale, losses would compound.

If, on the other hand, constant returns in A combine with increasing returns of the product B specialises in, global welfare, measured in the traditional way as more goods, must necessarily increase under Graham's assumptions. Finally, if both countries of the textbook world specialised in products enjoying increasing returns to scale this situation may be called Cockaigne or Paradise Regained. Compound positive effects would trigger a veritable welfare boom.

These clarifications seem to be necessary because rare references to Graham might otherwise be misleading. An example is Krugman (1990, p. 65), who writes: 'In a sense, the Marshallian approach to the analysis of trade under increasing returns goes back to Graham's famous argument for protection (Graham, 1923)', discussing then the case of increasing combined with constant returns. This, however, is, as already shown above, not at all Graham's problem, which emerges if and only if returns to scale decrease sufficiently.

Viner tried to find explicit counter-arguments to defend free trade. His most important point is that by moving to Specialisation II producers in B would lose 400 watches to get 250 units of corn at a time when 400 watches could buy 457 C in the international market (Viner, 1937, pp. 479f). Thus no resources would be transferred from watchmaking to corngrowing in B.

There is, however, one important flaw in this argument. According to standard microeconomic theory, producers maximise profits rather than volumes. The usual assumptions of perfect factor mobility within each country and perfect competition must have brought about equilibria with one single rate of profit for both industries in each country. According to the perception of classical economists, such as Ricardo, this would be a positive percentage of capital invested. Neoclassicists, by contrast, would think of a mathematically more elegant long-run equilibrium where marginal costs equal average costs and the rate of profit is zero. Be that as it may, the new option of selling at $P_{intl} > P_b$ allows producers in B (extra) profits inducing them to trade. As long as this difference between domestic and international prices widens – as it does in Viner's presentation – the incentive to export will increase. Under the assumptions of a perfectly competitive and free global market, where one product cannot be traded at two prices, and a constant P_{intl}, domestic prices will, of course, finally disappear, leaving P_{intl} as the only price in the market. This damaging export drive in B can only be stopped by government intervention – which is exactly Graham's point.

Regarding North–South trade, which closely resembled Graham's pattern of manufactures traded for raw materials, the line of argument presented earlier led economists initially to expect NBToTs of the South to improve, although not merely because of industrial economies of scale, but also because of stronger technical progress in the North. Regarding price relations, economies of scale and technical progress have the same effect: both reduce costs, which must lead to lower prices in a functioning market. As Spraos (1983, p. 21) pointed out, this was 'the dominant a priori view' on NBToTs. It necessarily results from the neoclassical model, which was not challenged until 1949. As was shown above, increasing NBToTs of the South would even have allowed outweighing not too large Graham-type specialisation losses. So one could conveniently assume that actual trade was in fact as beneficial as its academic model.

The Prebisch-Singer Thesis (PST) rocked the boat of professional complacency, exposing an apparent contradiction between theoretical expectations and practical outcome. Secularly deteriorating NBToTs of the South as documented by the seminal work of Prebisch (1949) and Singer (1950) destroy the whole established logic based on a beneficial world market (see Raffer, 1986). Unfortunately, however, the PST was reduced to a purely statistical debate on freight rates and the reliability of data, while Prebisch's main point – that the world market does not allow the periphery to benefit appropriately from technical progress – quickly vanished from sight.

It remains to be asked why critics usually did not bother to note that those criticised had themselves been aware of these problems. Both Singer (1950, p. 477) and Prebisch (1949, p. 360) drew attention to quality problems in their historic data. Many of the criticisms brought forward 'were already acknowledged at some length in the United Nation paper ... which Prebisch had indicated as the source of British data.' (Spraos, 1980, p. 107).

While the discussion of whether a negative trend can be proved statistically is both interesting and important, one must not forget that secularly falling NBToTs of the South are a sufficient, not a necessary condition for the loss of productivity gains, or what may be called the core of the PST. If international markets and trade behaved according to academic predictions and models NBToTs would have had to improve for SCs. As productivity has grown faster in the North, global income relations (DFToTs) can only remain constant *if* NBToTs move against the North, distributing the fruits of technical progress equally (see Prebisch, 1949, p. 360). In this case it really would not matter what product a country specialises in. If trade is expected to narrow wage differences, as the factor price equalisation theorem suggests, NBToTs would have to increase even more in favour of the South. At constant NBToTs, however, DFToTs deteriorate, that is global disparities in factor incomes increase. Trading disadvantages the periphery. Export earnings are lower than they should be according to neoclassical theory, and resources needed to finance development are lost. This is the core of the PST so perfectly obfuscated by the discussion which followed. A declining trend of the periphery's NBToTs merely reinforces the fall of DFToTs (see Raffer, 1986). There is, however, no statistical underpinning at all for improving NBToTs of the South.

This unequalising drive of foreign trade, or the siphoning off of income by the North as Prebisch called it, is only theoretically possible if factor incomes increase in accordance with technical progress in the centre. Again, Prebisch and Singer pointed out that exactly this had happened, helping to create the enormous capacity to save and hence to finance technical progress in the centre.

To explain how the North could siphon off productivity gains the authors offered perfectly traditional explanations, mostly excess demand and excess supply. Factors contributing to falling NBToTs – sometimes wrongly called different 'versions' of the PST – are:

— the *low income elasticity of commodity exports:* Northern demand for raw materials increases less than GDP-growth, limiting growth prospects of Periphery Country (PC) exports. While this view was hotly attacked initially, it has since been generally accepted (see for example IMF, 1987, p. 218; or IBRD, 1987, p. 18). Strong expansion of raw material exports thus tends to create excess supply;
— *low elasticities of demand:* lower prices of periphery exports do not stimulate demand sufficiently to make up for lost revenues;
— *necessary imports* to promote development, such as machinery, and so on, can only be imported from the centre. In contrast to the centre the periphery's income elasticity of imports is high. Developmental needs result in excess demand;

— *cultural dependence*, or the waste of resources for luxury consumption, increases total Southern demand but imports products of little or no use for the country's development;
— *oversupply of labour* in PCs keeping wages down;
— *(absence of) market power of factors of production:* workers (trade unions) and entrepreneurs in the North have sufficient market power to keep Northern prices from falling along with technical progress. The lack of such power in PCs forces their prices down. This 'para-market' assumption of the Prebisch-Singer Thesis (PST) was strongly attacked by critics of the PST (cf. Spraos, 1983, pp. 23f). Considering that orthodox economists had blamed the Great Depression of the 1930s on union power and stickiness of wages in Northern economies this is certainly surprising;
— *protection by the centre* restricts export outlets, increasing the pressure of surplus labour in SCs, giving additional force to the deteriorating trend. Because of the lower income elasticity of demand for imports in the centre (compared with the periphery), protectionism in the centre increases market disequilibria created by the disparity of export possibilities and import needs of SCs.

More recently Singer (1991) has added *debt pressure*, the need to service debts forcing PCs to export at any cost as an important factor depressing the NBToTs of indebted countries.

Important arguments of Prebisch's and Singer's can be traced back to Graham. Defending his point of disadvantageous trade he argues that there is no reason to suppose that A's falling unit costs and B's increasing costs would be reflected in a shift of NBToTs in favour of B. Driven by the play of reciprocal demand NBToTs may well move against B (Graham, 1923, pp. 210f; pp. 215f). Graham (1923, p. 217) already mentions decreasing income elasticities of demand for raw materials 'in the last century and a half' as one reason for deteriorating NBToTs of raw material exporters. Or:

> It may well be disadvantageous for a nation to concentrate in production of commodities of increasing cost despite a comparative advantage in those lines; it will the more probably be disadvantageous to do so if the world demand for goods produced at decreasing costs is growing in volume more rapidly than that for goods produced at increasing costs, while at the same time competition in the supply of the former grows relatively less intense as compared with competition in the supply of the latter. For in this case the operation of the law of reciprocal demand will throw the terms of exchange of commodities more and more to the

> disadvantage of the country producing the goods of increasing cost. (Graham, 1923, pp. 213f)

Expressed in modern jargon, excess supply of B's exports and excess demand by B may tilt NBToTs against B. Graham does not fail to point out that A producing less corn becomes more productive in corn as well and can more easily check a movement of NBToTs in favour of B, while increased unit costs of watches in B work against country B as well (ibid., p. 216).

Graham does not forget to mention that real wages will rise in A, or A's factors of production will keep prices from falling along with costs; 'This movement of wages will prevent any tendency towards readjustment of the terms of exchange ... in favour of the increasing costs good' (ibid., p. 215). By keeping NBToTs constant Viner has implicitly but quite clearly underlined this point of Graham's.

The fall of B's NBToTs and DFToTs is facilitated by the widening of the Ricardian limbo. Thus Graham's case provides a theoretical underpinning of the PST on the basis of the theorem of comparative costs. Furthermore it combines extremely well with the more recent non-Marxist approach to Unequal Exchange (Raffer, 1987).

Graham as well as the PST focused on raw material exporters, even though Prebisch (1976, p. 66) clearly stated that there is no inherent or irreversible intrinsic quality of raw materials dooming them to deteriorating NBToTs. Deterioration occurs when increases in production outstrip the growth of demand – that is, the periphery wants to sell more than the centre wants to buy. This, of course, could equally well happen in the case of manufactures (cf. Prebisch, 1959, p. 258f), but Prebisch never brought manufactures fully into his analysis. Singer has recently extended research on the PST to manufactures (Sarkar and Singer, 1991).

Unequal Exchange theory does not differentiate between raw materials and manufactures either. The main argument of non-Marxist Unequal Exchange theory (for details see Raffer, 1987a; 1987b) is that exports – be they raw materials or manufactures – have different specific importance, depending on how urgently a product is needed and how easily it can be replaced. The exporter who has specialised in the more important product or service can change both NBToTs and DFToTs in his/her favour. It therefore matters what a country specialises in. PCs are characterised by exports which are either easily substituted for – at least for a longer period than a PC would afford not to sell – or amenities on which the smooth running of Northern economies does not depend, while Southern economies depend crucially on imports from the North. Individual problems of PCs, such as urgent need of foreign exchange to service debts, and different forms of substitution limit possible price increases. These constraints impose an upper barrier to improvements in NBToTs and DFToTs, which can best be illustrated by the example of raw materials. Substitution may take the form of:

— *country substitution:* a PC trying to increase its export prices substantially and persistently will simply lose its market share to another country offering the same product at lower prices;
— *product substitution:* the product whose price increase is substituted by another product. Copper by fibreglass, cane sugar by beet sugar, or jute by plastics are good examples;
— *technical change:* recycling or ocean-floor mining are good examples in the field of raw materials;
— *stocks:* this is the most important short-run instrument to stop attempts to raise prices. It has been frequently used by industrialised countries to fight price strategies of Southern exporters;
— *domestic production capacities,* protected if uncompetitive.

The best index to measure the specific importance of a product is its producer's pricing power or the reaction of the purchaser – more technically the specific elasticity of demand. If demand is highly elastic upwards a seller cannot increase the price without losing income. As the reaction of purchasers depends on the market share of the seller and substitution possibilities the index for the capacity to increase prices proposed by Raffer is

$$- |\eta_i| = \left[- |\eta_{wi}| - \sum_j e_{rij} \; s_{rj} \right] s_i^{-1} \qquad (2)$$

Verbally: the specific elasticity of demand of a product exported by country i equals the cross elasticity of global demand for this product (η_{wi}) plus the sum of all cross elasticities of supply from all other sources (e_{rij}) times their respective shares (s_{rj}) divided by the share of the exporter (s_i). Equation (2) differs from usual econometric estimations: first, it uses arc-elasticities because quantity reactions are not independent of the size of price changes; second, reactions of demand are inferred from potential substitution at higher prices rather than by extrapolating past experience from 'business as usual'.

Demand for raw materials is, on the other hand, usually rather inelastic downwards, that is, *vis-à-vis* price reductions (Raffer, 1992), as already observed by Prebisch and Singer. Substantially higher prices are excluded, but not lower prices. Excess supply and excess demand, very much as with the PST, are possible reasons. PCs are thus locked in the worst of all possible worlds. Excess supply might also be the result of debt pressure or the routine advice by the Bretton Woods Twins to increase exports.

Graham explained why B should adopt protection as a rational policy, but not why the industrialised country A reaping all advantages of trade might do so. There is a need for an explanation of actual trade policies of industrialised countries, especially protectionism in agrarian trade. Combining Graham's case with Raffer's Unequal Exchange provides it. Food (corn) is apparently a product with a high specific importance – it is easier to survive one month without watches than without food. If A became dependent on importing corn B could increase the price of corn, even beyond the Ricardian limbo, for example if corngrowing skills were forgotten in A after some time. By safeguarding some domestic production, A can avoid this danger as well as shocks resulting from repeated substantial changes of a less than perfectly and instantly malleable production structure.

This conclusion should not be misunderstood as implying that any protectionist measure makes sense – the EEC's or the US agrarian policies would disprove this perception most forcefully. It does, however, caution that protectionist measures are not by necessity economically unsound. Like free trade, protection has positive and negative aspects. Analysing the merits and pitfalls of both more fully and objectively is a task economists have still to turn to.

After elaborating Graham's case further this paper has integrated it with two other, independently developed, dissenting views on the effects of trade – the PST and non-Marxist Unequal Exchange theory – into a logically consistent theoretical framework. It has not exposed logical contradictions within the body of present neoclassic theory but shown the sensitivity of its welfare and policy conclusions to the assumptions made, especially constant returns to scale. Applying traditional tools of economic analysis this framework allows a more critical, and possibly more realistic analysis of trade and trade policy. Providing economically rational explanations for protectionism, it also helps bridge the often glaring gap between actual policies in international trade and policy advice given by most economists.

References

Amin, S. (1976) *Unequal Development, An Essay on the Social Transformations of Peripheral Capitalism* (Hassocks, Sussex, Harvester Press).

Graham, F. D. (1923) 'Some Aspects of Protection Further Considered', *Quarterly Journal of Economics*, vol. 37.

Helpman, E. (1984) 'Increasing Returns, Imperfect Markets, and Trade Theory' in R. W. Jones and P. B. Kenen (eds).

IBRD (1987) *World Development Report 1987* (New York: Oxford University Press).

IMF (1987) *IMF Survey*, July 13.

Jones, R. W. and P. S. Kenen (eds) (1984) *Handbook of International Economics*, vol. I (Amsterdam: North-Holland).

Jones, R. W. and J. P. Neary (1984) 'The Positive Theory of International Trade' in R. W. Jones and P. B. Kenen (eds), op. cit.

Krugman, P. R. (1990) *Rethinking International Trade* (Cambridge, Mass./London: MIT Press).

List, F. (1920) *Das nationale System der politischen œkonomie*, (3rd edn Jena: G. Fischer; originally published in 1841).

Mill, J. S. (1976) *Principles of Political Economy, with Some of Their Applications to Social Philosophy*, Reprints of Economic Classics, (ed.) with an introduction by Sir W. Ashley (Fairfield: A. Kelley).

Pareto, V. (1927) *Manuel d'Économie politique*, 2nd edn (Paris: Giard).

Prebisch, R. (1949) 'El desarrollo economico de la America latina y algunos de sus principales problemas', *El Trimestre Economico*, vol. XVI, no. 3 (Julio–Sept.) (English version published by UN-ECLA in 1950).

—— (1959) 'Commercial Policies in the Underdeveloped Countries' *American Economic Review, Papers and Proceedings*, (May) vol. 49.

—— (1976) 'A Critique of Peripheral Capitalism' *CEPAL Review*.

Raffer, K. (1986) 'Siphoning-Off Resources from the Periphery: The Relevance of Raúl Prebisch's Thinking for the Eighties', *Development & South-South Cooperation*, vol. II, no. 3 (December; Special Issue: 'Homage to Raúl Prebisch'), Reprinted in H. W. Singer, N. Hatti and R. Tandon (eds) (1991) *New World Order Series*, vol. 9: Aid and External Financing in the 1990s (New Delhi: Indus Publishing).

—— (1987a) *Unequal Exchange and the Evolution of the World System, Reconsidering the Impact of Trade on North – South Relations* (London/New York: Macmillan/St. Martin's Press).

—— (1987b) 'Unfavorable Specialisation and Dependence: The Case of Peripheral Raw Material Exporters', *World Development*, vol. 15, no. 5.

—— (1992) 'Structural Adjustment' or Debt Relief – The Case of Arab LDCs' in K. Raffer and M. A. M. Salih (eds), *The Least Developed and the Oil-Rich Arab Countries – Dependence, Interdependence or Patronage?* (London: Macmillan) (forthcoming).

Samuelson, P.A. (1976) 'Illogic of the Neo-Marxian Doctrine of Unequal Exchange' in D. Belsley et al. (eds), *Inflation, Trade and Taxes: Essays in Honour of Alice Bourneuf* (Columbus: Ohio State University).

Sarkar, P. and H. W. Singer (1991) 'Manufactured Exports of Developing Countries and Their Terms of Trade since 1965', *World Development*, vol. 19, no. 4.

Singer, H. W. (1950) 'The Distribution of Gains between Investing and Borrowing Countries', *American Economic Review, Papers and Proceedings*, vol. XL.

—— (1991) 'Terms of Trade – New Wine and New Bottles?', *IDS Sussex*, 5 June 1991 (mimeo).

Spraos, J., (1980) 'The Statistical Debate on the Net Barter Terms of Trade Between Primary Products and Manufactures', *Economic Journal*, vol. 90.

—— (1983) *Inequalising Trade? A Study of Traditional North/South Specialisation in the Context of Terms of Trade Concepts* (Oxford: Clarendon Press in co-operation with UNCTAD).

Viner, J. (1937) *Studies in the Theory of International Trade* (London: Allen & Unwin).

6 Development and Standard of Living

ALEXANDRE RANDS BARROS[1]

INTRODUCTION

An enormous effort is made in economic theory to understand the process of economic development. The dramatic disparities in standards of living among nations is a major concern for researchers, while the fact that such disparities have not tended to decrease is an even more disturbing problem, which economists struggle to understand.

There are two basic approaches to the problem of disparities in the development literature. The first tries to justify them based on the standard concepts of economic theory, without attributing to developing countries any special feature that is not part of the theoretical framework used. Good examples of this approach may be found in recent works by Lucas (1988), Romer (1986 and 1990), and Becker and Murphy (1990). In this type of approach, no differences in the structure of the economies exist. Differences in the development level result from quantitative differences in some variables, such as stock of capital. It is maintained that since economic variables are intertemporally related, these differences arise from the historical behaviour of the economy.

The second approach relies on structural differences of the economies to explain the distinct levels of development. These differences affect not only variables which are considered exogenous to the economic dynamics, but also those determining the dynamic relations of the economy. Some of these differences are commonly associated with the way developed and developing countries are integrated in the world economy. Some well-known examples of this approach are the centre–periphery model, developed by Prebisch and other Latin American structuralists, the dependency theories, originally developed by Cardoso and Faletto (1970) and Frank (1966 and 1967) and the North-South trade approaches, such as those presented by Taylor (1981), Burgstaller and Saveedra-Rivano (1984) and Darity (1990).

While the first approach is more connected with the neoclassical tradition, the second is commonly associated with non-orthodox economic theories. In this chapter, a non-orthodox interpretation of the causes of the disparities in economic development among nations, based only on quantitative differences of variables, will be presented. It uses the idea of failure in the labour market, which is a widespread idea in neo-Keynesian macroeconomics, and the role of demand in GDP determination, as emphasised by Latin American structuralists, to explain the existence of different levels of economic development. It stresses that some recent macroeconometric results, which sometimes challenge orthodox economic theory, give support to the theory outlined here.

Following the theoretical presentation in the next three sections, some empirical examples are then discussed, and followed by a critique of the Economic Commission for Latin America's (ECLA) and dependency theories. This critique may help understanding of the ideas put forward in this paper, since they have been a starting point for these developments.

EFFECTIVE DEMAND AND ECONOMIC GROWTH

The most widespread explanation of business cycles nowadays is that they are generated by the accumulation of the effect of small autonomous changes in GDP. The idea is incorporated in the models of the two currently major schools in macroeconomics, namely neo-Keynesian and neoclassical. These autonomous changes lead to the typical business cycles behaviour because of the intertemporal relation among variables. This conception of business cycles was originally proposed by Slutsky (1937) and has recently become very popular (see Gordon, 1986). The autonomous changes mentioned, also called innovations, result from exogenous changes in economic variables which affect output. The oil price shocks of 1973/74 and 1979/80 well exemplify such changes. They originated politically (cartel decision by exporters) and imposed readjustments in developed countries which contributed to the subsequent recessions.

Recent empirical developments in macroeconometrics have shown that the old tradition of using different approaches to analyse short- and long-run dynamics may be misleading. The changes which determine long-run economic growth also affect short-run cyclical fluctuations. Studies on the existence of a unit root in GDP gave empirical support to this idea, which was already used theoretically by neoclassical macroeconomists and more recently by neo-Keynesians.[2]

While the neo-Keynesians emphasise the role of demand innovations on GDP fluctuations, at least in the short-run (Solow, 1988), the neoclassicals give a prominent role to supply innovations, which originate mainly from productivity (Lucas, 1987). Empirical tests were not able to deny an important role for demand innovations in GDP fluctuations. Shapiro and

Watson (1988) and Blanchard and Quah (1989) provide examples of empirical tests on these lines. Therefore, from the recent debates in macroeconomics, one is left with the idea that changes in demand are important in explaining GDP fluctuations. While these studies refer mainly to the United States, recent studies by Barros (1990a, chs. 3 and 4) and Cribari (1990) showed that these relations also hold for Brazil.

Neo-Keynesian macroeconomics normally attributes a special role to demand only in short-run macroeconomic fluctuations and accepts the idea that long-run growth results strictly from supply innovations (see Shapiro and Watson, 1988; Blanchard and Quah, 1989). Empirical tests, however, do not support this hypothesis.[3] Barros (1990c) and Lutkepohl (1990) investigated this empirically and found a sizeable persistence of innovations in consumption, which are generally accepted as demand innovations. Sims (1992), Bernanke and Blinder (1990) and Christiano and Eichenbaum (1991) found evidence that monetary disturbances, which are also agreed to have a demand effect, have a persistent effect on GDP. Stadler (1990) developed a model with optimal behaviour of agents in which demand shocks are allowed to have a permanent effect on GDP. To obtain this result, he introduced technology as endogenously determined. In his model, monetary shocks account for demand innovations, but consumption shocks could easily replace them and produce the same results (see also Christiano and Eichenbaum, 1992). Barros (1992) developed a structuralist growth model which justifies the long-run persistence of autonomous changes in consumption.

Recent aggregate consumption theory has emphasised that the dynamics of consumption is largely independent of GDP fluctuations. Hall (1978) suggested that, under rational expectation of agents, consumption should be completely independent of disposable income. Subsequent studies showed that this was not the case,[4] either theoretically or empirically, although they could not dismiss the idea that a large proportion of consumption was independent of GDP. Campbell and Mankiw (1989) arrived at the conclusion that the best representation would be to split the consumers into two groups, one whose consumption was determined by their income and another for which it was determined independently of their disposable income. Therefore, much room was left for an autonomous component in consumption. Moreover, the rational expectations approach led to the conclusion that the autonomous component of consumption is not stationary, but rather integrated of order one.[5]

Recent developments in the literature of co-integration have emphasised the co-integration between consumption and income. Engle and Granger (1987), using some simple tests on co-integration, showed that these two variables are co-integrated of order one for the American economy. Barros (1990a, ch. 4) used a more elaborate test developed by Stock and Watson (1988) and confirmed this hypothesis.

When this result on co-integration of income and consumption is combined with the conclusion that there is an autonomous component of consumption which is integrated of order one, the obvious implication is that innovations in this autonomous component have a permanent effect on income. Otherwise these two variables would not be co-integrated.

REAL WAGES AS A SOURCE OF DEMAND INNOVATIONS

The behaviour of the labour market has been a major source of disagreement among the two mainstream macroeconomic theories. Neoclassical macroeconomics assumes wages to be determined by supply of and demand for labour, which determine real wages, employment and GDP, given the production function. Neo-Keynesians argue that wages are sluggish and consequently there is no equilibrium in the labour market. The recent experience of developed countries, mainly in Europe, has shown that these disequilibria are persistent, without any endogenous mechanism leading to a long-run equilibrium.[6] Insider–outsider models, the efficiency wages hypothesis and the fair wage-effort hypothesis are tentative explanations of this problem.[7] Empirical tests of these two confronting views are more in line with the neo-Keynesian views supporting the hypothesis of failure in the labour market, although the results also pose some challenges to the neo-Keynesian models (Greenwald and Stiglitz, 1988; Kniesner and Goldsmith, 1987).

Two empirical conclusions found in many studies are that there is an important autonomous component in wage determination and that shocks to wages have a high persistence (Sargent, 1978; Kennan, 1988a and 1988b). Therefore, estimated models for the real wage can only explain a small part of the movements in wages, if they do not emphasise the intertemporal correlation of wages. These conclusions favor the hypothesis that real wages have a unit root and that a large share of wages shocks are not explained by other economic variables. Therefore, real wages closely resemble a random walk (Ashenfelter and Card, 1982; Kennan, 1988a).

The autonomous component of changes in real wages may be linked to changes in the idea of fairness, in line with the fair wage-effort hypothesis, as in Barros (1991), but in this approach it is still not determined by economic variables. Changes in the autonomous component have an important permanent effect on wages, as a consequence of the permanent effect of shocks on wages.

It is an accepted idea in economic development that the propensity to consume from wages is higher than that from profit and incomes accruing from wealth.[8] This is a consequence of the fact that, on average, wage earners have a lower income than the earners of these other sources of income. As a consequence, an increase in demand will result from a redistribution of income in favour of wages. Since this redistribution has a high permanent effect on wages themselves, a new level of permanent higher demand will result. If GDP is able to respond, this new level of demand will produce a new GDP flow. Recent findings in consumption theory and unit root econometrics support the view that this new GDP could be sustained, otherwise consumption and GDP would have a high degree of trend-reversing, which is a possibility rejected by the data.

In addition to this effect on demand, as a consequence of the growth of the average propensity to consume, real wage increases also lead to the substitution of capital for labour. This has a transitory expansive effect on GDP too, since it fosters investment, one of the components of demand. The substitution of capital for labour is not only a consequence of changing the optimal choice of technology, but also of new technical developments which arise from changed incentives. A constantly increasing real wage could create a tremendous pressure for technical progress, if this increase does not go beyond the capacity of the economy to absorb it. This could lead to a high economic performance, as was the case in Sweden in the golden age of the Swedish model (Lundberg, 1985).

The impulse that technical change receives from wages does not flow smoothly. Therefore, in dynamic macroeconometric models, wages innovations do have a larger role in economic growth than indicated by variance decompositions. Part of the effect of wages innovations on GDP comes through subsequent random changes in productivity, which would enter these dynamic models through autonomous shocks in productivity.

There are limits to wage increases which have a positive effect on income. If wages rise excessively, employment may fall and more than compensate for the additional demand from higher wages. Stagnation would be the consequence of the wage increase in this case. The fall in the average propensity to save could also lead to inflationary excess of demand, if the economy reaches its full capacity. Inflation would be the final outcome of the rise in wages in this case.

In the framework of an open economy, with the ability to borrow from abroad, a country could respond to a domestic rise in real wages by increasing the inflow of consumption and capital goods, which could be traded for future exports. The experience of the sixties and seventies, when most of the developing world had a net inflow of resources from abroad, shows that this strategy is possible for some time.[9] Therefore, international economic integration widens the range of potentially positive wage rises.

WAGES AND STANDARD OF LIVING

In this chapter, I emphasise causation going from the social idea of fairness to real wages, and from this to income distribution and growth. The relation between wages and growth resulting from this causality has already been suggested in the literature and tested empirically. The main argument in the literature comes from the Latin American Structuralists and relies on the differences in the propensity to consume out of incomes accruing from profits and wages,[10] as argued by Cambridge economists.

Most of the empirical tests have used general equilibrium models and did not reach a definite conclusion.[11] These tests have the shortcoming that no substitution effects are allowed and the hypothesis that the economy operates at full capacity is ruled out by assumption. Barros (1990b) used a vector-autoregression framework, which does not contain these shortcomings, and confirmed the hypothesis of a positive effect from wages to growth.

Many of these studies consider real wages to be endogenously determined.[12] Therefore, the policy options to increase real wages are limited and may differ radically from those which would follow the interpretation given here. It is generally assumed that a causation exists from income to wages and from these to the standard of living of the population. Even though this chapter does not deny this possible direction, it emphasises the reverse causation as an important determinant of economic development.

SOME EXAMPLES

In this section, the role of an autonomous component in real wage determination will be considered side by side with other important sources of economic growth, namely, the Schumpeterian factor, human capital growth, the Weberian factor and the accumulation of capital, to explain the differences in the development level of some countries.

The socially accepted standard of living can be more adequately considered in conjunction with the Schumpeterian and Weberian factors, to form a group of development factors which do not require intertemporal substitution of welfare. If, at any time, these sources of economic growth operate, social hardship need not increase in one period in order to improve the welfare in another.[13] On the other hand, both human and physical capital accumulations foster development at the expense of welfare while the accumulation takes place.

Technical progress is certainly a major factor explaining economic growth and has been strongly emphasised in the recent literature on economic growth (see for example Romer, 1990; Grossman and Helpman, 1991). Its flow from one country to another, however, when there is an appropriate environment, limits its role as a source of disparities in economic development (Lucas, 1988, pp. 15–16). Therefore, this factor was not included among the major factors explaining disparities.

The Development of British Ex-Colonies

In some of the British ex-colonies, the local population was largely composed of British citizens and their descendants, as in the United States, Canada, Australia and New Zealand; in other cases, the native people still constituted the majority of the population, as in India and Kenya. These different types of colonisation had important consequences for the development-level of the country. Those countries in which the British population became a majority have become developed, while the others are underdeveloped.

All the major sources of economic growth aforementioned can help explain these differences. The capital accumulation hypothesis uses the fact that in those colonies with a majority of British descendants, the surplus generated domestically was invested locally, rather than expatriated. The Schumpeterian and Weberian factors are closely linked in this case, since they depend on institutions and culture. An argument on these lines would use the idea that the culture of the British people led to institutions that provided the necessary environment for the development of hard-working and innovative ideologies. The human capital hypothesis tends to emphasise the fact that the British migrants had a higher level of human capital than the native populations of the colonies. Therefore, the larger their share in the population, the higher the development level of the country.

An additional element to some (or all) of those already cited is the fact that in those colonies in which there was a close cultural identification with Britain, the pressure to incorporate within the country the changes affecting the standard of living of the population in Britain were stronger. Therefore, real wages tended to rise faster than in those countries which did not have a labour class identified with that in England.

The imitative standard of living hypothesis is important in order to understand why Australia and New Zealand developed while Argentina and Brazil did not. These British ex-colonies did not diversify their production much more than did Brazil and Argentina. The most important difference in performance among these countries is the faster-rising expected standard of living of the population, which forced constant increases in productivity and structural adjustments to meet the demands.

Sweden

Before the take-off of capitalist relations of production and productivity, Sweden was already a country with strong cultural integration and a large share of its population enjoying a similar standard of living, well integrated in communities (Rojas, 1991). When an emerging capitalist class started to increase its welfare, the pressure from workers to reduce the gap in standards of living was strong because of the cultural identification between workers and capitalists. The constantly increasing real wages following gains in productivity, forcing wages up through a profit squeeze, is the root of the Swedish model, which kept wages constantly rising at fast rates (see Lundberg, 1985). The real exchange rate was continuously adjusted downward to offset losses in international competitiveness and to avoid imbalances in foreign trade. Such a model led Sweden from a relatively backward stage of development, in comparison with other European countries, to the position of a country with one of the highest standards of living in the world (Table 6.1).[14]

Table 6.1 Levels of GDP per capita in some European countries: 1913, 1950, 1973 and 1989

Country	*1913*	*1950*	*1973*	*1989*
Austria	2667	2852	8644	12 585
Belgium	3266	4228	9416	12 876
Denmark	3037	5224	10 527	13 514
Finland	1727	3480	9072	13 934
France	2734	4149	10 323	13 837
Germany	2606	3339	10 110	13 989
Italy	2087	2819	8568	12 955
Netherlands	3178	4706	10 267	12 737
Norway	2079	4541	9346	16 500
Sweden	2450	5331	11 292	14 912
Switzerland	3086	6556	13 167	15 406
UK	4024	5651	10 063	13 468

Source: Maddison (1991, pp. 6 and 7).
Note: At 1985 US dollars and US prices adjusted for purchasing power of currencies.

Brazilian Regional Disparities

Brazil has a large regional disparity in its level of development. The population in the South and South-East regions has a reasonably high standard of living, in contrast to the North-East and North. The most developed regions received many European (from Italy and Germany) and Japanese immigrants, while the North-East was mainly populated by native people and Africans. When the Europeans and Japanese went to Brazil, Europe and Japan were already fast-growing economies and soon the standard of living of these regions started to rise. These migrants, as they arrived in Brazil, had already a higher standard of living than the local workers and were affected by the demonstration effect coming through the remaining contacts they had with their original countries.

The native people and Africans, who composed the majority of the population of the less-developed regions, had a tribal social organisation, with very low standards of living. Therefore, pressure to increase their standard of living was very limited. The ruling class of Portuguese origin never identified themselves with these poor segments and always justified the disparities in standards of living on the basis of origin. Consequently, they never made any effort to increase the standards of living of the poor.

The immigrants to Brazil settled in two different regions. In the South-East they entered society as workers employed by an existing ruling class, and constituted a social stratum between the poor slaves or ex-slaves (Africans and native people) and the élites. In the South they went to populate the region, which was largely unpeopled; they soon became the ruling class themselves and nowadays they constitute a large share of the population.

Today the South, which has a larger share of immigrants, is the region with the highest standard of living among the poor population, while the region with a well-settled ruling class (South-East) is the most economically powerful of the country, but with a lower standard of living among the poor population than the South. The region in which the natives and Africans constituted the majority of the population and where there was no cultural identity between the ruling class and the poor is the poorest region in the country (see Albuquerque, 1991).

Many other factors have also certainly contributed to the regional disparities in Brazil, but the socially accepted standard of living of the poor, which determines the wages (and the earnings of the peasants) had an enormous importance in mapping the development of the country.

THE THEORY OF UNDERDEVELOPMENT OF ECLA

In the early 1950s, the Economic Commission for Latin America (ECLA) proposed a new interpretation of economic development which greatly influenced the field afterwards.[15] As some of the ideas put forth in the present chapter are in direct conflict with ECLA's theory, it is worthwhile to specify where discordancies lie, as this can clarify some important aspects of the hypothesis presented here.

For Prebisch and his associates development is a consequence of capital accumulation only and the roots of the disparities of development level in the world are in the specialisation of each country in international trade.[16] Developing countries specialised in exporting primary products, which have low dynamism in markets and in technical progress, and imported industrial goods, characterised by high technological and market dynamisms. In addition to these specialisations, which by themselves could explain the lower growth of developing countries, there was also transfer of surplus from the periphery to the centre, as a consequence of an adverse long-run trend in the net barter terms of trade.

The idea in this theory is that the Latin American economies started to develop from the 'traditional stage', a situation of reproduction characterised by low productivity and low dynamism. The low expansion of foreign demand and the importance of its role in shifting resources from the traditional to the modern sector restricted the growth of developing countries. The fall in the net barter terms of trade further accentuated this constraint, since the necessary accumulation effort to maintain a given level of growth, measured in terms of social labour, became higher over time.

Industrialisation by means of import substitution was seen by these economists as the solution which could bring about productivity growth, overcoming the constraint imposed by international demand. The idea was to expand production to satisfy an already existing demand for industrial goods. In this strategy, developing countries could grow at the expense of their international integration and could catch up with developed countries, since a high rate of growth would become possible. The catching up of the standard of living would result from the higher growth of demand for labour in the periphery and subsequent increases in wages.

According to these economists, comparative advantage determines the specialisation of each country and the international market determines the relative prices of the goods traded, through supply and demand. Technical relations of production, or a production function, and the net barter terms of trade determine the productivity of labour, in both the modern and the traditional sectors, as well as the demand for labour. In the labour market, this demand is combined with the supply to establish the wages. Therefore, the low wages prevailing in developing countries are a consequence of the low demand for labour, *vis-à-vis* its supply. Wages will only increase when the demand for labour rises. This will follow a sufficiently fast and sustained expansion of the modern sector.

The fundamental difference between this theory and the hypothesis presented here is the causal relations put forward. I argue that instead of wages being mainly determined by supply and demand for labour, it is the socially accepted standard of living for workers which plays a more important role. If it increases, the technical relations of production and the comparative advantages adjust, so that the economy may reach a new equilibrium level with this different structure and higher wages. In terms of development policy implications, this would mean that not only the productivity and the relative size of the modern sector should be fostered, but it should also be recommended to establish a long-run policy of wage increase which would force the adjustments in the technical relations of production. Specialisations in international trade would also change according to the new comparative advantages.

According to the theory of ECLA, an important loss of productivity growth in the periphery is explained by falls in the net barter terms of trade. These falls reduce the potential accumulation in the periphery, the growth of labour demand, the amount of industrial goods which may be paid to workers in exchange for their labour and, consequently, the real wages.

In line with the ideas of this chapter, an alternative interpretation would be that the rate of profit is to some extent constrained by competition. Therefore, the lower rise of the socially accepted standard of living and of wages in the periphery *vis-à-vis* that of the centre, leads to a deterioration of the terms of trade, since the prices of each good should cover the costs, including wages and profit. The causation is, therefore, reversed in this case: the adverse long-run trend in the net barter terms of trade is a consequence, not a cause, of underdevelopment.

THEORY OF DEPENDENCY

Dependency theories can be divided into two groups. One emphasises the role of domestic relations in determining the dynamics of dependent societies, in addition to international relations (Cardoso and Faletto, 1970; Sunkel, 1971), while the other emphasises only the role of international relations (Baran, 1962; Frank, 1967).

In the framework of Baran (1962) and Frank (1967), development is caused by capital accumulation. Underdevelopment is caused by unproductive allocation of the surplus in the periphery, and transfer of an important part of the surplus generated in the periphery to the central economies through trade. The transfer was caused by undervaluation of the labour used in these areas, which was a consequence of market rules. The unproductive allocation of the retained surplus resulted from the consumption style of the élites in the periphery, which tried to copy the standards of those in the central economies.

This theory differs from our interpretation in one of the central assumptions. It assumes that the peripheral economies operate at full capacity all the time and that development follows accumulation of capital, which should be obtained by using the surplus. From the framework of Baran and Frank, one may easily conclude that growth of wages has a negative effect on the development process. As in Prebisch's approach, wage growth is seen as a consequence of the process of development, and will eventually reduce the level of growth.

Cardoso and Faletto (1970), on the other hand, emphasise the need to interpret the dynamics of domestic class relations to explain the development of a dependent society. In their framework, dependency is a consequence of the relations among the domestic social classes and the capitalist groups of the central economies, which may impose restrictions on the possibilities of development in the periphery. In the latest phase of the development of Latin America, namely, that of dependent industrialisation, these restrictions arise mainly from the technology and investment decisions of multinationals, made in the centre, according to a strategy of expansion pre-established there, rather than in the periphery. Another restricting factor has its roots in the fall of the net barter terms of trade, which reduces the surplus generated in the periphery and its expansion.

The economic interpretation of development given by Cardoso and Faletto emphasises the role of surplus generation and its use, as well as the negative effects on development when wages are raised. Therefore, their view of the mechanics of economic development is the opposite of the approach presented here. Their economic interpretation, however, is not the most important aspect of their dependency theory, which is more concerned with a sociological method of interpretation of development, rather than with particular economic conclusions.

As far as the interpretation of economic development presented here is concerned, Cardoso and Faletto's approach would still have a crucial role, which is to explain, at the sociological and political level, why the relations between groups and classes in each underdeveloped country prevented improvement in income distribution and consequently restricted economic development in these societies. Class relations, the nature of the economic activities, ethical factors and cultural integration are some of the aspects which play important roles in these analyses.

An attempt to develop the economic ideas of the dependency theory further was made by Tavares and Belluzzo (1982), Tavares and Serra (1971) and Cardoso de Melo (1982), among others. They emphasise the structural deformation of dependent economies, which results in a very weak capital goods sector. On this basis, they argue, the dynamics of the economy is limited. Therefore, some income concentration is needed to increase the demand for durable consumption goods. This is the only way long periods of sustained growth may be achieved, since the durable consumption goods sector is said to have a high multiplier effect and is believed to be the only sector which, in the absence of a capital goods sector, is able to sustain expansion over a long period. Therefore their main conclusions on the effect of autonomous changes in real wages on economic growth are opposite to those presented here.

CONCLUSIONS

This chapter has shown that some recent results in macroeconometrics can be brought together to support the hypothesis that an autonomous increase in the standard of living, which is an important force behind wage fluctuations, may have a positive effect on growth. This contradicts the standard neoclassical conclusion that wage increases reduce accumulation of capital, but is supported by empirical analysis.

The emphasis on autonomous wage increases, which have a political and ideological source rather than being driven by other economic variables, may have important policy implications regarding the improvement of income distribution in the process of development.

It has also been shown that although the relationship between wages and growth suggested here had already been introduced by Latin American Structuralists, it is absent from the major theories of economic development prevalent in Latin America.

Notes

1. The author gratefully acknowledges Analice Amazonas and Duilio Berne for helpful comments on a previous draft of this paper. Needless to say, remaining errors are solely the author's responsibility. The views expressed

in this chapter are those of the author and do not necessarily represent those of the International Sugar Organisation.

2. There is already an enormous literature on the existence of unit roots in GDP, which does not necessarily agree with the long-run effect of short-run autonomous changes in GDP, although generally no one is able to refute the idea of a large persistence in these effects. See for example Stock and Watson (1988), Diebold and Rudenbusch (1989), Blanchard and Quah (1989) and King, Plosser, Stock and Watson (1991). For a neoclassical theoretical model which incorporates this idea, see Kydland and Prescott (1982). For a neo-Keynesian version, see Stadler (1990) and Christiano and Eichenbaum (1992).
3. Blanchard (1989) tested this hypothesis explicitly, but was not able to refute the alternative.
4. See Hall (1989) for an extensive survey of the discussion which followed his proposition of the Random Walk Hypothesis.
5. A variable integrated of order one has a stochastic trend. Changes in this trend have a permanent effect in the variables.
6. See Coe (1988).
7. Krueger and Summers (1988) and Akerlof and Yellen (1986) present good surveys of the efficiency wages hypothesis. A helpful presentation of the insider-outsider model can be found in Lindbeck and Snower (1988). For a detailed explanation of the fair wages-effort hypothesis, see Akerlof and Yellen (1990). Solow (1990) and Blanchard and Fischer (1989, ch. 9) bring good reviews of these models.
8. This is an old idea originated by classical economists which recently played an important role in theories by Kalecki, Kaldor and Joan Robinson. See Tobin (1989).
9. The debt problem that arose from this strategy was a consequence of insufficient adjustments in these countries to balance the flow of resources across borders in the long run. It was not caused by any intrinsic problem with the strategy of borrowing for some period.
10. See Taylor (1990) for a recent formalisation of this hypothesis.
11. Cline (1975) surveyed this empirical literature and showed that the results are not very conclusive.
12. See for example the papers in Taylor et al. (1980).
13. In Schumpeter's (1926 and 1939) presentations, the expansionary activities of the entrepreneurs increased the share of the total product directed to investment, reducing consumption, as a consequence of the full-employment hypothesis used. If less than full capacity is allowed, no reduction of current consumption would be necessary.
14. According to the *Human Development Report* of the United Nations Development Programme (1990), Sweden had the second highest Human development index, second only to Japan.
15. The leading paper presenting this theory is Prebisch (1962). Recent surveys were made by Floto (1989) and Di Filipo (1988).
16. See Singer (1991).

References

Akerlof, G. and J. Yellen (1986) 'Introduction' in G. Akerlof and J. Yellen (eds), *Efficiency Wages Models of the Labour Market* (New York: Cambridge University Press).

Akerlof, G. and J. Yellen (1990) 'The Fair Wage-Effort Hypothesis and Unemployment', *Quarterly Journal of Economics*, vol. 55, no. 2, 255–83.

Albuquerque, R. (1991) 'A Situação Social: O que diz o Passado e o que Promete o Futuro' in IPEA, *Perspectiva da Economia Brasileira 1992*, (Rio de Janeiro: IPEA).

Ashenfelter, O. and D. Card (1982) 'Time Series Representations of Economic Variables and Alternative Models of the Labour Market', *Review of Economic Studies*, vol. 49, no. 5, 761–81.

Baran, P. (1962) *The Political Economy of Growth* (New York: Monthly Review Press).

Barros, A. (1990a) *Wages, Growth and Cycles in the Brazilian Economy*, PhD dissertation (Illinois: University of Illinois at Urbana-Champaign).

Barros, A. (1990b) 'The Role of Real Wages on Income Determination: An Empirical Test' in *Anais do XIIo Encontro Brasileiro de Econometrica*, Brasília: Sociedade Brasileira de Econometria, 337–60.

Barros, A. (1990c) 'Keynesians vs. Kaleckians on the Aggregate Consumption Theory', *Série Textos para Discussão*, Recife: PIMES-UFPE.

Barros, A. (1991) 'A Marxian Theory of Real Wages' in *Anais do XIIIo Encontro Brasileiro de Econometria* (Curitiba: Sociedade Brasileira de Econometria).

Barros, A. (1992) 'Consumption and Economic Growth: Confronting the Structuralist and the Neoclassical Approaches' Manuscript (London: ISO).

Becker, G. and K. Murphy (1990) 'Economic Growth, Human Capital and Population Growth', *Journal of Political Economy*, vol. 98.

Bernanke, B. and A. Blinder (1990) 'The Federal Funds Rate and the Channels of Monetary Transmission', *NBER Working Paper*, no. 3487.

Blanchard, O. (1989) 'A Traditional Interpretation of Macroeconomic Fluctuations', *American Economic Review*, vol. 79, no. 5, 1146–64.

Blanchard, O. and S. Fischer (1989) *Lectures on Macroeconomics* (Cambridge, Mass: MIT Press).

Blanchard, O. and D. Quah (1989) 'The Dynamics Effects of Aggregate Demand and Supply Disturbances', *American Economic Review*, vol. 79, no. 4, 155–73.

Burgstaller, A. and N. Saveedra-Rivano (1984) 'Capital Mobility and Growth in a North–South Model', *Journal of Development Economics*, vol. 15, no. 1, 213–37.

Campbell, J. and N. Mankiw (1989) 'Consumption, Income, and Interest Rates: Reinterpreting the Time Series Evidence' in O. Blanchard and S. Fischer (eds), *NBER Macroeconomics Annual 1989* (Cambridge, Mass.: MIT Press).

Cardoso, F. and E. Falleto (1970) *Dependência e Desenvolvimento na América Latina* (Rio de Janeiro: Zahar).

Cardoso de Mela, J. (1982) *O Capitalismo Tardio* (São Paulo: Brasiliense).

Christiano, L. and M. Eichenbaum (1991) 'Identification and the Liquidity Effects of a Monetary Shock' in A. Cuikerman, L. Hercowitz and L. Leiderman (eds), *Business Cycles, Growth and Political Economy* (Cambridge, Mass.: MIT Press).

Christiano, L. and M. Eichenbaum (1992) 'Liquidity Effects and the Monetary Transmission Mechanism', *NBER Working Paper*, no. 3974.

Cline, W. (1975) 'Distribution and Development', *Journal of Development Economics*, vol. 1, 359–400.

Coe, D. (1988) 'Hysteresis Effects on Aggregated Wage Equations' in R. Cross (ed.) *Unemployment, Hysteresis and the Natural Rate Hypothesis* (Oxford: Basil Blackwell).

Cribari, F. (1990) 'A Teoria da Renda Permanente e os Movimentos Estocásticos do Consumo' in *Anais do XIIo Encontro Brasileiro de Econometria*, Brasília: Sociedade Brasileira de Econometria, 79–112.

Darity, W. (1990) 'The Fundamental Determinants of the Terms of Trade Reconsidered: Long-Run and Long-Period Equilibrium', *American Economic Review*, vol. 80, no. 4, 816–27.

Diebold, F. and G. Rudenbusch (1989) 'Long Memory and Persistence in Aggregate Output', *Journal of Monetary Economics*, vol. 24, no. 2, 189–209.

Di Filipo, A. (1988) 'Prebisch's Ideas on the World Economy', *Cepal Review*, 34, 153–63.

Engle, R. and C. Granger (1987) 'Co-integration and Error Correction: Representation, Estimation, and Testing', *Econometrica*, vol. 55, no. 2, 251–76.

Floto, E. (1989) 'The Centre-Periphery System and Unequal Exchange', *Cepal Review*, 39, 136–54.

Frank, A. (1966) 'The Development of Underdevelopment', *Monthly Review*, 18.

Frank, A. (1967) *Capitalism and Underdevelopment in Latin America* (New York: Monthly Review Press).

Gordon, R. (1986) 'Introduction: Continuity and Change in Theory, Behaviour, and Methodology' in R. Gordon (ed.), *The American Business Cycle* (Chicago: University of Chicago Press).

Greenwald, B. C. and J. E. Stiglitz (1988) 'Examining Alternative Macroeconomic Theories', *Brookings Papers on Economic Activity*, no. 1, 207–60.

Grossman, G. and E. Helpman (1991) *Innovation and Growth* (Cambridge, Mass.: MIT Press).

Hall, R. (1978) 'Stochastic Implications of the Life Cycle–Permanent Income Hypothesis: Theory and Evidence', *Journal of Political Economy*, vol. 86, no. 6, 971–87.

Hall, R. (1989) 'Consumption' in R. Barro (ed.), *Modern Business Cycle Theory* (New York: John Wiley).

Kennan, J. (1988a) 'An Econometric Analysis of Fluctuations in Labour Supply and Demand', *Econometrica*, vol. 56, no. 2, 317–33.

Kennan, J. (1988b) 'Equilibrium Interpretations of Employment and Real Wage Fluctuations', *NBER Macroeconomics Annual*, vol. 3, 157–205.

King, R., C. Plosser, J. Stock and M. Watson, (1991) 'Stochastic Trends and Economic Fluctuations', *American Economic Review*, vol. 81, no. 4, 819–40.

Kniesner, T. J. and A. H. Goldsmith (1987) 'A Survey of Alternative Models of the United States Labour Market', *Journal of Economic Literature*, vol. 25, no. 203, 1241–80.

Krueger, A. and L. Summers (1988) 'Efficiency Wages and the Inter-Industry Wage Structure', *Econometrica*, vol. 56, no. 2, 259–93.

Kydland, F. and E. Prescott (1982) 'Time to Build and Aggregate Fluctuations', *Econometrica*, vol. 50, no. 6, 1345–70.

Lindbeck, A. and D. Snower (1988) *The Insider–Outsider Theory of Employment and Unemployment* (Cambridge, Mass.: MIT Press).

Lucas, R. (1987) *Models of Business Cycles* (Oxford: Basil Blackwell).

Lucas, R. (1988) 'On the Mechanics of Economic Development', *Journal of Monetary Economics*, vol. 22, no. 1, 3–42.

Lundberg, E. (1985) 'The Rise and Fall of the Swedish Model', *Journal of Economic Literature*, vol. 23, no. 1, 1–36.

Lutkepohl, H. (1990) 'Asymptotic Distributions of Impulse Response Functions and Forecast Error Variance Decompositions of Vector Autoregressive Models', *Review of Economics and Statistics*, vol. 72, no. 1, 116–25.

Maddison, A. (1991) *Dynamic Forces in Capitalist Development* (Oxford: Oxford University Press).

Prebisch, R. (1962) 'The Economic Development of Latin America and its Principal Problems', *Economic Bulletin for Latin America*, vol. 7, no. 1, 1–22.

Rojas, M. (1991) "The 'Swedish Model' in Historical Perspective", *Scandinavian Economic History Review*, vol. 32, no. 2, 64–74.

Romer, P. (1986) 'Increasing Returns and Long-Run Growth', *Journal of Political Economy*, vol. 94, no. 5, 1002–37.

Romer, P. (1990) 'Endogenous Technological Change', *Journal of Political Economy*, vol. 98, no. 5, 71–103.

Sargent, T. J. (1978) 'Estimation of Dynamic Labour Demand Schedules Under Rational Expectations', *Journal of Political Economy*, vol. 86, no. 6, 1009–44.

Schumpeter, J. (1926) *The Theory of Economic Development* (Cambridge, Mass.: Harvard University Press).

Schumpeter, J. (1939) *Business Cycles: A Theoretical, Historical and Statistical Analysis of the Capitalist Process*, 2 vols (New York: McGraw-Hill).

Shapiro, M. and M. Watson (1988) 'Sources of Business Cycle Fluctuations' in S. Fischer (ed.), *NBER Macroeconomics Annual 1988* (Cambridge, Mass.: MIT Press).

Sims, C. (1992) 'Interpreting the Macroeconomic Time Series Facts: The Effects of Monetary Policy', *European Economic Review*, forthcoming.

Singer, H. W. (1991) 'Terms of Trade: New Wine in Old Bottles', Presented in a seminar at Queen Elizabeth House, Oxford, June.

Slutsky, E. (1937) 'The Summation of Random Causes as the Source of Cyclic Process', *Econometrica*, vol. 5, 105–46.

Solow, R. (1988) 'Growth Theory and After', *American Economic Review*, vol. 73, no. 3, 307–17.

Solow, R. (1990) *The Labour Market as a Social Institution* (Oxford: Basil Blackwell).

Stadler, G. (1990) 'Business Cycle Models with Endogenous Technology', *American Economic Review*, vol. 80, no. 4, 763–78.

Stock, J. and M. Watson (1988) 'Variable Trends in Economic Time Series', *Journal of Economic Perspectives*, vol. 2, no. 3, 147–74.

Sunkel, O. (1971) 'Capitalismo Transacional y Desintegración Nacional en la América Latina', *Trimestre Económico*, 150, 571–628.

Tavares, M. and L. Belluzzo (1982) 'Notas sobre o Processo de Industrialização Reciente no Brasil' in L. Belluzzo and R. Coutinho (eds), *Desenvolvimento Capitalista no Brasil* (São Paulo: Brasiliense).

Tavares, M. and J. Serra (1971) 'Mas Allá del Estancamiento: Una Discusión sobre el Estilo de Desarrollo Reciente', *El Trimestre Económico*, vol. 33, no. 4, 905–50.

Taylor, L. (1981) 'South–North Trade and Southern Growth: Bleak Prospects from a Structuralist Point of View', *Journal of International Economics*, vol. 11, 589–602.

Taylor, L. (1990) 'Real and Money Wages, Output and Inflation in the Semi-Industrialized World', *Economica*, vol. 57, no. 227, 329–53.

Taylor, L., E. Bacha, E. Cardoso and F. Lysy (1980) *Models of Growth and Distribution to Brazil* (Oxford: Oxford University Press).

Tobin, J. (1989) 'Growth and Distribution: A Neoclassical Kaldor-Robinson Exercise', *Cambridge Journal of Economics*, vol. 13, no. 1, 37–45.

UNDP (1990) *Human Development Report 1990* (New York: Oxford University Press).

7 The Appraisal and Evaluation of Structural Adjustment Lending: Some Questions of Method

JOHN TOYE[1]

THE APPRAISAL OF STRUCTURAL ADJUSTMENT LENDING (SAL) PROGRAMMES

The difference between appraisal and evaluation is that appraisal is *prospective:* looking forward to anticipate what might happen as a result of undertaking a project or making an adjustment loan, while evaluation is *retrospective:* looking back at what has happened after a project has been completed or an adjustment loan made. Because, before 1980, most development aid was for *projects*, various methods of appraising and evaluating projects were the great priority of the 1970s. For projects, the methods of appraisal and evaluation are relatively well known, and closely connected with each other. World Bank methods are described by Ray (1984) and ODA methods by ODA (1988). They involve the calculation of a prospective economic rate of return in advance for appraisal purposes, and then calculating an actual economic rate of return for purposes of evaluation. Both of these calculations can be done with and without information on the distribution of the net benefits of the project across the affected population.

The methods of project appraisal and evaluation are microeconomic in their theoretical basis, make special simplifying assumptions concerning the constancy of variables in the economy beyond the project itself (the so-called *ceteris paribus* assumption) and are too detailed to be applied to anything broader in scope than the individual project. They are, therefore, not appropriate for post-1980 lending for structural adjustment, although SAL finance demands appraisal and evaluation no less than individual projects.

Parenthetically, it is questionable whether they are appropriate for project lending either, or whether they merely create an illusion of precise appraisal and evaluation. The question is whether aid finances the project to which it is nominally attached, which is the one appraised and evaluated, or another project which would not have been undertaken if the aid finance had not been available. Aid donors tend to like to finance attractive projects, and therefore to give aid money to projects which probably would have been implemented anyway by the recipient government in the absence of aid. But if they do this, they are really making it possible for the government to undertake a different and truly marginal project which could not have been afforded without the aid flow. This feature of aid money is given the name 'fungibility', meaning 'capable of being put to uses different from the ones formally stated'.

Structural adjustment lending (or SAL finance) differs from project lending in the following three important ways:

(a) *It is programme aid*
Programme aid is official development assistance (ODA) which is given as general balance-of-payment support and not to finance specific investment projects.

(b) *Policy conditionality is attached to the loan*
Policy conditionality is a set of loan conditions which require stated policy reforms, and not merely actions designed to secure the servicing and repayment of the loan.

(c) *Policy conditions are economy-wide or sector-wide in scope*
The scope of the required policy reform is that of the entire macroeconomy, or at least an entire sector. If it relates to a particular institution, (for example, the operation of the Ministry of Finance), it does so because of the economy- or sector-wide impact that is anticipated.

When aid is given as programme aid, it is often acknowledged as fully fungible, that is it can be used for any purpose that the recipient government determines without the further permission of the donor being required. That is so unless the donor explicitly inserts restrictions into the programme aid agreement, in an attempt to restrict the degree of fungibility. Donors may insert restrictions to prevent their aid being used entirely freely for two major reasons.

The first reason is that adjustment lending normally combines programme aid with economy-wide or sectoral policy conditionality. This is usually directed to promoting not only macroeconomic stabilisation but also a liberalisation of the supply side of the economy. A potential conflict exists between the supply of programme aid and the implementation of the policy conditionality. That is to say, the recipient may use the aid inflow to postpone, rather than to facilitate, the required policy changes. The donor, in deciding whether to provide adjustment lending, may wish to avoid financing sectors of the economy which embody a misallocation of resources supported by the unchanged policies of the recipient government. The donor may also positively wish to be seen supporting activities generally believed to be beneficial to development – such as health and education services.

The second reason is that donor agencies are politically sensitive about aid money being seen to finance certain categories of imports. Firearms, drugs, tobacco and alcohol are among the types of imports which donors refuse to finance. More generally, 'luxury items' like limousines, aircraft, air conditioning are sometimes also regarded as inappropriate imports to be financed by donors whose remit is to assist development and alleviate poverty. Methods of appraising SAL finance concentrate on trying to avoid luxury imports, as well as trying to avoid funding economically distorted sectors or activities. But, from an economic point of view, the attempt to avoid using aid to import luxuries does not make sense. If luxuries cannot be bought domestically, the rich will find ways of buying them either illegally or by travelling abroad. It is better policy to permit the import of luxuries and then tax their consumption heavily.

In the appraisal of SAL programmes, most donors still rely very heavily on the conditionalities adopted by the IMF and World Bank. When their structural adjustment finance is in support of a Fund/Bank adjustment programme, they rarely seek any further restrictions on their aid than those requested by the Fund and Bank. They presume that the economic and policy analysis which underlies the programme designed by the Fund and Bank is adequate in its understanding of the distortions in the economy and the recipient government's propensity to misuse aid.[2]

Some of the relevant considerations in determining whether programme aid is desirable (with or without Bank/Fund conditionality) are:

(a) Whether the form of exchange rate determination is:
administered but with a degree of flexibility and adjustment;
market determined – either partially or fully, by auction, and so on;
unified or two tier.

(b) How far the exchange rate is over-valued on the basis of real exchange rate or other tests.

(c) The nature of the licensing system for imports:
type of system; criteria; degree of arbitrariness;
scope for and evidence of corruption, etc.

(d) The nature of the tariff structure and quantitative restrictions on imports:
degree and variability of protection, taking as a crude yardstick of acceptability an average effective rate of protection of less than 25 per cent.

(e) The structure of subsidies, including implicit subsidy in pricing policy of public sector enterprises.
(f) The degree of monopoly power among producers (and hence users of imports) as well as distributors/marketers of products and imports.
(g) The priorities for allocation of resources, as set out in the public sector budget, capital and recurrent.
(h) The existence of other distortions to allocative efficiency, for example controls on credit and interest rates, labour-market freedom, policies with regard to income distribution.[3]

The precise manner in which the efficiency of the foreign trade sector can be investigated is by calculating the *effective rate of protection* (ERP) which applies to the anticipated final user of the programme aid. For example, if aid were being given to support the rehabilitation of a country's mining industry, one could calculate the level of protection that the trade regime provided for the value added generated in mining. The ERP is determined not just by the nominal height of the tariff on the industry's final product, but also by the nominal tariff on its material inputs and the share of value added in the final product. Algebraically,

$$ERP = \frac{n - mx}{v}$$

where n = nominal rate of duty on final product;
m = nominal rate of duty on material imported input;
x = coefficient of material input;
v = proportion of value added to final output.

The ERP provides an indication of the *potential* efficiency or inefficiency of resource use in the sector concerned. When the ERP exceeds 25 per cent, this can be interpreted as indicating that potential inefficiency is high, and then a further calculation of the sector's *actual* economic efficiency can be undertaken. This is done by estimating the *domestic resource cost ratio* (DRC) of the industry or sector which will receive the programme aid. The DRC ratio is defined as:

$$DRC_X = \frac{W^0 L_x + r^0 K_x}{V_x^*}$$

where W^0 = the shadow wage of labour
r^0 = the shadow price of capital
L_x = the proportion of labour in x
K_x = the proportion of capital in x

V_x^* = domestic value added in x at world prices

The relationship between the DRC ratio and the ERP is as follows:

$$ERP_X = \frac{V_X}{V_X^*} - 1$$

where V_x is domestic value added at domestic market prices.

Substituting for V_x^* in the first equation gives the relationship:

$$DRC_x = \frac{W^0L_x + r^0K_x}{V_x/1 + ERP_x} = \frac{(W^0L_x + r^0K_x)(1 + ERP_x)}{V_x}$$

There are two slightly different methods of making this calculation, one derived from the seminal work of Corden (1966) and the other from the work of Balassa (Balassa and Schydlowsky, 1972). In principle these methods are equivalent, but in practice they may produce somewhat divergent numbers.

Apart from trying to estimate the degree of economic distortion in the sectors to benefit from the aid credit, donors may also monitor whether aid is being used to provide 'luxury' goods. This is partly a political concern – the donor's taxpayers will not support the use of aid to provide luxury items for people who are supposed to be poor, and partly a policy concern, to direct aid to those whose basic needs are unmet in circumstances where better policies (taxation of luxuries or redistribution of income) are deemed to be not feasible. Donors have to decide, when considering a proposal for adjustment lending, whether to allow their aid to be added to the pool of foreign exchange which, under liberalisation conditionalities, the adjusting country is usually required to auction. If it does this, it will have no control over the goods purchased by those who bid successfully in the foreign exchange auction. No formulas can help here. It is essentially a pragmatic judgement that has to be made.

In their appraisal methods, few donors appear to address specifically issues concerning the sequencing of the different measures within a Structural Adjustment package. This may be because economic theory does not provide any easy diagnostic tools for this purpose. The 'theory of the second best' proves that to remove one distortion in the presence of any other distortion, or distortions, may not lead to an increase in economic welfare. It thus points to the possibility of trade-offs in welfare when liberalisation measures are taken in sequence. But what economic theory does not do is to provide the basis for a theory of optimal sequencing, that is the demonstration of a correct order for liberalisation actions to be taken, either universally or in any particular case.[4]

Appraisal of proposed reform sequences rests on a basis of experience and common sense. Stabilisation of the macroeconomic balances is usually taken to be a priority compared with supply-side reforms, because doing both at the same time could be too deflationary, and doing supply-side reform first could be aborted by unmanageable balance of payments and budget deficits. Nevertheless, adjustments to producer prices, interest rates and import regimes will be needed if stabilisation is to be achieved. Liberalisation of the current account of the balance of payments is usually regarded as necessary long before the liberalisation of the capital account, to avoid channelling foreign investment to inefficient industries. Liberalisation of interest rates and elimination of the fiscal deficit are also thought to be a precondition of liberalising the capital account. In some cases, cutting the fiscal deficit is hampered by trade liberalisation, as revenues from import tariffs decline (Smith and Spooner, 1992; Greenaway and Milner, 1991). One has a series of 'rules of thumb', but no inviolable rank order of policy priorities.

THE EVALUATION OF SAL IMPLEMENTATION

We now turn to the methodological problems of evaluating SAL finance. In the early 1980s the Overseas Development Administration ODA began to evaluate its own programme aid. The purpose of these early studies was to investigate certain issues of aid management. They were important mainly because they demonstrated how tricky some of the methodological problems of this kind of evaluation were (see Thomson (1984, pp. 83–92) for details). But the ODA has also funded research into an evaluation methodology. A proposed method has recently been designed and applied by Mosley, Harrigan and Toye (1991) funded by ODA research funds.

The impact of a structural adjustment programme derives from the interaction of three things:

1. The initial situation of the economy before structural adjustment is attempted;
2. The inflow of programme aid;
3. The policy changes that are made as a result of the conditionality of the programme aid.

The third factor breaks down into two components, reflecting the different time phases of an adjustment programme. When adjustment finance is negotiated, a set of policy changes is promised in exchange for a certain amount of borrowing. When it is time to implement this set, a certain number of reforms will prove to be infeasible, or feasible but no longer desirable, and these will not be implemented. The promised reforms which are not implemented can be called 'slippage', because the expected reforms have slipped behind to some extent. The net effect of the conditionality of the loans is, therefore, the promised set of reforms minus the slippage.

The method of evaluation employed by Mosley, Harrigan and Toye (1991) starts out by concentrating attention on SAL implementation, the third factor in our list above. The relationship between implementation of reforms, the initial economic situation and the effects of the aid inflow are discussed later on.

The first step is to make a comprehensive survey of the policy reform conditions agreed to by the country whose programme is being evaluated. In principle, this is fairly straightforward. Many, but not all, of these conditions are written down in the loan agreements between the Fund and the Bank and the country concerned. The task then is to assemble the relevant documents and abstract the relevant passages. Practical difficulties with this task may arise because the international financial institutions (IFIs) and/or the country government may not, for various reasons, be eager for their agreements to be inspected by third parties.

Assuming that this difficulty can be overcome, what are the other problems? They are that not all conditions may be formally written into the loan documents. They may either be omitted because a gentlemen's agreement exists, but may be too sensitive to commit to paper, or because the Bank wants to retain the discretion to ask for fresh policy conditions even during the disbursement of the loan. These omitted conditions are as much a part of loan conditionality as those written down. By the same token, some of the written conditions may be included as much because the country's government wants to shift responsibility for them on to the IFIs, as because the IFIs regard them as essential to structural adjustment. It is important to test for the existence of these cases before proceeding on the assumption that the abstracts of the loan agreements tell us everything that is relevant.

The second step is to try to estimate the amount of slippage that has occurred in the implementation of the agreed policy conditions. In principle, this can be done by interviewing the ministers and officials in those parts of the government responsible for the matters which have been identified as subject to loan conditionality. Either by submitting a written questionnaire or by undertaking a more unstructured personal interview, reports on the progress of implementation may be sought. Relevant published documents, plus any internal documents which the informant is willing to release should also be collected.

Almost certainly, however, the interpretation of some of this information will pose problems. These arise for a variety of reasons. Some conditions are stated more vaguely than others. Some are stated very explicitly, for example the removal of subsidies on petrol and fertilisers by the end of the current year. But others merely ask for satisfactory progress towards a policy objective, or that the policy issue should be studied in detail. In these cases, it is hard to tell whether the reported progress on implementation represents any slippage or not.

Another difficulty of interpretation derives from the possibility of countervailing action. Using the example of removal of subsidies again, a government may comply with the condition and eliminate budgetary subsidies to entrepreneurs in a given industrial sector. But simultaneously it may also relax the credit ceiling for the same sector, and thus offset by monetary policy the effect of implementing the loan condition. Unless countervailing action is also reported on, the existence of slippage can easily be misjudged. Compliance plus countervailing action should clearly be counted as slippage.

Finally, some slippage is not culpable. Both IFIs and the government may have agreed on policy reform actions which cease to be desirable as economic circumstances change. This is particularly likely when conditions are highly quantified and time-bound. A change in the external trading environment, such as an unexpected fall in the cocoa price, may make compliance with a previous agreed policy condition (for example, to raise the producer price of cocoa to x per cent of the world price) inappropriate. Cases of non-culpable slippage ought to be excluded from the measurement of slippage. At the same time, the condition itself ought to be excluded from the set of relevant policy conditions, along with conditions where it is simply not clear whether they have been fulfilled or not.

One might wish to extend the idea of non-culpable slippage to include the situation in which the Fund and the Bank have underestimated the difficulty of sustaining the reform programme politically. Almost by definition, the recipient government knows more about the requirements of political sustainability than do the international financial institutions. If slippage is allowed by the government as a method of lowering resistance to reforms in order to prevent them being abandoned entirely, there is little difference between this case and the previous case where economic conditions are inappropriate because of a misestimation by the Fund and Bank of international economic trends.

It is possible to construct a simple index of implementation indicating the percentage of agreed policy conditions where no slippage has taken place. But in the light of the problems of vagueness, offsetting action and fluctuating circumstances of performance, it is very easy to make measurement mistakes. The wide variation of the importance to be attached to different policy conditions creates an additional hazard. A simple index may show high implementation percentages because many unimportant conditions have been fulfilled while a few absolutely critical conditions have not. Likewise, a low implementation score is possible when the few critical policy changes have been made but little else has been done. The only remedy here is a weighting system which discriminates numerically between conditions by the degree of their importance, or separate indices for trivial and critical conditions.

Let us assume at this point that all the problems of measuring slippage and weighting the importance of conditions have been solved. We are left, ideally, with a measure of the extent to which the agreed programme of policy reform has been implemented in a particular country. Comparing different countries that are undergoing structural adjustment, we can now distinguish between those that have received the inflows of structural adjustment lending and adopted reforms fully and those that have received the aid flows but failed, in differing degrees, to adopt the policy changes that were promised. This is vital information for the next stage of the evaluation.

THE EVALUATION OF SAL EFFECTIVENESS

The measurement of policy changes that are implemented as a result of SAL conditionality are only one part of the complex process of evaluating the effectiveness of SALs. We shall come back to them once we have developed an overview of the entire evaluation process. This breaks down into three stages – the specification of the criteria for evaluation; the specification of a valid method of measuring the socioeconomic changes associated with the implementation of SAL policy reforms; and the drawing of correct inferences about causality.

No evaluation can be performed without explicit criteria. With SAL finance, the changes that are supposed to be caused are 'structural changes' in the economy that are necessary to correct severe balance of payments deficit and to restart a process of sustainable economic growth with distributional equity. It is worth emphasising two points about such structural changes, which make the criteria for evaluating such changes difficult to define.

The concept of 'sustainability' cannot be a very precise one because it often includes within itself political judgements. Even very serious balance of payments disequilibria do not become unsustainable automatically, when some percentage of GNP is exceeded. They do so when the political authorities of the day decide that they are unsustainable. Once a decision is taken to embark on structural adjustment, the sustainability of the economic growth which it produces also depends on political factors – the strength of the opposition, the determination to persevere of the government, and the willingness of external donors to continue to supply net additional finance. It is hard to estimate any one of these factors singly, and even harder when they are all interacting with each other.

The concept of 'distributional equity' is also problematic. The information available about income distribution in poor countries is often very sparse, and governments often do not regard equity in distribution as a priority goal. It is often far from clear *whose* concept of equity is supposed to be attended to. Often it is the aid donors' concept which appears to be the guiding one. But donors' views on this matter are notoriously volatile and subject to the pressures of ideological fashion.

Such concepts are needed as ultimate criteria, despite the continuing debate about what they really mean. In practice however, they have had to be replaced in the evaluation process by more easily definable intermediate criteria. Obvious examples of purely economic intermediate criteria are the growth of GNP, the growth of exports, the state of the current account of the balance of payments, and the size of the fiscal deficit. Average real incomes in the urban and rural sectors have also been used by some evaluators (Gaiha, 1988, pp. 30–8). Social indicators of nutrition, child mortality, school enrolment, female literacy could also, in principle, be used as intermediate criteria. There is, however, no 'fixed list' of such criteria. The criteria to be used vary with what policy-makers and evaluators believe is important. That changes from time to time. Instead of being able to summarise evaluation findings through one or two summary statistics, the use of multiple intermediate criteria produces for each country a variegated pattern of outcomes. It remains for the evaluator to make a judgement as to how far these demonstrate an outcome of 'sustainable economic growth with distributional equity' in the particular case under review. There is no way in which this final judgemental element can be eliminated from an evaluation.

Once criteria have been established, the next task is that of deciding how to establish a valid association between the implementation of SAL policy changes and changes in the chosen intermediate criteria. It is generally accepted that two of the possible methods are not satisfactory. One of these is to compare the values of the criteria in the initial position of the economy with those prevailing at some period after the implementation of the SAL policy changes. This is called the 'before and after' approach. The reason why this approach is not satisfactory is obvious. It is possible, indeed almost inevitable, that other influences, additional to the SAL policy changes, will also affect the values of the chosen criteria. For example, if one of our evaluation criteria is the size of the deficit on the balance of payments, the SAL policies may have had a positive beneficial effect in reducing the deficit at the same time as falling export prices may have had a larger effect in increasing the deficit. The net deficit would have increased in the 'after' position. But it would be a mistake to associate the introduction of SAL policies with a deterioration in the balance of payments. The use of the 'before and after' method is valid only when the influence of all other variables is controlled for. Given the complexity of the economic system, simple comparisons rarely include all the necessary controls.

Another unsatisfactory method is called the 'plan versus realisation' method. This involves a comparison of the 'after' position, that is, the actual or realised value of the criterion compared with that which was initially planned. Going back to the previous example of the balance of payments, the actual position after the introduction of SAL policy changes would be compared with the size of deficit that was anticipated when the policy changes were introduced. The procedure makes allowance for the effect of non-policy influences, such as falling export prices. But is does so only to the extent that they were correctly anticipated. Only if the planned or target value of the criterion embodies perfect foresight of the effects of non-policy influences will a comparison of actuals with plans or targets for the criterion provide a true measure of the degree of association between policy changes and changes in the criterion. In a world characterised by uncertainty, such perfect foresight is impossible, and thus all plans and targets have an irreducible element of arbitrariness. One can take this argument even further. In a world from which uncertainty had been eliminated (if that were possible) the entire problem of evaluating the impact of policy changes would disappear. We would know this impact in advance, and would not need to search for an elaborate methodology to discover it!

In principle, only one method is correct for estimating the correlation between policy changes and changes in the chosen criteria. This is the method of 'with and without'. The 'after' position, or the actual state of affairs after the policy changes, represents the 'with' side of the comparison, and this is relatively easy to measure. The 'without' side of the comparison is more difficult, because it requires the elaboration of the state of affairs that would have existed if the policy changes had not been made. The 'without' scenario is hypothetical and counterfactual. But it also has to be plausible or reasonable. It must be a disciplined speculation about what might have happened if the policies subject to SAL conditionality had *not* been changed, but had stayed as they were originally.

The counterfactual is, by definition, not observable. This is no single counterfactual that is right or correct. Attempts to construct a counterfactual are various, and their plausibility and reasonableness are a matter of discussion and judgement. In a sense, all that we are saying by describing the 'before and after' and the 'plan versus realisations' methods as unsatisfactory is that the counterfactual that they imply is not at all reasonable. But what might be more reasonable?

CROSS-SECTION METHODS OF CONSTRUCTING COUNTERFACTUALS

Counterfactuals may be constructed by cross-section ('aggregative') or time-series ('single-country') methods. One cross-section method is that of comparison between SAL and non-SAL groups of countries. The underlying idea of such comparisons is that the non-SAL countries represent a control group of similar countries *without* structural adjustment programmes. The limitations of this method centre on the extent to which the necessary similarity is in fact present in the countries chosen as the control. The required similarity in the control group may be absent for various reasons. If the structures of production are significantly different, as between the control group and the SAL group of countries, so the trading opportunities of the control group may be better or worse. The same is true if there is a significant difference in the average size of foreign exchange holdings. As well as these two examples, many other factors may differ and lead to a comparison which gives misleading results (for example, balance of payments deficits, growth and inflation rates).

The way to try and eliminate the differences that distort the comparisons is to compose the two groups on the basis of close initial pairwise comparison of the countries concerned. In other words, for every SAL country placed in the SAL group, a non-SAL country is placed in the control group which has been pre-tested for similarity in major characteristics which would distort the comparison. These characteristics are its general level of development measured by per capita GNP; its recent rate of per capita growth of real output; and its recent changes in terms of trade, as well as later changes during the period after the initial position. The availability of statistics limits the number of characteristics for which pair wise comparisons are possible. But in any case no pairing can be perfect: it is often simply not possible to guarantee to find a country which is identical in the relevant respects. However, to the extent that we intend to compare the average of the performance of the two groups, one can rely on the assumption that some of the unavoidable remaining differences will cancel each other out.

There remain other sources of potential distortion in these group comparison exercises. One is the fact that not all the SAL countries performed equally well in terms of the implementation of the required policy changes. Here we need to have recourse to the indices of implementation which have already been discussed in the previous section. These enable the formation of a smaller high-implementation SAL group, with a smaller control group using only the relevant paired control countries. This approach provides a considerable refinement of the approach (used by the World Bank and others in the 1980s) of comparing the performance of countries receiving SALs with the performance of all non-oil exporting developing countries.

If the group comparisons are based on a common time period, some further refinement may still be necessary. Not all SAL programmes started at the same time. So within any fixed time period, some will be more advanced than others; it may therefore be necessary to drop from the SAL group countries whose SAL programme began only late in the fixed time period, because their values of the criterion variables cannot reflect very much of the impact of SAL policy changes. Obviously, if this is done, the paired countries must also be dropped from the control group.

Even after all these refinements have been made, however, it is hard to interpret the results obtained – countries 'with structural adjustment packages' may (or may not) have out-performed those 'without'. But since not all such packages are identical, what have we learned that is useful for policy?

CROSS-SECTION COUNTERFACTUALS: AN ECONOMETRIC APPROACH

Another major source of difficulty also remains unresolved. It is that in the SAL countries policy conditionality and programme aid accompany each other. It is hard to say whether the better or worse performance of the SAL group in terms of the criteria should be attributed to the SAL policy changes (when these have been implemented) or to the inflows of programme aid. In order to be able to discriminate between the many influences which may have contributed to the performance of the SAL countries, it is useful to undertake multiple regression analysis.

The general form of the analysis is to take each of the chosen intermediate criteria as the dependent variable in a separate regression equation. The independent variables to be regressed fall into three categories:

(1) financial flows, separating out World Bank flows from those of the IMF and (where relevant) domestic flows;

(2) indicators of the degree to which policy changes have been made as a result of loan conditionality;
(3) other relevant variables, such as the state of the weather and the movement of the external terms of trade.

The lag structure of the independent variables is an important consideration. This is especially so in categories (1) and (2), because these are the influences whose effects it is a priority to disentangle. Once the regression equations have been estimated and the coefficients tested for statistical significance, it is possible to estimate the strength and timing of the effects of the different categories of influence – finance, on the one hand and policy changes on the other. This is important because the regressions enable us to throw light on situations where no difference in performance exists between the SAL and the control countries. We can see the extent to which this situation arises because the effect of the aid inflows and the effect of the policy conditionality operate in contrary directions and cancel each other out. Such findings can have powerful implications for the redesign of adjustment lending modalities.

CONSTRUCTING THE COUNTERFACTUAL: THE SINGLE-COUNTRY MODEL

We have discussed so far two versions of the 'with and without' methodology. We have looked at the country group comparison method. Here the counterfactual is represented by the performance of similar countries that do not have SAL programmes. The problems of this counterfactual centre on how similar the two groups of countries really are. We have also looked at the econometric approach. Here the counterfactual is represented by zero values of the SAL component of the financial flows variables and of the compliance index for SAL conditions. This counterfactual, too, fails to eliminate the possibility of biased results, because the zero value countries may differ systematically in some other respects from the positive value countries.

The use of a single-country model overcomes the problems that arise from using other (possibly dissimilar) countries in the counterfactual. A model itself constitutes a well-defined causal structure for the main aspects of macroeconomic activity. This structure is the same for the 'with' and 'without' cases, *except* to the extent that precisely defined changes are inserted into different runs of the model to simulate the effects of alternatives to SAL finance and policies. This represents a very substantial advance in constructing the counterfactual.

A second major advance is the fact that a simulation model can explore the effects of SAL policies in a more disaggregated way than either the country group comparisons or the econometric approach. Both of these rely on capturing the effects of SAL policies by use of the compliance index, which is a single number. It is a proxy for the implementation of SAL-related policies. But SAL-related policies, though broadly similar between countries, actually vary in their detail. Also, as has been explained previously, no single number can fully represent the extent to which a complex package of policies has been implemented. Dispensing with the compliance index is, therefore, another very attractive feature of the single-country model approach. In its place, the effect of an individual policy instrument within the conditionality package of policies can be analysed separately. We can ask what would have happened if a condition relating to devaluation had not been implemented while other conditions for policy change had been implemented. Thus, in principle, the modelling approach provides a much more sensitive and disaggregated method of examining the consequences of policy.

Despite both these advantages, the single-country model approach has been relatively little used, because it also has big problems attached to it. They may be listed as:

(1) the definition of the counterfactual;
(2) the design and calibration of a suitable model;
(3) the integration of economic and social variables.

Each of these is discussed below in turn.

The model is normally made of a country which has accepted SAL finance and conditionality. The actual performance of the economy thus gives the 'with' part of the 'with and without' comparison. The 'without' part, however, is less straightforward, because of the need to define what policies would have been adopted if the SAL policies, as well as the SAL finance, had been rejected. It can often be quite unclear what the alternative policies would have been. The easiest case, perhaps, arises when the decision to accept SAL finance and conditionality has been preceded by an informed public debate in which a feasible alternative is clearly spelled out. One can then assume that the alternative programme is the counterfactual against which the with-SAL performance should be evaluated. Another easy case is when one can safely assume that rejection of structural adjustment would have been followed by policy paralysis, that is, no changes would have been made in the economic policy instruments. However, it is obvious that there are many stopping places between policy paralysis and the implementation of a feasible alternative programme.

Because the situation never did arise in fact, it is hard to say what is the most reasonable counterfactual assumption to make.

Designing and calibrating an economic model, too, is rarely as easy as the textbooks make it seem. The minimum content of a macroeconomic model is a set of national accounts identities, which ensure the internal consistency of the numbers in the model. This is absolutely necessary, but at the same time fairly straightforward to design. Choosing how to focus the model, that is, which sectors or markets to model in greater detail, usually follows from the type of policy measures one is trying to evaluate. It would be hard to evaluate, for example, a fiscal stabilisation policy without a reasonably detailed government sector in the model design.

The real problem arises in specifying the 'well-defined causal structure' which has been cited as a key advantage of the modelling approach. Where does this come from? In many models, it comes from the econometric estimation of functional relationships using data which embody many years of previous experience ('time-series'). Developing countries often do not have sufficient statistics of the required quality for this method to be usable. At the same time, it has to be asked whether it is sensible to rely on historical functional relations to evaluate performance during a period when extensive structural change is being attempted. The econometric method is also very costly in terms of the researcher's time, and therefore also in terms of money. For all of these reasons, econometric estimation tends to be abandoned, in favour of writing in a causal structure which corresponds with the researcher's intuition and calibrating the model with the most recent year's data. Inevitably, such an intuition-based simulation model is more subjective in the results it produces than an econometrically estimated model. On the positive side, it is cheaper, more timely, and easier to use.

One way of simplifying the modelling task is not to use an economy-wide model, if that is not necessary. A model of one sector of the economy may be sufficient to evaluate those forms of adjustment lending that are sectorally focused. This yields further savings of time and money. The drawback is that a sectoral model only provides a partial equilibrium analysis. It assumes that whatever happens within the sector being modelled has no effect on any other sectors and hence no feedback effects on to the modelled sector itself. The realism of this partial analysis will need to be checked against reality.

Another short cut, particularly when it is necessary to evaluate economy-wide measures, is to adapt an economy-wide model that has already been constructed for another purpose. One type of model that can be adapted in this way is the computable general equilibrium model (or CGE model). The basic idea of general equilibrium models is that they calculate the feedback effects between decisions taken in all types of market until all markets finally clear. For practical purposes, the number of different markets has to be kept quite small (for example, goods, labour, money and foreign exchange). The agents in these markets also have to be categorised fairly broadly (for example, key sectors, key types of households, the government and the banks). Computable production and consumption functions have to be defined (including inter-industry demand). 'Closure' rules have to be specified to define the manner of market clearing. A recent development of the CGE-type model has been the addition of a financial sector (despite the theoretical oddity of the existence of money in a general equilibrium system). This development is of obvious importance for evaluating policies which include those of financial liberalisation.

CGE models allow the exploration of the effects of different structural adjustment policies which have economy-wide effects. Examples are taxation policies, foreign trade regimes and financial liberalisation. When they employ a disaggregated household sector, they can throw light not only on questions of growth and internal and external balance, but also on distributional issues. The effects of adjustment policies on the level of employment, on the number below a poverty line and on the degree of income inequality can all be estimated.

In elaborate models of the CGE type, unevenness in the quality of design and articulation is usually evident. It is rare to find an example which does not contain some features which contradict normal economic logic, or at the very least embody crude and arbitrary assumptions. Areas where assumptions are especially problematic are supply elasticities and the speed with which markets clear. Even when the model can reproduce the statistical path of the economy quite accurately (and by no means can all models do this), the presence of imposed assumptions will give misleading results for policy purposes. The model-builders themselves are usually very conscious of where and how their model designs are most unsatisfactory. They recognise that their craft is still rather under-developed (see for example, Gaiha, 1988, pp. 36–7). It is interesting to note that Ghana, though a leading example of successful structural adjustment, does not yet have a CGE model of its economy.

Despite the fact that some indications of the impact of adjustment on employment, poverty and inequality can be derived from a CGE model, such models are not good at evaluating many aspects of socioeconomic policies. These are originally static models which find long-run investments in human resources, such as health and education spending, hard to incorporate. Apart from the difficulty of introducing dynamic considerations such as these into equilibrium models, it is much easier for a researcher to define a causal structure among pure economic variables, than it is among the variables that affect human resource development. Many factors impinge on health. The provision of health services is important, but so too is the level of education, the position of women in society and the quality of the external environment. It is much harder to specify all these complex interrelations than it is to specify the links between income, demand, supply and price. The social economy is more resistant than the economy itself to the modelling approach. At present, we have only partly verified the microeconomic mechanisms which link structural adjustment measures to household welfare (Gaiha, 1988, pp. 57–60). This is an important consideration as 'adjustment with a human face' has successfully established itself on the development agenda.

We should also note that single-country models by definition do not deal with the effects that structural adjustment in one country may have on other countries. One such effect is the reduction in price of other countries' exports which can follow from measures to increase the adjusting country's volume of exports. Some studies (see De Rosa and Greene, 1991) suggest that this effect is significant for beverage tree crops (tea, coffee and cocoa) and certain non-ferrous metals (copper). To measure the consequences of several countries undertaking adjustment simultaneously, it is necessary to construct a multi-country applied general equilibrium model, such as the RUNS model of the OECD Development Centre, Paris (for details, see Evans, Goldin and van der Mensbrugghe, 1991).

As the above discussion suggests, none of the evaluation methods reviewed – country group comparisons, econometric equations or single-country models – is without difficulties and deficiencies. This does not necessarily mean that they are useless for evaluation purposes. Rather than use none of them, one should use them all. If certain results emerge from all or most of the methods applied, it is possible to be confident that they are fairly robust. Our mirrors of reality may be cracked and distorted, but if we have enough of them, we may still be able to pick up some of the key features of what we are trying to observe.

CONCLUSIONS

The Appraisal of SAL Programmes

(a) Different methods are required for aid appraisal, on the one hand, and aid evaluation on the other. Appraisal is the assessment of a future proposal; evaluation is the assessment of past events in relation to some hypothetical alternative scenario (what has been called here 'the counterfactual').

(b) The methods used for appraisal and evaluation of *project* aid are by now quite well defined. But these methods are not appropriate for the appraisal and evaluation of *structural adjustment lending*, whose key features are the combination of programme aid with policy conditionality or an economy-wide or sectoral basis.

(c) In the appraisal of adjustment lending, donors rely, usually heavily, on the economic analysis and policy conditionalities of the IMF and the World Bank. But occasionally they may place further restrictions of their own on their co-financing.

(d) The method for determining whether any further restrictions are imposed is based on calculations of the effective rate of protection and the domestic resource cost ratio for the sector of the recipient country's economy which will finally use the aid finance. Sequencing of policies can be important, but there is no proven method to determine the optimal sequence for reforms.

The Evaluation of SAL Programmes

(a) The ex post evaluation of adjustment lending is a relatively new area of research. A methodology has recently been designed and applied by Mosley, Harrigan and Toye (1991).

(b) The first step is to develop indicators of the degree of implementation of the policy conditionalities of the adjustment loans. Single-number indicators can only be very approximate because of the many conceptual problems attaching to the idea of 'slippage' in implementation.

(c) The second step is to develop the criteria of evaluation. 'Sustainable growth with distributional equity' is too vague to be operational. Intermediate (and usually economistic) criteria have to be defined instead.

(d) Evaluations of adjustment based on comparison of economic performance before and after the implementation of adjustment measures or of planned performance with actual performance will be misleading because the implied counterfactuals are not credible.

(e) Cross-country comparisons can have a more credible counterfactual if the sample and the control group of countries are closely matched pair-wise both for similarity of economic characteristics and for the degree of implementation of conditionality.

(f) Cross-country comparisons using econometric techniques permit the separation of the effects of policy reforms from the effects of the aid inflows themselves. But this requires a proper specification of lags in the estimating equations.

(g) A single-country model provides a well-defined causal structure which can help to provide a reasoned counterfactual for the adjustment performance of a particular economy analysed in isolation. The effect of particular parts of the package of policy conditionalities can also be analysed separately with such a model.

(h) Nevertheless, three major problems obstruct the use of the modelling approach. It can often remain quite unclear what the government would have decided to do if it had not adopted the policy conditionalities attached to an adjustment loan. The cost of building a properly specified model is very great and its justification debatable. Finally such models are not well-developed for the purpose of evaluating socioeconomic policies, because the functional relations in areas of health, education and social welfare are much more difficult to specify than ordinary demand, supply and price relations. Nor do single-country models capture the effects of one country's adjustment measures on the economic performance of *other* countries. For that purpose, large multi-country general equilibrium models are needed.

Notes

1. I am grateful to Charles Harvey, Ike Inukai and Kohiti Sakamoto for comments on an earlier draft. The usual disclaimer applies.
2. The European Community assistance for structural adjustment under Lomé IV implies some criticisms of the Bank/Fund programmes of the 1980s – their conditionalities and their neglect of social dimensions. But little of this has yet generated a new EC approach to appraisal. The Japanese have also begun to voice criticism of Bank/Fund policies (see OECF, 1992, pp. 11–18).
3. In making this list, I have been heavily influenced by the practice of the British ODA during the late 1980s (see ODA, 1987). The ODA has been much more in support of Bank/Fund programme design than other donors.
4. 'Our (economic) theories ... do not provide us with a satisfactory analysis of timing and sequencing. That is not a subject which can be analyzed very easily and it is not one on which economic theory has progressed very far. It deserves our attention.' (Stern, 1989, p. 21).

References

Balassa, B. and D. M. Schydlowsky (1972) 'Domestic Resource Costs and Effective Protection Once Again', *Journal of Political Economy*, vol. 80, pp. 63–9.

Corden, W. M. (1966) 'The Structure of a Tariff System and the Effective Protective Rate', *Journal of Political Economy*, vol. 74, pp. 221–37.

De Rosa, D. and J. Greene, (1991) 'Will Contemporaneous Devaluation Hurt Exports from Sub-Saharan Africa?' *Finance and Development*, vol. 28, no. 1, March.

Evans, D., I. Goldin and D. van der Mensbrugghe (1991) 'Trade Reform and the Small Country Assumption', Paris, OECD Development Centre, mimeo.

Gaiha, R. (1988) 'Structural Adjustment and Rural Poverty in Developing Countries: a Survey', University of Delhi (Faculty of Management), mimeo.

Greenaway, D. and C. Milner (1991) 'Fiscal Dependence on Trade Taxes and Trade Policy Reform', *Journal of Development Studies*, vol. 27, no. 3, pp. 95–132.

Lipton, M. and J. Toye (1990) *Does Aid Work in India?* (London: Routledge).

Mosley, P., J. Harrigan and J. Toye (1991) *Aid and Power: The World Bank and Policy-based Lending* (London: Routledge).

ODA (1987) 'The Assessment and Design of Programme Aid: Guidance Note for Economists' (London: ODA) mimeo.

—— (1988) *Appraisal of Projects in Development Countries* (London: HMSO).

OECF (1992) 'Issues Related to the World Bank's Approach to Structural Adjustment', *OECF Research Quarterly*, 1992/2, no. 73.

Ray, A. (1984) *Cost-Benefit Analysis: Issues and Methodologies* (Baltimore: Johns Hopkins University Press, for the World Bank).

Smith, L. D. and N. J. Spooner (1992) 'Sequencing of Structural Adjustment Policy Instruments in the Agricultural Sector' in C. Milner and A. J. Rayner, 1992 (eds) *Policy Adjustment in Africa* (London: Macmillan).

Stern, N. (1989) 'Prices in Planning', *China Programme No. 1*, LSE, STICERD Development Economics Research Programme.

Thomson, B. P. (1984) 'Programme Aid' in *The Evaluation of Aid Projects and Programmes* (London: ODA).

8 Education and Adjustment: The Experience of the 1980s and Lessons for the 1990s

FRANCES STEWART*

INTRODUCTION

The 1980s was a decade of adjustment for much of the Third World, especially for most countries in Africa and Latin America. The stabilisation and adjustment policies followed – mainly under the auspices of the IMF and World Bank – were necessitated by major imbalances that developed in the early 1980s and persisted for much of the decade. Many countries suffered very large deficits in their external accounts, with the value of imports plus payments due on their debt greatly exceeding the value of their exports, while budget deficits were also pervasive.

Stabilisation and adjustment policies were intended to reduce the imbalances, correct some of the policy biases and establish the basis for sustainable growth. The policies were adopted – with more or less effective implementation[1] – in many countries, often almost continuously throughout the 1980s, dominating policy-making and displacing most long-run development policies (Table 8.1). Because of the pervasiveness, dominance and prolonged nature of stabilisation and adjustment policies, they had wide-ranging medium-term consequences, not only for the macro-economy but also for the social sectors and for vulnerable groups.[2]

This chapter reviews the impact of the policies on the *education* sector. As discussed below, any adverse effect on education is of great significance for long-term development efforts, as well as for the immediate welfare of children, since human capital, it is now recognised, is among the most important factors for economic growth and transformation, while female education especially also has much wider significance, through its effects on household health, nutrition and family size. Moreover, education represents the only chance for children from poor households to break out of the cycle of poverty.

*This is a revised version of a paper prepared for the Commonwealth Secretariat. I am grateful for their permission to publish it here, and to Robert Cassen for comments on an earlier draft.

Table 8.1 Incidence of stabilisation and adjustment policies, 1980s*

	Number of countries with programmes			
	5 or more years		*2–4 years*	
	IMF	*WB*	*IMF*	*WB*
Sub-Saharan Africa	13	2	9	21
Latin America and Caribbean	5	2	12	10
Rest of the world	5	4	11	5
Total	23	8	32	36

* Data from IMF for 1989 incomplete.
Sources: World Bank (1990) RAL II; Khan (1990).

In order to understand how policy changes associated with stabilisation and adjustment affect education, it is necessary to show how supply and demand for education services fit into the macroeconomy. The next section provides a brief overview of the interconnections between macro and meso developments and education, followed by a discussion of the likely impact of major policy changes associated with adjustment. Following this the empirical evidence of how the main variables relevant to supply and demand for education were affected over this period is reviewed. The chapter then considers whether and to what extent changes in supply and demand led to changes in the quantity and quality of education. Some evidence on the importance of education for development, and why adverse changes matter is then presented. Finally some lessons from the experience of the 1980s for adjustment policies in the future are considered.

THE MACROECONOMY AND THE EDUCATION SECTOR

Education encompasses formal schooling of both children and adults, in specially designated educational institutions, training associated with economic enterprises, and informal education of children and adults in the home and community. Over their lifetime people learn more from informal sources than from formal, but in this review attention will be focused on formal education mainly because of data availability, but also because informal sources of education are generally complementary to and to some extent dependent on the formal education system (as for example, the education imparted by mothers, which is heavily dependent on the formal education they themselves have received).

Like many other commodities, the quantity (and quality) of education depends on both supply and demand. But both supply and demand have peculiar features. In most societies, supply is dominated by the public sector. Education is demanded largely as an investment good (for the future income it makes possible); demand for education is affected by the economic costs and benefits from attending school.

Changes in the macroeconomy affect both supply and demand. The links are illustrated in Figures 8.1 and 8.2.

Supply

The national income provides the resources from which all expenditure – including that on education – comes. The proportion of national income allocated to education can be viewed as the product of a series of decisions: first, how much of national income is allocated to public expenditure, which we shall describe as the *expenditure ratio*; second, the proportion of government expenditure going to education, or the *education allocation ratio*. Together the expenditure ratio and the education allocation ratio determine the total public resources available for education as a proportion of national income. But this leaves open how the education budget is spent, which can make a great difference to the equity and efficiency of the system. A critical set of decisions therefore concern *education expenditure patterns* within the sector. We describe the proportion of educational expenditure going to primary education as the *education priority ratio*; the proportion going to recurrent costs as the *recurrent ratio*.

The impact of stabilisation and adjustment policies on the supply of public education can thus be seen as depending on the impact on the level of GNP per capita, the expenditure ratio, the education allocation ratio and education expenditure patterns.

Demand

There are important cultural and social factors determining the demand for different levels of education in any society. But economic factors also play a part (Figure 8.2). Education involves some quite heavy costs to the household – both direct costs, consisting of transport, money for books, uniforms and fees, and indirect costs (or opportunity costs) consisting in the incomes the children might have earned if they were not at school, and also non-income earning activities they might perform, like working on the family farm and looking after younger children. Both types of costs bear more heavily on poorer households. These costs are compared with the benefits the

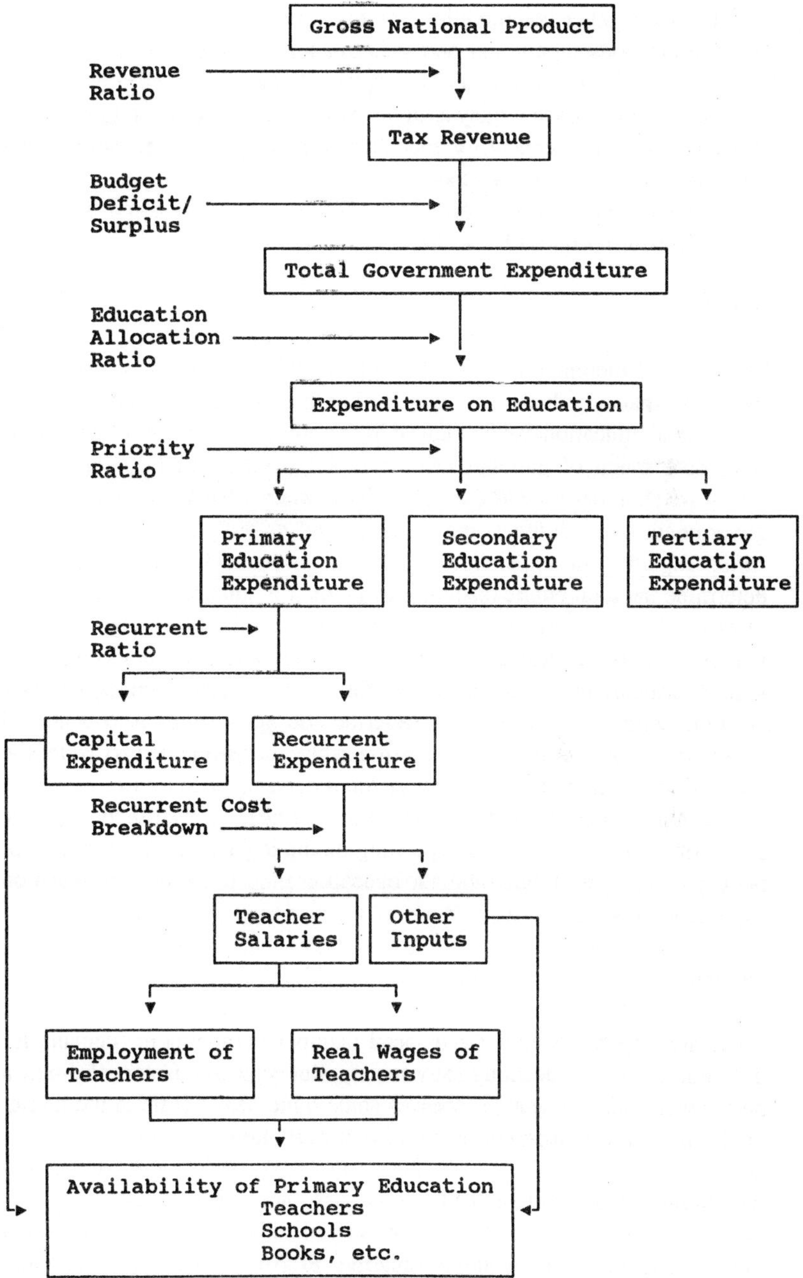

Figure 8.1 Factors affecting supply of education

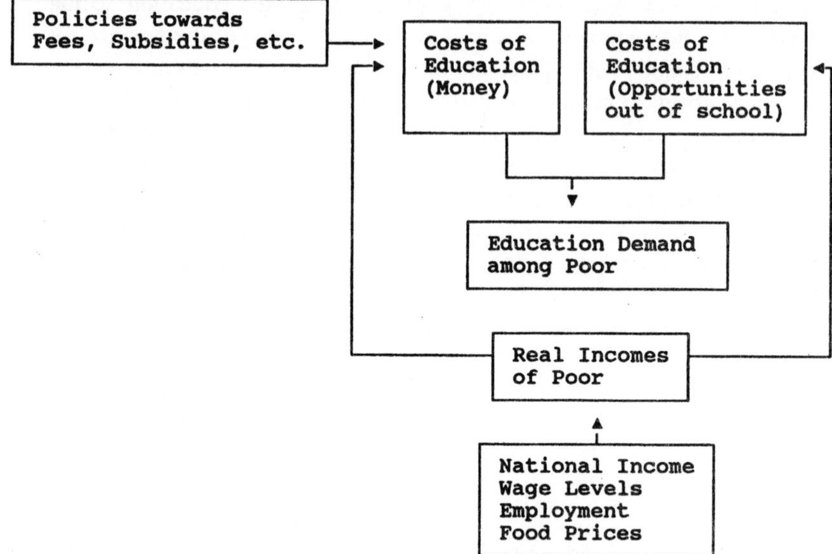

Figure 8.2 Factors affecting demand for education

individual or household is expected to receive, economic and non-economic, in determining demand for education. The economic benefits to the individual are the additional earnings more educated people are expected to earn.

Changes in the economic system affect both costs and benefits. On the cost side, a critical factor is the real incomes of the poor, since the lower the income, the greater the costs appear. There is evidence that the direct costs of education alone can be quite high in relation to incomes of poor households: for example, in three West African countries, parental costs of primary education amounted to 7–14 per cent of average per capita GNP.[3] This would be equivalent to 30 per cent or more of the income of low-income households. Thus any reduction in incomes of the poor can be expected to reduce demand for education. Moreover, the indirect costs, or loss of income from children's work, may be of greater importance to poor households, although this can be offset by lesser economic opportunities for children in these households.[4] In general, then, we can expect demand for education to vary positively with income and to fall if real incomes of the poor fall.

Stabilisation and Adjustment Policies

The stabilisation and adjustment policies of the International Monetary Fund and the World Bank are mainly directed at the macroeconomy, but nonetheless they have important implications for the education sector. Until 1987, little attention was paid to the implications of the policies for the social sectors or for vulnerable groups. Since then, however, the Bank has made efforts to monitor developments and adapt some of its policies.

The content of Fund stabilisation programmes is, by now, well known.[5] There are three elements: demand restraint, with emphasis on public expenditure reductions, credit control and real wage restraint; switching policies, especially emphasising exchange rate reform and devaluation; and long-term supply policies including financial reform and trade liberalisation. Analysis indicates that demand restraint policies dominate, being a universal feature, while over half the programmes include switching policies and a somewhat lower proportion long-term reforms.[6]

The WB structural adjustment policies also include demand restraint, switching and long-term supply, but the main elements of macroeconomic stabilisation are left to the Fund. About 85 per cent of Bank adjustment conditions relate to efficiency. In these reforms, the Bank shares the market-oriented philosophy of the Fund. Areas covered include trade policies (usually import liberalisation), industry, energy and agricultural policies (with emphasis on reforming and deregulating the price system), reforms of the financial sector, rationalisation of government and administration, public enterprise reforms (with emphasis on privatisation) and social policy reforms.[7] Social policy reforms accounted for just 2.9 per cent of all adjustment lending conditions by the Bank, pre-1987, and only 6 per cent in the post-1987 era.[8]

The policies can be expected to affect the education sector in the following way:

(1) Through any impact on levels of GNP, which, as shown above, would potentially affect both supply and demand for education. Stabilisation policies are liable to involve depressed incomes in the short run, while adjustment policies are intended to lead to acceleration in the growth of GNP.

(2) Through affecting the real income levels of the poor, and therefore demand for education. Stabilisation and adjustment policies which reduce public sector employment levels and hold down real wages are likely to reduce the real incomes of the poor in the short run, as will abolition of food subsidies, but this can be offset by improved rural incomes and (in the longer run) new employment opportunities.

(3) Through impacts on direct costs of education (for example if fees are introduced or raised, as is sometimes the case in education sector adjustment loans).

(4) Through changes in the supply ratios described above. The most obvious effect is through stabilisation policies, which tend to involve reduced government expenditure ratios. Changes in allocation and priority ratios may occur in a way that accentuates or offsets this effect.

DEVELOPMENTS IN THE 1980S

Below, I describe what happened to the major variables relevant to the education sector and to the outcome in terms of the performance of this sector over the period. But to describe what happened is not to attribute responsibility for these events. In a sense the economic crisis was responsible for developments – the policies were a reaction to this crisis. Had these policies not been adopted some other set of policies would have been introduced, which in turn would have affected the outcome. Thus to attribute responsibility to the adjustment policies is only legitimate if it can be shown that the effects that followed were different from those that would have occurred without them. Yet this poses an impossible task because we cannot know for sure what would have happened. Quite complex methodologies have been developed to try to hypothesise what would have happened,[9] none completely satisfactory. In the analysis below, I stick mainly to a description of actual developments, making occasional attempts to present a contrast with what might have been. This approach is legitimate given the basic aim of the chapter – which is to identify actual developments and point to preferable options.

The Supply Side

Macro Developments: The Course of GNP

The most disappointing outcome of the adjustment policies of the 1980s was the very poor performance of GNP per capita, especially in Sub-Saharan Africa and Latin America. There was considerable variation in macro performance among adjusting countries: on the one hand, there is the experience of Indonesia, Burkina Faso and Mauritius, for example, which combined adjustment with economic growth and rising rates of investment; on the other, countries such as Zambia and Argentina which had sharply declining per capita incomes and falling investment, and, despite successive programmes, have not reduced the imbalances in their economies, either budgetary or external.

Despite this variation, in Sub-Saharan Africa and Latin America – the two major adjusting areas – the balance of experience in the 1980s was undoubtedly negative, as indicated in Table 8.2; each region exhibited falling per capita incomes in the 1980s, falling investment and accelerating inflation. The balance of payments current account showed some improvement

Table 8.2 Macro performance of adjusting countries

	GNP per capita[a] *1980–88*	*Budget*[b] *deficit (–) surplus (+) as % 1989*
Sub-Saharan Africa		
Early-intensive adjusters		
Cote d'Ivoire	–3.7	n.a.
Ghana	–1.4	+0.4
Kenya	–0.2	–4.4
Madagascar	–3.4	n.a.
Malawi	–0.6	–6.0
Mauritania	–1.3	–4.2
Mauritius	+5.1	–1.5
Nigeria	–4.3	–10.5
Senegal	+0.3	n.a.
Tanzania	–1.3	n.a.
Togo	–2.8	–2.6
Zambia	–4.9	–4.6
Average	–1.5	–4.2
Other adjusting	–0.7	n.a.
Whole SSA	–2.2	–6.1[d]
Latin America		
Early-intensive adjusters		
Bolivia	–4.3	–1.6
Brazil	+1.2	–14.9
Chile	–0.1	–0.2
Colombia	+1.2	–0.7
Costa Rica	+0.2	–2.3
Jamaica	–2.1	n.a.
Mexico	–1.4	–4.8
Average	–0.8	–4.0
Other adjusting	–1.9	–2.9
Whole LA	–0.4	–8.3[d]

continued

Table 8.2 (continued) Macro performance of adjusting countries

	GNP per capita[a] *1980–88*	*Budget*[b] *deficit (–) surplus (+) as % 1989*
Other Areas		
Early-intensive adjusters		
Korea	+7.7	+1.6
Morocco	+0.8	–4.6
Pakistan	+3.0	–7.0
Philippines	–2.4	–2.8
Thailand	+3.8	+3.1
Turkey	+3.0	–4.6
Average	+2.7	–2.4
Asia	+7.5	n.a.
Middle East	+0.4	n.a.
All developing	+3.8	–5.8[a]

Sources: a UNDP, *Human Development Report (1991)*;
b World Bank, *World Development Report (1991)*;
c These are countries which have had the longest experience of World Bank adjustment programmes (see RAL II, World Bank);
d Budget deficit as per cent GNP, 1988 (UNDP, 1991).

(substantial in the case of Latin America) but was still in large deficit, despite rescheduled debt and restricted imports; the budget deficit showed no improvement in Sub-Saharan Africa, but a marked improvement towards the end of the decade in Latin America; the inflation rate was stable in Sub-Saharan Africa, but accelerated greatly in Latin America. Thus for the two regions taken as whole the macro adjustment measures of the 1980s were associated with deterioration in macro performance, while the adjustment process was not completed, as indicated by the persistent imbalances. There is evidence especially for Latin America, however, of improvement in the latter half of the decade.

The weak macro performance was shared by countries with IMF and World Bank programmes, as well as those without them (Table 8.3).

More sophisticated analysis of the macro effects of IMF and World Bank policies suggests that Fund stabilisation policies alone had some negative effects on growth, Bank adjustment policies had a small positive effect, while each had negative effects on the investment rate, compared with some hypothesised counterfactual (see World Bank (1990); Mosley et al. (1991); Khan (1990)). Outside Sub-Saharan Africa (SSA) and Latin America (LA) actual growth performance has, on balance been positive among adjusting countries. But in SSA and LA, there was falling income per capita among adjusting countries (as well as non-adjusting) *reducing the resources available to meet educational needs.*

Resources for the Education Sector

As shown earlier, for any given level of national income, the resource flows to the publicly funded education sector depend on the proportion of national income going to public expenditure and the proportion of public expenditure going to the education sector (Table 8.3 and 8.4).

The adjustment programmes – especially those of the IMF – tended to emphasise expenditure reduction rather than tax increases in order to reduce the budget deficit.[10] Among twenty-one adjusting countries is SSA, only four increased their expenditure ratio over these years; the rest showed a decline. About half the adjusting countries in SSA showed a decline in the education allocation ratio, with a higher proportion in Latin America (60 per cent), and a lower proportion (40 per cent) in the rest of the world. The rest of the world tended to have more positive changes on both ratios.

As a result of these changes, in Africa, the proportion of national income devoted to education fell in 12 cases and rose in only four. In Latin America, it fell in seven out of ten cases. In the rest of the world, it fell in three out of five cases. Thus on balance *meso policies* had a negative effect on the education sector. For the most part, the worsening per capita income, as a result of poor macro performance, combined with negative meso policies to lead to a fall in education expenditure, as shown in Table 8.5. In Africa, education expenditure per head fell in eleven out of sixteen cases. In some cases, the fall was quite catastrophic – as for example, in Tanzania, Zambia and Zaire – where there was adverse movement in each of the three variables. But some countries managed to protect and even increase education expenditures through meso policies, even when income was falling – Ghana's success was most spectacular, increasing education expenditure per head[11] by more than 40 per cent, as a result of an increase in both expenditure ratio and education allocation ratio. It should be noted that this was achieved while the budget deficit was reduced.

In Latin America, the fall in education expenditure per head was equally pervasive, though no falls were as drastic as the worst Africa cases. Only countries with positive GNP changes managed to increase education

Table 8.3 Changes in expenditure on education as per cent of GNP, 1981–89: Sub-Saharan Africa

	Expenditure ratio %		*Education allocation ratio %*		*Public expenditure on education as % GNP*	
	1981	*1989*	*1981*	*1989*[a]	*1981*	*1989*
Sub-Saharan Africa						
Early-intensive adjusters						
Cote d'Ivoire	32.2	22.1[d]	16.3	22.6[b]	5.2	5.0[e]
Ghana	10.1	14.0	22.0	25.7	2.2	3.6
Kenya	28.4	28.0	20.6	22.1	5.9	6.2
Madagascar	n.a.	18.9[d]	14.1	18.5[b]	n.a.	3.5[c]
Malawi	35.3	29.5	11.1	12.3	3.9	3.6
Mauritania	35.8[e]	42.0[d]	n.a.	14.3[b]	n.a.	6.0[c]
Mauritius	33.0[e]	24.2	15.8	15.3	5.2[e]	3.7
Nigeria	25.4[e]	28.1	7.8	2.8	2.0[e]	0.8
Senegal	29.3	22.3[d]	21.3	16.9[b]	6.2	4.6[c]
Tanzania	33.3	20.0[d]	12.1	8.5[b]	4.0	1.7[c]
Togo	35.3	32.5	n.a.	19.9	n.a.	6.5
Zambia	39.9	20.0	11.9	8.6	4.7	1.7
Other adjusters						
Burkina Faso	14.6	11.2	15.8	14.0	2.3	1.6
Burundi	21.2	18.1[d]	n.a.	15.5[b]	n.a.	2.8[c]
Central African Republic	23.5	31.5[d]	16.9	16.8[b]	4.0	5.3[c]
Congo	54.6	20.0[d]	n.a.	14.0[b]	n.a.	2.8[c]
Mali	25.9	28.9	15.7	9.0	4.1	2.6
Niger	25.9	17.5[d]	18.0	22.9[b]	4.7	4.0[c]
Sierra Leone	27.2	16.6[d]	14.3	18.1[b]	3.9	3.0[c]
Zaire	33.8	18.4	20.2	6.1	6.8	1.1
Zimbabwe	31.3	40.8	19.5	23.4	6.1	9.5

Notes:
a WDR, 1991.
b HDR, 1991: data for 1987–88.
c HDR, 1991; for 1986.
d Estimated.
e % GDP.

Sources: World Bank, World Development Report (1991); UNDP/World Bank *African Economic and Financial Data (1989);* UNDP, *Human Development Report (1991).*

Table 8.4 Changes in expenditure on education as per cent of GNP: Latin America and rest of world

	Expenditure ratio %		*Education allocation ratio %*		*Education as % GNP expenditure*	
	1981	*1989*	*1981*	*1989*	*1981*	*1989*
Latin America						
Early-intensive adjusters						
Bolivia	12.7	16.8	24.4	20.3	3.1	3.4
Brazil	19.5	30.6	3.8	4.2	0.7	1.3
Chile	31.0	32.5	14.4	10.1	4.5	3.3
Colombia	n.a.	n.a.	n.a.	n.a.	n.a.	n.a.
Costa Rica	23.7	27.8	23.7	17.0	5.6	4.7
Jamaica	44.9	42.1[a]	14.2	13.3	6.4	5.6
Mexico	20.8	21.2	18.2	12.3	3.8	2.6
Other adjusters						
Argentina	23.6	15.5	7.3	9.3	1.7	1.4
Ecuador	17.1	14.2	30.1	23.4	5.1	3.3
Peru	36.1	31.7	12.8	19.1	4.6	6.1
Uruguay	24.9	25.8	7.7	7.9	1.9	2.0
Other intensively adjusting countries						
Korea	19.0	18.5	17.9	16.9	3.4	3.1
Morocco	39.8	29.1	16.5	17.0	6.6	4.9
Pakistan	17.7	21.5	3.1	5.0	0.5	1.1
Philippines	12.8	17.1	14.2	15.7	1.8	2.7
Thailand	18.5	15.1	19.3	19.3	3.6	2.9
Turkey	23.3	23.7	16.8	15.7	3.9	3.7

Note: a: 1988.
Source: As Table 8.3.

expenditures per capita. The reason lies in the poor performance on the education allocation ratio, which is largely a reflection of the rising share of interest payments in the government budget.

To summarise, in Latin America and Africa, despite some exceptions, macro and meso policies combined to generate negative effects on education expenditures. In the rest of the world, positive growth of per capita income, together with more favourable ratios, led to rising expenditure per head on education in all but one case.

Table 8.5 Expenditure per capita on education

	GNP per capita	*Expenditure ratio*	*Education allocation ratio*	*Education expenditure per capita, 1989 (1981=100)*
Sub-Saharan Africa				
Early-intensive adjusters				
Cote d'Ivoire	–	–	+	0.73
Ghana	–	+	+	1.46
Kenya	–	–	+	1.03
Madagascar	–	n.a.	+	n.a.
Malawi	–	–	+	0.88
Mauritania	–	+	n.a.	n.a.
Mauritius	+	–	–	1.06
Nigeria	–	+	–	0.28
Senegal	+	–	–	0.76
Tanzania	–	–	–	0.38
Togo	–	–	n.a.	n.a.
Zambia	–	–	–	0.24
Other adjusters				
Burkina Faso	+	–	–	0.84
Burundi	+	–	n.a.	n.a.
Central African Republic	–	+	–	1.25
Congo	+	–	n.a.	n.a.
Mali	+	+	–	0.65
Niger	–	–	+	0.60
Sierra Leone	–	–	+	0.65
Zaire	–	–	–	0.14
Zimbabwe	–	+	+	1.44

continued on facing page

Other investigations have analysed the impact on education expenditure among adjusting countries, as compared with some counter factual. The most comprehensive is that of Kakwani et al. (1990) and World Bank (1990) which apply econometric analysis, allowing for differences in initial conditions and exogenous developments, differentiating between adjusting and non-adjusting countries. Both studies find that countries that were intensively adjusting had worse performance on three educational indicators – the education allocation ratio (here defined as a proportion of 'discretionary' – that is, non-interest – expenditure), education expenditure per capita and gross primary school enrolment rates – as compared with other countries.[12]

Table 8.5 (continued) Expenditure per capita on education

	GNP per capita	*Expenditure ratio*	*Education allocation ratio*	*Education expenditure per capita, 1989 (1981=100)*
Latin America				
Early intensive adjusters				
Bolivia	–	+	–	0.77
Brazil	+	+	+	2.04
Chile	–	+	–	0.73
Costa Rica	+	+	–	0.85
Jamaica	–	–	–	0.84
Mexico	–	+	–	0.61
Other adjusters				
Argentina	–	–	+	0.72
Ecuador	–	–	–	0.59
Panama	+	–	+	1.34
Uruguay	–	+	+	0.94
Rest of World, intensively adjusting				
Korea	+	–	–	1.65
Morocco	+	–	+	0.79
Pakistan	+	+	+	1.27
Philippines	–	+	+	1.23
Thailand	+	–	0	1.12
Turkey	+	+	–	1.20

Source: As Table 8.3.
Note: + = increase;
– = decrease.

Education Expenditure Patterns

(i) The priority ratio – the share of resources going to primary education
There is wide variation across countries in the proportion of education expenditure going to primary education ranging from 21 per cent (Venezuela) to 83 per cent (Chad), suggesting considerable scope for reallocation of education expenditures in some countries. Evidence on changes in the ratio over the adjustment period for the most part suggests an *improvement* in this ratio – that is the proportion of expenditure going to primary education on balance increased in adjusting countries for which we have evidence.

Table 8.6 Changing priority ratios in selected countries

Primary as % total education expenditure		
Africa[a]	*1980*	*1987*
Ethiopia	42.0	52.8
Malawi	38.9	47.0
Tanzania	45.0	59.1
Madagascar	41.4	42.3
Burkino Faso	32.3	39.2
Burundi	42.7	45.0
Mali	38.8	48.4
Ugunda	16.2	20.1
Zambia	45.3	44.2
Rwanda	67.1	68.0
Central African Republic	63.1	51.2
Lesotho	38.6	35.7
Latin America	*1980*	*1986*
Argentina	46.2	10.0 (85)
Bolivia	64.0	64.0 (85)
Brazil	18.4	49.0
Chile	45.7	51.1
Costa Rica	33.0	37.0
Dominican Republic	43.4	53.6 (87)
Jamaica	38.0	35.0 (87)
Venezuela	28.3	43.5

Note: *a* Proportion of total recurrent expenditure spent on primary education.
Sources: WCEFA Background Document, Table 3, 1990; Grosh (1990).

Among 23 African countries, only seven *decreased* the proportion of recurrent expenditure allocated to primary education, while 15 increased the proportion between 1980 and 1987.[13] Among eight Latin America countries, five increased the proportion going to primary education and only two reduced it[14] (Table 8.6).

To some extent, the improvement in the primary school ratio was at the expense of secondary education, not tertiary. Thus among the African countries reported on by Dougna (1987), more countries decreased their allocation to secondary education (10) than to tertiary education (8), and more increased their allocation to tertiary (9) than secondary (5).[15] Among Latin American countries, six out of seven countries decreased their allocation to secondary schools, while only three out of seven decreased the allocation to tertiary education.[16] While the reallocation towards primary education is desirable both for equity and efficiency, the changing balance between secondary and tertiary education is likely to have worked in the opposite direction. Evidence for Sri Lanka shows that the poorest 20 per cent of the population receive 27 per cent of the benefits from primary education, 17 per cent of those from secondary education and 12 per cent from tertiary, while the richest 20 per cent receive 14 per cent of the benefits from primary education, 25 per cent from secondary and 32 per cent from tertiary.[17] There is also evidence for a few countries that *adult* education has been squeezed over these years: for example, in Tanzania, the share of adult education in recurrent expenditure fell from 7.5 per cent (1982–3) to 3.8 per cent (1986–7).[18]

(ii) The recurrent ratio – the share of educational expenditure going to recurrent costs There is consistent empirical evidence that capital expenditure tends to be cut more than recurrent when there are aggregate cuts in public expenditure, in general and also in the social sectors.[19] This was also indicated for the education sector over the 1980s.[20] This tendency is partly due to bureaucratic and political pressures, but it is also a rational response to a crisis that can be expected to be temporary. However, if the crisis is prolonged – as was the case over the past decade – then heavy cuts of capital expenditure may have seriously adverse effects over the long run.

Despite the relative protection of expenditure on recurrent costs in total education expenditure, recurrent costs per pupil fell in 18 African countries, 4 Asian, 13 Latin American and 5 Arab countries between 1980 and the latest available date, with severe cuts (over 5 per cent) in 22 countries.[21]

(iii) The recurrent cost breakdown It is often suggested that when government expenditure is cut, the heaviest cuts fall on material inputs, as wages are relatively protected, although evidence for government expenditure as a whole is conflicting on this point.[22] It has been suggested that material inputs were also most acutely affected in the education sector,[23] but the very limited evidence is not conclusive. A report on Africa argues that 'supplies of key inputs (especially books and other learning materials) are critically low and the use of these inputs has declined in relation to the use of teachers' time and of physical facilities'.[24] For Latin America, where expenditures on materials are very low (for example, less than 1 per cent of the recurrent budget in Bolivia and Costa Rica), a fall in the proportion of the recurrent budget going to teaching materials was noted in Argentina and Jamaica, but a rise in Chile, Costa Rica and Venezuela. The proportion also increased in the Philippines.[25]

Cuts in the budget inevitably mean cuts in the wage-bill which is much the largest element in recurrent costs. This may be achieved by cutting numbers of teachers, or by cutting wage levels, or some combination. The evidence suggests the major burden was borne by teachers' real wage levels. Numbers of primary school teachers continued to grow (albeit at a slower rate) in every region in the 1980s.[26] Teachers' salaries declined – often quite dramatically – in those countries for which evidence is available. For example, in Tanzania the 1987 level of a starting teacher was just 29 per cent of the 1977 level; that of someone at the top of the scale was only 23 per cent of the 1977 level. In Kenya, teacher salaries fell by 30 per cent, and in Zimbabwe by 40 per cent, but the falls were much smaller in Malawi and Zambia. In Costa Rica, the salary level of a primary school teacher fell by 30 per cent and a secondary school teacher by 35 per cent, 1980–87.[27] Data for real recurrent expenditure per teacher (a broad indicator of teacher wage-levels) show declines in 40 countries, especially concentrated in African and Latin American countries.[28]

Anecdotal evidence suggests that the declines in real wage-levels had some deleterious effects on teacher efficiency, for example increasing moonlighting. But it undoubtedly meant that pupils were relatively insulated against the fall in resources, while the teachers' levels of living bore a large proportion of the burden of the cuts.

The Supply Side: Summary

To summarise our findings: for many adjusting countries, negative movements in national income per capita were not offset, and were sometimes accentuated, by movements in the expenditure ratio and the allocation ratio, leading to a fall in education expenditure per head in the 1980s in 11 out of 16 adjusting countries in Africa for which we have evidence, and in eight out of ten adjusting countries in Latin America. But in the rest of the world, positive trends in GNP led to an increase in education expenditure in five out of six cases.

Changes in the priority ratio tended to protect primary education relatively, but secondary education suffered most. Capital expenditure also tended to be cut more than recurrent expenditure. Within recurrent expenditure, the brunt was born by the real wage levels of teachers. Teacher numbers were generally sustained.

The Demand Side

Many of the factors determining the demand for education (shown in Figure 8.2) were adverse in the 1980s.

Incomes

The downward movement in per capita incomes in many countries has already been noted in the earlier discussion (and Table 8.2). The income elasticity of demand for schooling is likely to be greatest among low-income households, and therefore special attention needs to be focused on the incomes of the poor. The adjustment policies were associated with cuts in employment (or a reduced rate of increase) and substantial cuts in real wages. For Latin America real wages fell significantly in eight out of 11 countries, often to below 50 per cent of their 1980 level. Similar falls were recorded in at least 16 African countries, with an average cut of 25 per cent, 1980–85. For some countries the cuts were much more severe – for example in Tanzania the real wage in 1986 was just 35 per cent of its 1980 value. As the rate of expansion of the formal sector slowed or reversed, open unemployment rose and the proportion employed in the informal sector – with much lower remuneration – rose in both regions.[29]

There is evidence of a significant rise in the proportion of the urban population in poverty in many adjusting countries. In Latin America, where the data are more extensive, urban poverty rose in ten out of eleven countries. This poverty was made worse by the fact that food prices rose faster than the general price level in most countries, due to deregulation, reduced food subsidies, increased agricultural producer prices and devaluation.[30] The rural poor were less badly affected by the adjustment policies, and in some cases the improved terms of trade for agriculture helped raise rural incomes. But this was sometimes offset by reduced fertiliser subsidies, while many poor households did not benefit from improved prices because they did not produce export products. In Latin America the (rather weak) evidence suggests that rural poverty decreased slightly in six countries, and rose in two. In Africa, detailed data shows rising rural poverty in the Ivory Coast, but elsewhere there are no reliable data.

Educational Charges

The introduction of 'user' chargers is a near-universal aspect of the adjustment policies. For the education sector, this means the introduction of school fees, and shifting of responsibility of finance of books, etc. onto parents. An analysis of a sample of World Bank loans showed that in 51 loans, there were 87 conditions relating to financing in the education sector, of which 60 per cent concerned the reallocation of resources, and 40 per cent resource mobilisation. Introducing/raising book and tuition fees accounted for nearly half of the resource mobilisation measures. Stevenson (1991) states that while cost recovery measures included the primary level in the early 1980s, only limited cost recovery is currently recommended at this level.

Systematic evidence on the introduction or increase in educational charges is not available. But evidence suggests parental costs were increased in a wide range of countries, often including the primary level. Primary school fees for tuition and/or books were introduced in Malawi, Zaire, Mali and parts of Nigeria, in each case followed by lowering of school attendance. Book fees were introduced in Ghana, including at the primary level, while at the secondary level the subsidy for food and boarding was withdrawn. In Burkina Faso, the state stopped providing school supplies, which became the responsibility of parents and the community. In Zambia, fees were introduced for secondary boarding schools, placing a particular burden on rural families for whom the only option is boarding. In Sierra Leone, school authorities 'have had to supplement their low incomes by imposing a multiplicity of hidden charges on parents and pupils' and it is estimated that parental cost per student has quadrupled.[31]

Opportunity Costs of Education

These can be divided into two – lost earnings from paid employment, and the use of children's time for domestic duties. As far as the first is concerned, the reduced opportunities for employment and remuneration reduced the money value of what the children might earn in paid employment. On the other hand, for families on the verge of survival, the value of children's earnings to the family may increase because of their vital role in family survival. In some countries female participation rates rose as women sought to offset declines in income by seeking paid employment,[32] increasing the need for children – particularly girls – to perform domestic duties.[33]

The Demand Side: Summary

Although the data are not comprehensive, the evidence shows that almost every relevant element tended to *decrease* demand for education – with falling incomes reducing families' ability to pay the expenses of education and increasing the need for children's earnings, greater pressure on women to work outside the home leading to the use of girls as substitutes in domestic duties, and, in some areas, increased direct costs of education as fees were introduced or raised and other costs were redistributed from the state to the parents.

PERFORMANCE OF THE EDUCATION SECTOR

The survey has indicated that both supply and demand were negatively affected by economic developments and adjustment policies in the 1980s. This section considers how far these negative influences were reflected in the performance of the education sector, both in quantity and in quality. There are two crucial aspects of performance of the sector: how many children it educates and how well it does so.

Quantity

The numbers going through education at all levels continued to expand, taking the world as a whole. But in some countries, progress in expanding education was reversed during the 1980s, while in others it was slowed. As Table 8.6 shows, 42 per cent of countries showed a fall in the primary school enrolment ratio, and a lesser proportion (21 per cent) a fall in secondary enrolment rates. The data for new entrants to primary schools for African countries show a much greater and more pervasive decline – out of 30 countries new entrants fell in 24, whereas total enrolment fell in only six[34] – suggesting that the change in aggregate enrolments understates the deterioration. In some countries the reduction in enrolment rates was large: for example, in Tanzania primary school enrolment dropped in absolute terms, as the gross enrolment ratio dropped by about a quarter. This is probably the first time since the Dark Ages that progress in extending education has been reversed on such a scale. As noted earlier, the intensively adjusting countries do quite markedly worse than other countries on the primary enrolment rate, with 56 per cent showing a fall.

School survival rates provide another indicator of reduced performance in quantitative achievements of the school system. Berstecher and Carr-Hill (1990) find that out of 57 countries, there was a decrease in 23 and an improvement in 18, while in 16 countries the rate remained broadly unchanged. The average number of years each student attends school showed a decrease in a similar proportion of countries (Table 8.7).

Indicators of Quality

There are a variety of indicators of educational quality, for which piecemeal evidence is available. Data for recurrent costs per student for 69 countries show that more than half experienced a decrease in the 1980s, 17 in Africa, 11 in Latin America and nine elsewhere. But as noted earlier, the effect on quality of education resulting from this was moderated by the declining salaries of

Table 8.7 Enrolment ratios, 1980s

	Gross primary enrolment	*Gross[a] secondary enrolment*	*Survival rate*	*Average length of study*
Number of countries decreasing	40	14	23	23
Number of countries increasing	55	62 (4)[b]	18 (16)[b]	19 (15)[b]
Number decreasing				
Africa	14	8	11	7
Latin America	10	2	5	8
Other	16	4	6	8
Intensively adjusting				
Number decreasing	14	n.a.	n.a.	n.a.
Number increasing	11			

Notes: a Source for the secondary ratios are *World Development Report,* 1984 and 1991. The data may be less accurate than the primary data.
b Figures in brackets are number of countries with no change.

Sources: Berstecher and Carr-Hill (1990); *World Development Report* (1984; 1991); World Bank (1990) RAL II.

teachers. The number of years required to complete five years' schooling increased in 12 countries in Africa, three countries in Latin America and four elsewhere out of a total of 57 countries. In 12 countries (out of 45), the proportion of girls in total primary school enrolment decreased.[35]

For other indicators, the evidence is less comprehensive. Table 8.8 summarises some evidence for 18 countries, all affected by economic difficulties and adjustment policies. Increased repetition rates (similar but not identical with the measure of years taken to complete five years schooling) worsened in seven countries out of 16; progression rates from primary to secondary school fell in six countries (out of eight); the (very limited) evidence on test scores showed worsening in three cases and improvement in five. The number of students per teacher increased in either primary or secondary level or both in six cases out of nine for which there is evidence. The ratio of girls to boys in primary school continued to increase in 13 countries, but fell in five.

These indicators show worsening quality in about half these adjusting countries. This does not mean, of course, that the situation is worse than non-adjusting countries, but does suggest some important failures on the education front among adjusting countries.

Table 8.8 Quality indicators for a sample of countries

	Recurrent expenditure per student	*Repetition rate*	*Progression rate*	*Test scores*	*Students/ teacher*	*Ratio of girls/total enrolment (primary)*
African countries						
Botswana	+	–	+	+	n.a.	–
Burkino Faso	–	+	+	–	–	+
Cameroon	+	–	–	+	n.a.	+
Ethiopia	+	n.a.	–	+	n.a.	n.a.
Malawi	–	–	–	n.a.	n.a.	+
Senegal	–	+	+	+	n.a.	+
Zambia	–	+	–	n.a.	n.a.	+
Latin America						
Argentina	0	+	n.a.	n.a.	–	+
Bolivia	–	–	n.a.	n.a.	–	+
Chile	+	+	n.a.	–	+(p)	–
Costa Rica	–	–	–	–	–(p) +(s)	–
Dominican Republic	0	+	n.a.	n.a.	+(p) –(s)	n.a.
El Salvador	+	+	n.a.	n.a.	+	+
Jamaica	–	0	n.a.	n.a.	+	+
Venezuela	+	?	n.a.	n.a.	+(p) –(s)	+
Other						
Morocco	?	+	n.a.	+	n.a.	+
Turkey	+	–	n.a.	n.a.	n.a.	+
Philippines	–	–	–	+	n.a.	–
Korea	+	0	n.a.	n.a.	n.a.	+

\+ improvement 0 no change (p) primary
– deterioration ? conflicting evidence (s) secondary

Sources: Berstecher and Carr–Hill (1990); Ogbu and Gallagher (1991); Grosh (1990); Noss (1991); World Bank, *World Development Report (1984)*; UNDP, *Human Development Report (1991)*.

There were thus serious reversals in the previous trend improvement in both quantity and quality of education in a large number of countries in the 1980s. But it must be emphasised that some countries succeeded in maintaining progress on major aspects: for example Botswana made significant advances on most indicators over this period, while increasing the enrolment rate at both primary and secondary level. Senegal and Morocco also showed progress on almost all indicators. Very few countries showed positive performance on every indicator, however, as Table 8.8 indicates.[36]

DOES THE WORSENING EDUCATIONAL PERFORMANCE MATTER?

If education were primarily for consumption purposes, it might be regarded as a luxury that countries could do without during crisis, to be resumed when the adjustment period was over. But – as is now widely recognised – this is not the case. Education is an extremely important type of investment, of major significance for economic performance. Moreover, female education improves the health and nutrition of children and also helps to bring down population growth by leading to reduced family size. There is a massive accumulation of empirical evidence on these issues: below I present a short summary and a few examples.

Economic Returns to Education

Numerous studies round the world have shown high economic returns to education. Private returns of over 30 per cent have been recorded in some places, while for developing countries as a whole the average returns for every level of education exceed 10 per cent – a common cut-off point for deciding whether to go ahead with physical investment. Many investigations show that returns to female education are greater than male education, while returns to primary education are usually greater than for secondary or tertiary.[37]

World Bank estimates of the social returns (which include costs and benefits not directly borne by the individual), are 24 per cent for primary education as a whole in developing countries (compared with an estimate of 31 per cent for private returns), 15 per cent for secondary (private returns 19 per cent) and 13 per cent for tertiary (private returns 22 per cent).[38] But these figures understate the true social returns because they do not allow for the positive effects on productivity and health associated with education.

Education and Productivity

Farming productivity

Evidence shows that the productivity of farmers *using modern technology* increases significantly with schooling. Farmers who use traditional technology are less affected. Analysis of farmer productivity in South Korea, Malaysia and Thailand – where modern technologies were in use – showed additional physical output of 3 per cent for every additional year of schooling among cultivators, while a comparison between productivity in the Punjab in India and Pakistan attributed the superior performance in the Indian Punjab to the greater education of farmers and institutional factors.[39]

Industrial Productivity

Education, supplemented by industrial training, has been established as an important determinant of industrial productivity, with the level of education needed depending on the type of technology. 'Basic numeracy and literacy are essential for all modern processes.'[40] As the complexity of technology increases, higher levels of education and vocational training are needed.[41]

Female Education and Health

Mothers are the most important health workers for their children. Female education increases mothers' information on health practices and improves household health behaviour; raises mothers' earning power and therefore household expenditure on the basic needs of the family; and enhances women's role in family decision-making, leading to greater emphasis on children's welfare.

Studies in every part of the globe have shown the close connection between female education and health. For example, studies in Colombia, Nigeria, Peru and Malaysia showed that infant death rates were significantly greater among the babies of uneducated mothers. A 17-country study showed that an additional year of schooling reduced infant mortality by 9 per 1000 live births.[42] Maternal education was shown to have a significant effect in improving child nutrition in Colombia, Jordan, Lebanon, Nepal, Nicaragua, Nigeria and the Philippines.[43]

Education and Fertility

Studies all over the world show that female education decreases fertility.[44] In Kenya, women with the highest education have two children less than women who have completed only primary education. In Colombia, there is a difference of four children.

The positive social and economic returns to education mean that the falling enrolment rates and declining quality of education observed so widely in the 1980s will have serious negative effects on economic growth potential and progress in health and nutrition over the years to come. Weakening the education system has more serious effects than cutting back on physical investment. The 'lost' physical investment can be replaced, when the crisis is over; but a generation whose education is deficient will suffer for the rest of their lives, and so will their children and their society.

LESSONS FOR THE FUTURE

The 1980s experience of developments in the educational sector was clearly unsatisfactory in many adjusting countries, with falling education expenditure per student, falling enrolment rates and some deterioration in quality. The intensively adjusting group of countries were on the whole worse affected than other countries. This is obviously undesirable, not only from the perspective of the lost opportunities of the children concerned, but also for the adverse effects this is likely to have on future social and economic conditions. The most obvious and clear-cut lesson for the 1990s, then, is that this situation should be reversed and the long-term progress in education resumed on a world-wide basis. The critical question is how?

It is not necessary to be speculative or fanciful to see how the situation could be improved. It is only necessary to record what actually happened in the countries that did succeed in maintaining educational progress. Each of the suggestions made here are reflections of experience in some countries in the 1980s. The main requirement is to increase the resource flow to the educational system. Something can, of course, be achieved by redirection of expenditures and raising the efficiency of resource use, but it is naive to believe that this type of measure can generally compensate for reduced resources.

Macro Policies

While the social sectors can be protected when GNP per capita falls, it is increasingly difficult to sustain over a long period. Thus the first necessity is to avoid excessively sharp and/or prolonged periods of deflation, but combine adjustment with growth. This was achieved in Indonesia, Korea, Columbia, Ghana and Botswana during the 1980s. To achieve this, the policies need to be less deflationary, and external financial support may be required, either in the shape of new lending, or in a reduced debt burden. The new debt initiatives and cuts in world interest rates may make this strategy easier to achieve in the 1990s.

The Expenditure/Tax Balance

Emphasis needs to be placed on raising government revenue rather than cutting expenditure. Some countries were very successful in this respect in the 1980s, and were able to raise government expenditure, while reducing the budget deficit: for example, Botswana, Burkina Faso, Colombia and Ghana. Most countries which placed prime emphasis on expenditure cutting also cut educational expenditure.

The Education Allocation Ratio

There is potential for increasing the share of government expenditure on education. In the 1980s this was very difficult to achieve because of the huge increase in the share of expenditure going to interest payments, but this may be reversed in the 1990s. Nonetheless, some countries – including Guatemala, Panama, Venezuela, Egypt and Zimbabwe – did raise the share of government expenditure on education. In countries, where defence preempts a large share of the budget there is strong potential for reducing this and increasing the education allocation ratio. In 1986 at least 36 countries were spending more on military purposes than on education.

Intra-Sectoral Allocation

Increasing the proportion of resources being spent on primary education is a way of protecting basic education, carried out by quite a number of countries in the 1980s. But there is a danger of achieving this at the expense of secondary education which also has important social and economic returns. However, countries spending a very low proportion of their budget on the primary sector may achieve much by reorientation, especially from tertiary education: for example, Venezuela, Mexico, Cuba, Nigeria and Guinea each spend less than one-quarter of total public education expenditure on the primary sector.[45]

Fees and Charges

Recently the World Bank has emphasised the introduction/raising of charges as a way of raising resources for the sector. However, charges rarely raise a large amount of revenue – in 1988 China and Nigeria raised most in this way, yet in both cases charges accounted for only 5 per cent of public expenditure on education.[46] Moreover, experience in the 1980s showed that fees and charges tended to discourage school enrolment. Tertiary education is the one area where fees do seem appropriate, combined with student loans.

Reducing Costs

The largest element of costs is teachers' salaries. In the 1980s, in many places costs were cut by quite drastic reductions in these salaries. In some places, salaries are now below an efficiency level, leading to poor quality and absentee teachers. But elsewhere teacher salaries remain very high in relation to per capita incomes: for example, in Burkina Faso, the average primary school salary is estimated at 13 times the average per capita.[47] The desirability and potential of further reductions in teachers' salaries thus varies with the situation in the particular country. In countries where salaries are high, the use of assistant teachers can help reduce costs – as for example, in Colombia. The Bangladesh Rural Advancement Committee (BRAC) introduced a new school system with basic education costing only $15 per pupil, partly as a result of using teachers who are not fully trained. Increasing class size (within limits) can reduce the teacher cost per pupil without affecting achievements.[48] This may be achieved by double shifts, which also reduces the capital costs per pupil. Zambia reduced capital costs by almost half through shifts; Senegal reduced costs, while raising enrolment by introducing shifts in its urban classes, also making greater use of assistant teachers.[49] These mechanisms can offer considerable savings in some countries, but cost-reducing measures alone are not likely to be sufficient to protect the sector when cuts in aggregate expenditure persist.

The Role of the Private Sector

Expansion in the private sector (encompassing both profit-making initiatives and community efforts) can reduce the impact of public expenditure cuts. The evidence suggests that the proportion of pupils in private schools increased in a number of countries in the 1980s.[50] This is a response to inadequate public provision. But while it increases the total resources going to education, it also leads to some problems. It is usually not a solution for children from poor households, who cannot even afford the out-of-pocket expenses of publicly provided schools. It also tends to be associated with a two-tier system of education and perpetuation of divisions within society.

CONCLUSION

The education sector is too important to become a casualty of adjustment, as it did in some countries in the 1980s. The evidence suggests that this was unnecessary and could have been avoided, by a number of different measures described above. In any particular country, the appropriate package of policies will depend on the particular circumstances: but in each case, there are feasible options which would protect and advance the sector, even during adjustment.

Notes

1. Mosley, Harrigan and Toye (1991) argue that many countries failed to implement the policies fully.
2. For an overview of the impact on vulnerable groups see Cornia et al. (1987); Stewart (1991 and 1992).
3. Berstecher and Carr-Hill (1990, p. 64).
4. In some areas of Africa decreases in demand for education were shown to be stronger in the regions where agriculture was flourishing and consequently opportunity costs of attending school were higher (Berstecher and Carr-Hill, 1990, p. 69).
5. See, for example, Killick (1984); Cornia in Cornia et al. (1987); Williamson (1983).
6. Cornia (1987).
7. See World Bank (1990, RAL II); Mosley (1987); Mosley, Harrigan and Toye (1991).
8. Chhibber et al. (1991).
9. See, for example, World Bank (1990) RAL II; Mosley, Harrigan and Toye (1991).
10. See Cornia and Stewart (1990).
11. This is not, of course, the same as education expenditure per student. Rising enrolment rates mean that this increased less fast in the Ghana case.
12. These two studies covered 86 (Kakwani et al., 1990) and 78 countries (World Bank, 1990). Two other studies with smaller coverage and using a simpler methodolgy found no definite effects (Sahn (1989); Gallagher (1990)).
13. Data from WCEFA Background Document.
14. Grosh (1990).
15. Quoted in Berstecher and Carr-Hill (1990).
16. Grosh (1990).
17. Alaihima (1984); see Grosh (1990) for similar evidence for a number of Latin American countries.
18. Wagao (1990).
19. See Hicks and Kubish (1984); Cornia et al. (1987); Hicks (1991).

20. Noss (1991); Ogbu and Gallagher (1991); Grosh (1990).
21. Berstecher and Carr-Hill (1990).
22. There is some support for this view in Pinstrup-Andersen, Jaramillo and Stewart (1987), but conflicting evidence in Hicks (1991).
23. Lewin (1987).
24. World Bank (1988), quoted in Berstecher and Carr-Hill (1990).
25. Colclough and Lewin (1990).
26. Berstecher and Carr-Hill (1990, Table 15).
27. Data from Wagao (1990); Zynelman and DeStefano, quoted in Noss (1991); Grosh (1990).
28. Berstecher and Carr-Hill (1990); Grosh (1990).
29. For more detailed evidence see Stewart (1991a, b).
30. For evidence see Stewart (1991); Reul and Garrett (1991).
31. Evidence from Stevenson (1991); Cornia et al. (1987); Toye (1991); Savadogo and Wetta (1991); Clarke (1988); Kamara et al. (1990).
32. Cornia et al. (1987).
33. Moser (1989).
34. Carr-Hill (1991).
35. Data from Berstecher and Carr-Hill (1990).
36. See also Berstecher and Carr-Hill (1990).
37. Schultz (1989).
38. World Bank (1986).
39. Jamison and Lau (1982); World Bank (1983).
40. Lall (1989).
41. Harbison and Myers (1964).
42. Cornia (1984); Caldwell (1979); Cochrane (1980).
43. Wray and Aguirre (1969); Wolfe and Behrman (1983); Barrera (1990).
44. See Cochrane (1980); Cassen (1981).
45. Though this only includes central government expenditure, so the picture could look different if other levels were included, especially in federal states.
46. UNDP, *Human Development Report* (1991, p. 66).
47. Savadogo and Wetta (1991).
48. Colclough and Lewin (1992).
49. Colclough and Lewin (1992); UNDP (1991, p. 62).
50. Noss (1991).

References

Alaihima, P. (1984) 'Fiscal Incidence in Sri Lanka 1973 and 1980', WEP Working Paper, WEP 2–32/WP 56 (Geneva: ILO).

Barrera, A. (1990) 'The Role of Maternal Schooling and its Interaction with Public Health Programs in Child Health Production', *Journal of Development Economics*, vol. 32, 61–91.

Berstecher, D. and R. Carr-Hill (1990) *Primary Education and Economic Recession in the Developing World since 1980* (Paris: UNESCO).

Caldwell, J. C. (1979) 'Education as a Factor in Mortality Decline', *Population Studies*, vol. 33, no. 3.

Carr-Hill, R. (1991) *Social Conditions in Sub-Saharan Africa* (London: Macmillan).

Cassen, R. (1981) 'Population and Development', *Recent Issues in World Development* (Oxford: Pergamon).

Chhibber, A. et al. (1991) 'Supporting Policy Change: The Interrelation between Adjustment and Sector/Investment Lending', processed (Washington DC: World Bank).

Clarke, J. (1988) *Debt and Poverty: A Case Study of Zambia* (Oxford: Oxfam).

Cochrane, S. (1980) 'The Effects of Education on Health', World Bank Staff Working Paper, 405 (Washington DC: World Bank).

Colclough, C. and K. Lewin (1992) *Educating all the Children: Strategies for Primary Schooling in the South* (Oxford: Oxford University Press).

Cornia, G. A. (1984) 'A Survey of Cross-Sectional and Time-Series Literature on Factors Affecting Child Welfare', *World Development*, vol. 12, no. 3.

Cornia, G. A. (1987) 'Economic Decline and Human Welfare in the First Half of the 1980s' in Cornia et al.

Cornia, G. A. and R. Jolly and F. Stewart (1987) *Adjustment with a Human Face* (Oxford: Oxford University Press).

Cornia, G. A. and F. Stewart (1990) 'The Fiscal System, Adjustment and the Poor', Innocenti Occasional Papers, EPS 11 (Florence: UNICEF).

Dougna, K. D. (1987) 'Crise economique et crise d'education en Afrique', IIEP/KD/87–06 (Paris: International Institute for Educational Planning).

Faini, R., J. del Melo, A. Senhadji-Semiali and J. Stanton (1989) 'Growth-Oriented Adjustment Programs: A Statistical Analysis', L d'A/QEH Development Studies Working Papers 14 (Oxford: Queen Elizabeth House).

Gallagher, M. (1990) 'Fiscal Duress and the Social Sectors in Developing Countries', Background paper for *World Development Report* (Washington DC: World Bank).

Grosh, M. E. (1990) *Social Spending in Latin America: The Story of the 1980s*, World Bank Discussion Paper, 106 (Washington DC: World Bank).

Harbison, F. H. and C. S. Myers (1964) *Education, Manpower and Economic Growth* (New York: McGraw-Hill).

Hicks, N. (1991) 'Expenditure Reductions in Developing Countries Revisited', *Journal of International Development*, vol. 3, no. 1.

Hicks, N. and A. Kubish (1984) 'Recent Experience in Cutting Government Expenditures', *Finance and Development*, vol. 21, 37–9.

Jamison, D. T. and L. J. Lau (1982) *Farmer Education and Farm Efficiency* (Baltimore: Johns Hopkins University Press).

Kakwani, N., E. Makonnen and J. van der Gaag (1990) 'Structural Adjustment and Living Conditions in Developing Countries', World Bank PRE Working Paper, WPS 467 (Washington DC: World Bank).

Kamara, S., M. T. Dahniya and P. Greene (1990) 'The Effect of Structural Adjustment Policies on Human Welfare in Africa South of the Sahara: Sierra Leone', mimeo, (Florence: UNICEF).

Khan, M. S. (1990) 'The Macroeconomic Effects of Fund-Supported Adjustment Programmes', *IMF Staff Papers*, 37.

Killick, T. (1984) *The Quest for Economic Stabilisation* (New York: St. Martins Press).

Lall, S. (1989) 'Building Industrial Competitiveness: New Technologies and Capabilities in Developing Countries' (Paris: OECD Development Centre).

Lewin, K. (1987) *Education in Austerity: Options for Planners,* Unesco, International Institute for Educational Planning.

Moser, C. (1989) 'The Impact of Recession and Structural Adjustment Policies at the Micro-Level: Low-Income Women and Their Households in Guayaquil, Ecuador' in UNICEF, *Invisible Adjustment*, 2 (UNICEF).

Mosley, P. (1987) 'Conditionality as Bargaining Process: Structural Adjustment Lending 1980–86', *Princeton Essays in International Finance*, no. 168.

Mosley, P., J. Harrigan and J. Toye (1991) *Aid and Power* (London: Routledge).

Noss, A. (1991) 'Education and Adjustment: A Review of the Literature', mimeo, (Washington DC: World Bank).

Ogbu, O. and M. Gallagher (1991) 'On Public Expenditures and Delivery of Education in Sub-Saharan Africa', *Comparative Education Review*, vol. 35, no. 2.

Pinstrup-Andersen, Jaramillo, M. and F. Stewart (1987) 'The Impact on Government Expenditure' in Cornia et al., op. cit.

Psachoropoulos, G. (1980) 'Return to Education: An Updated International Comparison' in 'Education and Income', World Bank Staff Working Paper 402 (Washington DC: World Bank).

Reul, M. and J. Garrett (1991) 'Economic Crisis, Health and Nutrition: Evidence from Central America', Paper for Workshop on 'Macroeconomic Crises, Policy Reform and the Poor in Latin America', Cali, October 1–4, processed (Washington DC: Cornell University Food and Nutrition Program).

Sahn, D. (1989) 'Fiscal and Exchange Rate Reforms in Africa: Considering the Impact Upon the Poor', (Washington DC: Cornell University Food and Nutrition Program).

Savadogo, K. and C. Wetta (1991) 'The Impact of Self-Imposed Adjustment: The Case of Burkina Faso, 1983–89', Innocenti Occasional Papers, 15 (Florence: UNICEF).

Schultz, T. P. (1989) 'Women and Development: Objectives, Frameworks and Policy Interventions', PPR Working Paper, WPS 200 (Washington DC: World Bank).

Stevenson, G. (1991) 'Adjustment Lending and the Education Sector: The Bank's Experience', mimeo, (Washington DC: World Bank).

Stewart, F. (1991a) 'The Many Faces of Adjustment', *World Development*, vol. 19, no. 12.

Stewart, F. (1991b) 'Protecting the Poor during Adjustment in Latin America and the Caribbean in the 1980s: How Adequate was the World Bank Response?', L d'A/QEH Development Studies Working Papers, 44 (Oxford: Queen Elizabeth House).

Toye, J. (1991) 'Ghana's Economic Reforms and World Bank Policy-Conditioned Lending 1983–88' in Mosley et al., op. cit.

UNDP (1990) *Human Development Report 1990* (New York: Oxford University Press).

UNDP (1991) *Human Development Report 1991* (New York: Oxford University Press).

UNDP/World Bank (1989) *African Economic and Financial Data* (New York: UNDP/Washington: World Bank).

Wagao, J. H., (1990) 'Adjustment Policies in Tanzania, 1981–89: The Impact on Growth, Structure and Human Welfare', Innocenti Occasional Papers, 9 (Florence: UNICEF).

Williamson, J. (ed.) (1983) *IMF Conditionality* (Cambridge, Mass.: MIT Press).

Wolfe, B. L. and J. R. Behrman (1983) 'Is Income Overrated in Determining Child Nutrition?', *Economic Development and Cultural Change*, vol. 31, no. 3.

World Bank (1983) 'Review of Comparative Agricultural Performance in East and West Punjab', South Asia's Project Department (Washington DC: World Bank).

World Bank (1984) *World Development Report* (New York: Oxford University Press).

World Bank (1986) *The Rate of Return on Educational Expansion*, mimeo, (New York: Oxford University Press).

World Bank (1987) 'Argentina: Social Sectors in Crisis', LAC Report No. 6900-AR (Washington DC: World Bank).

World Bank (1988) *Education in Sub-Saharan Africa: Policies for Adjustment, Revitalisation and Expansion* (Washington DC: World Bank).

World Bank (1990) *Report on Adjustment Lending II: Policies for the Recovery of Growth* (Washington DC: World Bank) [RAL II].

World Bank (1991) *World Development Report* (New York: Oxford University Press).

Wray, J. D. and A. Aguirre (1969) 'Protein-Calorie Malnutrition in Candelaria, Colombia', *Journal of Tropical Pediatrics*, 15.

9 Development Ethics – An Emergent Field?

A look at scope and structure, with special reference to the ethics of aid

DES GASPER

AN EMERGENT INTER-DISCIPLINARY FIELD?

'Development ethics' is attracting increasing attention. An association has existed since 1984 which now uses the acronym IDEA (International Development Ethics Association). Already fairly well established in the Americas, it is extending more widely. IDEA's president recently published a survey article in 'World Development' (Crocker, 1991a), citing a notable number of relevant publications.

Crocker's valuable survey reflects how interest in development ethics has arisen from many streams of work. Moral and social philosophers, like Crocker himself, have been prominent. They are the largest group in IDEA, whose flyer even defines the association as 'a cross-cultural group of philosophers and practitioners'. Perhaps it uses the terms 'philosophers' and 'practitioners' broadly. Equally or more important than the extension to professional philosophers is the interest that has emerged from practice in governmental, international and non-government development organisations and groups, and from work on human rights, international relations and law, environment, gender and other fields, not least development economics. Adoption of the title WIDER for the UN's World Institute for Development Economics Research has to date been matched by its work. Some of the most interesting research on ethics now comes from development economists such as Amartya Sen and Partha Dasgupta who combine formal analytical skills with a relatively wide cultural and practical experience and basis for comparison.

The first meeting of a UK Development Studies Association study group on development ethics, in 1991, gave an indication of the range of starting points and interests. A philosopher presented some basic conceptual issues in development ethics; an economist outlined options in assessing (primarily material) well-being, drawing on work for the UNDP Human Development

Report; and an international relations specialist spoke on national sovereignty and the debt issue. Finally an educational administrator looked at distinctive issues of administrative ethics which arise in many cases in poor countries. Official rules may be impossible to follow; and salaries are often wretchedly low and/or not paid or paid very late, so that civil servants survive only through networks of kin and clan which impose their own demands and ethics. What norms and sanctions should be imposed in such cases?

These concerns from experience on the ground need to be accommodated in development ethics, at the same time as academics extend the range of their theories. A study like Shawcross's 'The Quality of Mercy' (1984), on the emergency food supply operation to Cambodia in 1979–83, illustrates how fraught and complex experience can be. He records the quandaries in which humanitarian organisations were placed and the paradoxes with which they had to deal, when facing high stakes but with severely limited information in situations of intra- and international conflict. Development ethics requires more than philosophers and economists enriching each others' models.

I want to present some ideas on the scope and contours of this growing field. We need to consider: is the development ethics field underdefined and over-broad? What are its relations to other areas of work, including ethical theory, applied ethics and development practice? One issue that Crocker raises is whether development ethics should be seen as a unified discipline of 'normative development science (or studies)' (1991a, p. 468), or rather as an interdisciplinary forum for mutually enriching exchange between a number of streams of work. In my view, development ethics is an interdisciplinary field, not even a subdiscipline. I doubt if it will become a subdiscipline, except possibly for some philosophers; nor is that to be seriously regretted. We are unlikely to have more agreement on scope, let alone priorities, in this field than we have in defining 'development' or 'development studies'. These questions of the coverage of development ethics and some of the different streams of work which make an entry are introduced in the next section.

Not surprisingly, the shape of an interdisciplinary field may appear differently according to people's academic discipline and experience. The approach used here grows out of development economics, but with influences from the revival of political philosophy and from other lines of thought and practice. The necessary structure of a response to the criticisms by writers like Bauer, Lal and Seers to giving development aid or promoting redistribution in less developed countries (LDCs) is sketched. I will emphasise the range of considerations that arise beyond conventional economics, and comment in particular on the contributions by Riddell and

Mosley. This picture of structure is extended and the variety and styles of literature on the ethics of development aid are examined.

Development ethics as now surveyed by writers like Crocker and essayed within IDEA is wider yet and the penultimate section returns to how we might define and order this variegated field. One option is to distinguish core, background and specialisation areas. Another is to seek unifying themes. I will note a few reasons why it may yet be wise for the field to remain consciously plural and resist disciplinarity.

WHAT IS DEVELOPMENT ETHICS?

Denis Goulet, whom Crocker and others identify as the pioneer of a self-conscious development ethics (DE), defined it as work on 'the ethical and value questions posed by development theory, planning, and practice', by the method of 'an explicit phenomenological study of values which lays bare the value costs of various courses of action' (1977, cited by Crocker, 1991a, p. 458).[1] Goulet apparently saw this activity as a 'new discipline'. His own work is compatible with seeing it as an interdisciplinary field that draws on and influences various areas, rather than as a separate formalised discipline or sub-discipline, let alone a master-discipline prescribing development principles and practice.

Pioneers need not be very precise in drawing boundaries. Nor need an interdisciplinary field, for it aims to influence, energise and cross-fertilise, rather than distinguish itself from others. But more might be asked of a 'new discipline'. What precisely would it cover? The implications of Goulet's definition depend on how one sees the scope of 'development' and 'development studies'. Goulet's own work has been on economically poor countries and societies, including their relations with the rich. Others see 'development' as global.

We should speak of 'development studies' (DS) in the plural. Many modes of study are involved, shading into and cross-cutting other fields. Firstly, there are positive analyses of development processes. The scope of this area of work depends on the definition of 'development'. Thus secondly, we have analyses of the meaning of 'development'. Some are positive interpretations: such as economic growth, or its proposed institutional and social accompaniments ('modernisation': Berger, 1977), like urbanisation, or extension of the world market or of certain relations of production. Other definitions are normative. The broadest of these takes 'development' to mean all desirable change. Somewhat more narrowly one can refer to desirable growth and modernisation.

'Development' also connotes maturation to fulfil a potential. Segal (1986) speaks of development normatively as the fulfilment of desirable human potentials. Since death and decline are also maturation, one could add another descriptive sense – i.e. all societal maturation. These maturational definitions are very broad. With more historical specificity, 'development; in a normative sense can refer to fulfilment to some degree of the potential to greatly reduce human suffering and increase material welfare in 'the South'. This potential became increasingly apparent over the past century but dramatically visible in the last 45 years with decolonisation and accelerated Northern growth and hence the appearance of the new fields of DS, centring on economically poor countries and their relations with the rich, while drawing on many background fields.

Thirdly, DS can include work on normative theories of value. For as Gavin Kitching notes: 'the issues with which "development studies" deals are some of the great issues (of justice, of equality and inequality, of the nature of the "good" life) with which human beings have been preoccupied since the days of Plato and Aristotle' (1982: viii). This third area is an extension of that on normative interpretations of 'development'. It covers the principles behind any particular normative interpretation and the further considerations needed to assess changes. It includes for example views on basic human 'needs' and appropriate (or 'human') mouldings of human nature; and the relative claims of needs, rights and capabilities (the topic of IDEA's 1991 Montclair workshop; Aman, 1991).

And fourthly, we have attempts to assess particular activities, approaches or options, drawing on both positive and normative analyses. The activities can range from a project to a programme (like relief to Cambodia) to an organisation (like an aid agency).

Now let us look again at Goulet's definition of DE: work on 'the ethical and value questions posed by [first] development theory, [and second, development] planning and practice'. If one uses *only* a positive definition of 'development', the first part in DE so defined will be small – for development theory is seen as only positive – including just issues in research ethics, avoidance of ethnocentrism, and so on. And the second part, the ethical issues in planning and practice, might be seen as outside the discipline of DS, a matter for (mere) planners, consultants and practitioners. If one uses instead, or in addition, a normative definition of 'development', then the first part in DE will include work on normative theories of value and the debate on how to refine our interpretations and understanding of good development. The second part of DE will not be marginal and will also include issues in the assessment of particular activities and behaviour.

Note the danger, if one uses the normative definition which sees development as simply meaning desirable change, that DE expands to become social ethics *in toto*. More helpful, even if still very broad, is to say that DE tries to understand and assess what are desirable growth, modernisation and structural change, and their implications. A more modest coverage within that range can be set by emphasising the options and dilemmas for economically poor countries.

Interestingly, DE's boundaries seem to be widening rather than narrowing. Crocker's own recent definitions are, firstly, 'the normative or ethical assessment of the ends and means of Third World and global development' (Crocker, 1991a, p. 457). In an earlier version he spoke only of 'the ends and means of "developing" societies' (1988). Secondly, wider still: 'International development ethics is moral reflection on the ends and means of societal and global change' (Crocker, 1991b, p. 149). This extends beyond the Third World to view all societies as 'developing'. And finally the IDEA flyer drops all societal or national reference: 'International development ethics is ethical reflection on the ends and means of global development'. Should one perhaps instead call that global ethics?

We return to these issues later. Before more theorising on what DE is or should be, we need to refer to some of its work.

WIDENING ECONOMISTS' APPROACHES TO ASSESSING DEVELOPMENT AID

The Challenge from Critics of Redistribution and Foreign Aid

Distribution and redistribution have always been important motifs in development studies, as in its concerns with land reform or international aid. This is no accident: the questions are unavoidable political issues in poor countries and part of the moral charge and attraction of development studies in rich ones. But criticism emerged that these concerns have often been not merely politically naive, but worse: ignorant, muddled and even hypocritical in their supposed ethical thrust. In reviewing three presentations of the 1970s concern with distribution – Chenery et al. (1974); ILO (1976); Adelman & Morris (1973) – Deepak Lal argued that they 'show no evidence of having thought through the implicit ethical premises of their recommendations' (1976, p. 731), and that the 'ethical preconceptions underlying [the first two] are particularly shallow' (p. 737).

Two features which Lal claimed to find in this literature deserve note (whether or not they apply to the books he was reviewing; see Gasper,

1986). The first of these was the use of a primitive normative theory of distribution: notably a stress on remedying inequality, not only poverty, including through redistributive policies of all types, subject only to feasibility constraints, with no awareness of ethical constraints. Bauer argued similarly that: 'Many writers on development...express concern with income differences, and regard as self-evident the case for their substantial reduction or even elimination...without examining the reasons behind the differences and the process by which they are reduced' (1975, p. 393).

Lal's second objection was to the spectacle of authors situated in rich countries or international organisations ruling that poor country governments should give priority to effecting major internal shifts in the distribution of income and wealth. He made explicit the charges of double standards and hypocrisy that are often only silently voiced by recipients of such advice. Why not focus equally on international redistribution? Why presume the ethical and feasibility constraints on intranational redistribution apply less than internationally? Why do advisers not distribute their individual incomes in line with their theories? If the foreign rich claim the right to preach redistribution to the LDC rich, have they not an implied duty to make transfers to the LDC poor?

Issues of international redistribution were indeed debated in other fora, including those on the proposed New International Economic Order (NIEO). In an attack on NIEO, Lal (1978) raised the same issues. He queried certain influential 'Western' conceptions of distributive justice, here as applied internationally, and highlighted people's appeals to national rights, in this case not to proscribe poor countries' claims on rich countries but to reject as 'illegitimate intervention' the redistribution prescriptions given by the rich to the poor.

Debate in the West on foreign assistance intensified in the 1970s due to dissatisfaction with the impact of assistance of the earlier scale and types. Some groups pressed for greater concessional transfers, even for schemes of automatic transfer through international taxation. But on the other hand, and in the USA and UK with more influence, right-wing criticism of the ethical and instrumental justification of aid became prominent. (In contrast left-wing critics attacked aid's specific effects rather than its stated intentions.) Sumberg (1973, p. 60) 'looked for...without finding...[any] duty laid upon us. There is no such duty...[Aid] is purely discretionary'. Given such discretion, proponents of 'lifeboat ethics' advocated jettisoning 'basket case' countries (say Bangladesh) on the grounds that assisting them is hopeless and merely jeopardises the prospects of others on 'Spaceship Earth' (Hardin, 1974). Peter Bauer elaborated in a stream of papers and newspaper articles a series of claims against concessional dealings with

LDCs: present DC holdings are just, many LDCs do not deserve help, welfare goals are misconceived since there are no common needs and official aid is justified only insofar as it serves donor interests (e.g. Bauer, 1981, pp. 117–21).

Two subsequent defences of official aid accepted that rationales had never been sufficiently defined (Lewis, 1980; Healey and Clift, 1980). These studies therefore outlined a rationale in two parts: market imperfections justify official involvement, and ethical grounds imply a concessional element. However, neither provided much in the latter field. Lewis, chairman of the OECD aid committee, offered only a traditional call to human fraternity and the diminishing marginal utility of income. Streeten (1976) gave a similar but deeper argument including three sorts of moral claim: (a) again, the brotherhood of man; (b) that the poor are not fully responsible for their poverty; (c) that the rich are partly responsible for this poverty. Claims (a) plus (b), or (a) plus (c), might constitute a reasonable moral case. Whether (a), (b) or (c) alone do so is more dubious. This step towards formalisation already goes beyond Streeten but is not enough.

The critics needed a fuller response, for they disputed precisely the content, sufficiency and even relevance of traditional notions like fraternity, responsibility and welfare. Lewis had proposed that people are satisfied with a simple criterion of increasing long-run net welfare; but when we probe arguments and actions, both everyday and academic, we find many important and influential objections current. Even operationalising his criterion runs into major difficulties at some point. Further, when the late Dudley Seers, a pillar of development studies, came out against aid increases and existing aid budgets (e.g. Seers, 1983), he did so not only from doubts as to how recipients use aid, but with nationalist arguments of priority to domestic interests and of avoiding 'meddling' in ex-colonies for which the West no longer has responsibility. (Gasper, 1986, comments on Seers's views.)

An important philosophical literature has emerged on some of these issues, especially in the revival of ethics and political philosophy since the 1970s. From abstract and/or domestic concerns, as in John Rawls's work, interest extended to international issues. Peter Singer (1977) and others developed a utilitarian case for 'radical sacrifice' by the rich in a world of famines and malnutrition; while the lifeboat moralists advocated a different type of sacrifice (dropping the poor from the boat). Lal's own inspiration – '[allegedly showing] up the relative superficiality of the ethical underpinnings of RWG, AM and ILO' (1976: 731) – was Robert Nozick's libertarian treatise *Anarchy, State and Utopia* (1974). 'Nozick's book...[raised] some economists out of certain unreflective habits into which they had fallen. Indeed it has been said, however fairly, that it roused them from dogmatic slumbers' (Honderich, 1979:91). But to another economist: 'his case...[lacks] any systematic argument' (Arrow, 1978:265); and a different philosopher calls Nozick the leading representative of political philosophy as 'an expression of unjust American ideologies, which legitimates crass failures of humanity and elementary justice in the interest of class and national selfishness' (Richards, 1982, p. 924).

These last two judgements on Nozick have been echoed in much professional philosophy (Paul, 1982). He gained such attention, though, only because several of his points struck home. The attacks of Lal, Bauer and similar writers equally demanded examination. As Berger observed (1977) the relationship between rich and poor countries needs to be thought through – not considered on the basis of some psychological needs of the rich, whether for righteous sacrifice or for righteous rugged isolation. There are matters of appropriate degree in aid, beyond Singer's radical sacrifice and Nozick's radical rejection.

Any such assessment of aid requires attention to a set of issues beyond the traditional pastures of development economists. Until lately there has been a strange contrast: while positive theories of distribution and other matters were elaborated, many supposed policy analysts barely considered normative theories. They were presumed self evident, or arbitrary, or exogenous. As Lal implied, this was an intellectual scandal, perhaps even an ethical one. The critics have forced considerable enlargement of the debate.

In earlier work (Gasper, 1986) I examined the claims that much of development studies has been normatively primitive and looked at the range of conceptions of distributive justice available, including the New Right arguments against egalitarianism.[2] Here I will not essay further substantive argument, but look instead at the range of the recent literature on aid ethics and the structure and organisation of the wider emerging field of development ethics.

The Structure of the Argument on Justifying Aid

Riddell (1986, 1987) has concisely presented requirements of a moral case for intergovernmental foreign aid.[3] He argued that a complete case must establish all the following propositions:

1. the affluent have a (potential) moral obligation to help the poor (i.e. if they can, and subject to their other obligations);
2. this obligation affects governments, not just affluent individuals;
3. governments' obligations to help the poor extend across national boundaries;

4. such transnational obligations are not completely outweighed by governments' other obligations;
5. direct assistance is a good way to help, and indeed is
6. the best (feasible) way to help; and, lastly,
7. making such transfers via LDC governments is effective.

We can group these propositions under three headings: (a) no. 1 comes under the general normative theory of distribution; (b) nos. 2–4 concern the more concrete issue of whether *governments* in rich countries have any moral duty to help the (very) poor in *other* countries; and (c) nos. 5–7 look at the actual effects of direct government aid, especially if done via other governments, which, largely, it almost inevitably is.

Area (c), on the effects of aid, is well-trodden. We noted too that area (a), the general normative theory of distribution, has been intensively debated, with extensions to international relations and aid, and contributions by development economists such as Sen (e.g. Sen, 1981). In addition, development ethics must face the issues in area (b): why should governments try to help those in other countries? Very many people hold that even if every person has human rights, corresponding obligations lie only on his or her own government (Nelson, 1981).

Riddell's approach is more satisfactory here than are two other major contemporaneous studies by British economists: 'Does Aid Work?' by Robert Cassen et al. (1986), and 'Overseas Aid: Its Defence and Reform' (1987) by Paul Mosley. Both follow the tradition of little or no reference to the ethical issues under headings (a) and (b). Cassen et al. were constrained as consultants to the OECD Development Committee, an intergovernmental organisation which might inhibit embarrassing and controversial probing of moral claims on governments. Let us look at Mosley, originally one of the consultants, but who wrote his book independently.

Mosley gives a helpful analysis of current aid practice and of evidence on its more economic impacts. The opening chapter, though, seeks to establish the potential justification of aid and does not advance beyond the positions of Lewis or Healey and Clift. Following the categories of domestic public finance theory, which he transplants to the international arena, Mosley identifies three cases for official aid: (i) a redistributive case; (ii) an allocative case; and (iii) a stabilisation case. The last two concern possible defects of LDC, international and global market mechanisms, such that aid can support valuable investments in LDCs and help increase economic activity and employment worldwide, including in DCs (Mosley, 1987, p. 12).

The stabilisation case is an appeal to mutual interests and enlightened self-interest, since donor countries benefit too. For the redistributive case, Mosley speaks simply of a widespread value judgement that 'the conditions of life available to the poorer people of the Third World today are not acceptable, and should be relieved by transfers of income from those who have more' (p. 12). There are in fact two judgements here, of which the second must face the challenge of Bauer's taxpayers who object to compulsorily-raised taxes going to *non*-citizens for whose conditions they deny responsibility. One needs to supplement the judgements.

Similarly, for the allocative case, even if aid-funded investments do produce enormous benefits in LDCs, why should DC governments bother? And have they a right to use taxation for this when there are unmet demands or needs at home? So before the allocative case for aid can have force, we must tackle some of the other issues Riddell listed. The allocative case relies partly on the redistributive case. In domestic public finance, economists often treat the two as independent, because of utilitarian or other assumptions about domestic political community, so that it is enough to identify only potential Pareto improvements, that is, reallocations which increase total output (or welfare) are acceptable, regardless of whether some individuals lose (and whether they are compensated). A global utilitarian or an analyst who transplants domestic public finance presumptions to the world level, may assume that if resources can yield far greater benefits abroad, they should be allocated there. But the implied belief in some degree of global community is rejected by many nationalists and right-wingers, sometimes even for disaster aid. A thorough evaluation of aid must respond to those positions.

When he comes to sum up the arguments against aid that need to be assessed Mosley gives only two (1987, p. 14):

> To summarise, the right argue that the allocative case for aid is undone by side-effects on the supply of effort and on private investment in recipient countries, whereas the left argue that the redistributive case is undone by an improper focus by analysts on the distribution of income rather than on the distribution of power. The second of these propositions is a matter of differing priorities or value judgements, and as such not susceptible to empirical analysis. The first, however, is eminently a testable proposition.

So in Mosley's view, the right criticises the effects of aid, and the left argues that aid helps to sustain anti-people regimes (1987, p. 13). We saw though that many on the right strongly criticise the distributive rationale of aid, far more than the left have done. Secondly, some on the left do argue that aid which in the short-run palliates the position of the poor in LDCs, in the longer-run only helps maintain them in misery. But this is an argument about effects, not purely a value judgement (though values are involved in comparing short-term with long-term, and income with other goods). The left in general hold that if aid could have good effects, when appropriately judged over both short and long terms, then rich countries should give it. Many on the right reject this. Finally, we can note the sharp contrast between Mosley's degrees of faith in the power of empirical analysis to identify effects as opposed to informing value judgements. This positivism helps explain weaknesses in identifying the structure of the valuative arguments on aid.[4]

Riddell too is sometimes hampered by economistic presumptions and can confuse different theories of distributive justice.[5] He has difficulty, for example, in distinguishing the principles of entitlement and of desert (1987, p. 24). Nozick (and most legal systems) holds that people can be entitled to holdings, quite independently of their past actions and efforts, and hence of what they deserve, for instance they may legitimately inherit property. Economists' preoccupation with identifying the effects of actions, and with welfare as the criterion of relevant effects, make it harder for them to perceive Nozick's disinterest in both of these. His ethic refers to the past and to procedures of just acquisition. When economists do turn to look at past actions, they often assume these must be weighed according to their contributions to social welfare, that is, by a type of desert criterion – which is far from the Nozickian position.[6]

Since Riddell lays out the aid debate more adequately than many others, he enters wider areas and may sometimes run into problems. But we can appreciate and applaud his overview of the terrain.

SURVEYING THE LITERATURE ON ETHICS OF INTERNATIONAL AID

Method of Approach

This section supplements Riddell's schema with a framework for review of the literature on the ethics of international aid that has grown from the 1970s. The framework is quite simple and distinguishes core, background and specialist topics. A similar approach should be applicable, *mutatis mutandis*, to development ethics as a whole; but here I concentrate on the aid literature.

While the ethics of aid and of development are growing, they are not as prolific as the ethics of medicine, business or research. DE in general lacks a long self-conscious history or its own journals.[7] Standard computerised data bases have not yet captured a vast body of material, and the range of sources cited in major surveys (e.g.: Dower, 1983; Gasper, 1986; O'Neill, 1986; Riddell, 1987; Crocker, 1988, 1991a), while substantial, is not too dauntingly wide. Aid literature in particular has been dominated by economists, but most economics was traditionally cut off from ethics. We should add a proviso: the survey-writers may have been slightly biased to sources from conventional philosophy and not fully in touch with the working worlds of aid.

Writing as an economist, I will still propose that the work on aid ethics has a relatively small 'umbra' or core of literature. Having largely emerged since the mid-1970s, it lacks established boundaries defining it or some larger area as a sub-discipline (unlike the cases of medical and business ethics). A very large 'penumbral' zone also exists, containing topics which are undoubtedly relevant, but not unique to the ethics of aid or development, such as human rights, the history of colonialism, the effects of particular types of aid or the ethical issues associated with population policies, research, planning and consultancy. If one accepts the relevance of the penumbral areas, writing a survey would require significant time and judgement to define the field and justify one's selections. (Some work on DE does give space to general background on ethics, aid and so on; this reflects the varied audience, including donor and counterpart organisations, development studies and philosophy.)

From the literature on ethics, one needs to look at the current work that seeks to apply abstract theories of distributive justice onto the world stage. Besides the generalised debate on ethically appropriate volumes of international aid, several more concrete topics are important, including: (i) ethical issues in the actual operation of aid programmes, including the interpersonal and cross-cultural relations involved; (ii) issues in emergency aid (including famine relief, refugees, responses to wars and other disasters); (iii) the ethics of debt and repayment; (iv) the ethics of aid and environment. To take just the last of these, ethical analysis of environment and development has flourished from the mid-1980s (see Engel and Engel, eds, 1990), and was the theme of the 1992 IDEA conference in Honduras.

Crocker too, emphasises the limits to abstracted ethicising and calls for 'theory-practice', involving practical people and their concerns and knowledge (Crocker, 1991a). Related selection criteria in any survey of DE should include ensuring representation of Third World voices and work from disciplines other than philosophy and economics, including, when appropriate, literature and journalism.

The rise of practical or applied ethics is well summarised in DeMarco and Fox (eds, 1986), a set of essays directed not only to philosophers but to professionals in areas where ethical issues have become a pressing concern. It describes the recent emergence (or revival) of applied ethics as an active and self-conscious field, including intensive work on biomedical ethics, business ethics, reverse discrimination and equal opportunity, and the ethics of nuclear strategy. This work arose partly as a result of the revival in general ethics that we mentioned, but mostly in response to practical challenges.

With such points in mind, literature on (and for) aid ethics can be categorised as follows.

A – Background

(A1) Introductory: including discussion of 'what is the ethics of development aid?'
(A2) Background on development aid: history, types, volumes, distribution, organisation; reasons and motives for aid; conflicting perspectives on aid.
(A3) Background on ethics: the nature of ethical theory and of applied ethics; distributive ethics.

B – Core

(B1) The distributive ethics of international aid: especially applications of general normative theories of distribution to the case of international aid.
(B2) Nations and states, groups and individuals: locating responsibilities; (2a) the status of national boundaries; (2b) the respective roles (including obligations and rights) of governments, non-governmental organisations (NGOs) and individuals.
(B3) Reference to preceding events – the historical record: arguments for or against aid by reference to the past history of relations between countries now rich and those presently poor.
(B4) Reference to subsequent outcomes – assessing the effects of aid: including case studies (for example of food aid).
(B5) Applying conditions on future actions – leverage in aid: tying aid, such as to specific uses (project aid), or to satisfaction of more general conditions (as in much programme aid); including case studies (for example from population policies).

C – Special Topics

(C1) Ethics of 'technical assistance/co-operation', including of: international aid organisations and 'experts' aid-funded research, training and advice; cross-cultural and international interaction. (This topic might be in the core, for aid is always administered; but it includes special forms of aid and can also subdivide into a series of special topics.)
(C2) Emergency aid.
(C3) Ethics of debt.
(C4) Ethics of aid and environment. ... And so on.

Of course some literature, such as surveys, can span the categories.

We look next at this contents list in use, in a sketch of a cross-section of literature covering most of the headings. The aim is *not* a literature review, but aims to bring alive the great range, in both topic and approach, of current DE work. We start with two British economists whom we introduced earlier, and then spread our net wider.

The Range of Aid Ethics: Some Books and Articles from the 1980s

(A1) *Introductory.* We saw why Riddell (1986) is a helpful introduction to the scope of current discussions. Most people in Britain cite an ethical justification for aid when asked to comment; so did donor governments but none had rigorously spelled out their arguments. Riddell noted that a complete moral case for official aid requires several components, and looked at current criticisms of each. He then outlined a more systematic, as well as more qualified, justification of official aid than those made in the 1950s to 1970s.

(A2) *Background on aid.* Mosley (1987) gave a readable survey of many major aspects of overseas aid (in the British terminology). We commented earlier on his general economic case for official foreign aid. His history of aid and its distribution between recipient countries argue that while poorer LDCs tended to receive more aid as a percentage of their GNP than richer ones, there were two immense exceptions to this: India and China. In general, aid has been ineffective as an instrument of political leverage by governments. From an overview of the groups involved in each aid-donor community, their differing perspectives and conflicts, the processes involved in allocating aid budgets and the comparable groups and processes on the recipient side, Mosley suggested a set of likely biases in aid allocation: towards projects which are large, risk-avoiding and import- and capital-intensive; but also a rural bias.

(B1) *The distributive ethics of international aid.* What are the obligations to give, or rights to receive, aid? Two studies by British philosophers, Dower (1983) and O'Neill (1986), illustrate different theoretical approaches as well as different intended audiences. Dower's book was 'for the general reader who wants to explore the issues raised by our responses in the West to world poverty. It...deals with general moral principles and values, not their detailed application [and] in this sense it bears the stamp of a philosopher's mind' (p. vi). 'The book is concerned with ends, rather than with means, with [establishing] the central proposition that we ought to help, rather than with the wide variety of ways in which one [might be able to] help' (p. 11). It further discussed responsibilities, attitudes and possibilities at the level of the affluent individual in a rich country.

O'Neill's 'Faces of Hunger' gave a more dense and academic treatment of similar questions. She argued that while substantive ethical theory had definitively revived since the early 1970s, it remained disturbingly abstract and individualistic in method. She proposed steps towards a more adequate method and advocated a modified Kantianism, to take into account decision-makers' human limitations and constraints and to systematically consider the steps between general theory and practical application.

(B2) *Nations and states, groups and individuals.* Upon whom specifically lie any obligations to give aid? Some of the literature, probably too little, tries to clarify what could be the respective roles (and rights) of international agencies, rich country governments and individuals or private groups in rich countries, with respect to governments, groups or individuals in other countries. Perhaps not surprisingly, such analysis is quite often by those seeking to restrict their obligations.

At the level of nation states, an American philosopher, Nelson (1981), defended 'the standard assumption' that while each person has some general human rights, the corresponding obligations lie only on his or her *own* government. He argued that obligations must be attached to units which have adequate resources, internal sympathy and operational cohesion to act upon them; that the nation state meets these conditions but wider units do not; and that the nation state therefore has a self-enclosed moral status comparable to that often attached to the family.[8]

Much work looks at the public/private/NGO division of labour. Ethics enter Douglas's (1983) analysis of the rationale for the 'Third Sector', non-profit, non-governmental organisations, in interesting ways. The economic literature on market failure suggests necessary areas for activity by agents who are not private profit-seekers, but Douglas argued that the literature has a number of holes, reflecting inability to recognise and handle *altruistic and idealistic* behaviour. His parallel analysis of the limits on what can be achieved by governmental authority, given the constraints set by *democratic* norms, thus suggested necessary areas for the 'Third Sector'.

(B3) *The historical record.* Critics of aid coolly claimed corroboration from communist Eastern Europe, which rejected any duty to make the transfers to LDCs called for in the NIEO, on the grounds of having no colonial past (Lal, 1976, p. 732). Such claims about past events, as supposedly establishing *either* obligations for rich countries *or* their absence, cannot be avoided in debate on the ethics of aid. Literature on the balance sheet of colonialism is longstanding and immense, but for various reasons little of it makes systematic links to argumentation on aid. One factor is that what would have happened in the absence of particular past actions is inevitably hypothetical and open to dispute. But more recent, and equally germane, is the balance sheet of previous financial and technical assistance itself. Donors undeniably share responsibility for past mistakes.

(B4) *Assessing the effects of aid.* Most of the large aid impact literature is not distinctively ethical, but there are key value issues involved which demand attention (Hoksbergen, 1986).

Mainstream literature focuses on the impact of official aid on growth and investment. Mosley (1987) for example found no general statistical connection between aid flows and *aggregate* growth in recipient countries. Given the high average reported *project* returns, he argued that aid often allows diversion of domestic public resources away from investment into consumption and bids-up the price to the private sector of scarce local resources. (However he later noted that average aid impacts appear considerably more favourable in Asia than in Africa, which requires a modification of his general argument.) Several questions arise: how far should we generalise? how should we interpret imperfect data? which effects should we consider? who benefits? and whose views and perspectives should we include?

Concerning the types of effects to consider, one might for example agree that aid often does not increase LDC investment and growth, yet defend it as increasing current LDC welfare. But whose welfare? Mosley argued that the politics of aid processes have militated against investigation of whether poorer people benefit. From the few serious studies he identified, he suggested that 'aid projects can help the poor, but not the poorest' (p. 165) and that 'trickle-down' effects to the poor are 'virtually inoperative' (p. 178) in most countries. Reasons include the power of local élites, inappropriate technologies and leakage of benefits to richer areas; though these could, he argued, be reduced. (As to who benefits in donor countries, he found that aid given as export subsidies produced very few additional exports or jobs, but cushioned inefficient firms.)

Despite the limits of information, especially timely information, Riddell like Mosley believed not just in the pertinence of evidence on impacts, but that the aid debate 'is ultimately a controversy resolved by assessing the evidence' (Riddell, 1987, p. 58). How frequently do the forms of evidence and assessment in the social sciences resolve controversies? Often many actual and prospective effects remain far from clear, indeed open to profound debate. Riddell himself earlier noted: 'The total moral case for governments to provide development aid would seem to be dependent upon a blend of three interrelated factors: [i] narrow ethical beliefs (the basis for action), [ii] theories of development (constructs of how the world works) and [iii] an assessment of the performance of aid in practice' (1987, p. 16). These assessments are imperfect and theory-dependent; we would not otherwise need to mention factor [ii]. Faced with the limits to consequentialist assessment (that is, in terms of effects), we look for defensible principles of judgement, including reference to non-consequentialist criteria. Choice of these principles can be informed, but may not be fully resolved, by assessing the evidence.

For all the above reasons, it is important to obtain accounts of aid from a variety of viewpoints. As one example, 'Life and Death through Foreign Aid' by Kurien (1981), a Southern writer, has a significantly different scope and flavour from conventional Northern economic analyses. It illustrates recipient-country intellectuals' unease and dissatisfactions. Kurien discussed positive and negative impacts of the foreign aid channelled into India via churches, with special reference to Kerala. Suggested positive features of aid included provision of foreign exchange, jobs, training centres and hospitals (most of Kerala's 900-plus private hospitals in 1980 were run by churches and mainly set up with help from abroad); and in addition (in Kurien's view) the creation and expansion of churches. Negative features claimed included creation of attitudes of dependence and imitation, concentration on elites, proliferation of denomination-specific facilities (sometimes luxurious), promotion of corruption, demand for imports and scope for leverage and pacification of the oppressed. He drew a contrast with the case of a self-reliant mineworkers' group in Madhya Pradesh.

(B5) *Conditions attached to aid.* What conditions can or should be attached to aid to increase the chance of achieving desirable effects, despite possible interference with recipients' sovereignty and self-reliance? What of the other conditions that donors attach? Faaland (1981) exemplifies the mainstream literature here, in a set of accounts of experience from aid operations in Bangladesh. We find supplementary, rather richer, insights from an anthropologist, even in a topic like conditionality.

Harrell-Bond (1986) studied the programmes for Ugandan refugees in Southern Sudan in 1980–5 undertaken by the UN High Commission for Refugees and foreign NGOs. Thousands of refugees were interviewed, inside and outside the official settlements, as well as members of the indigenous population. Refugees helped determine the data to be collected and discussed its implications. Harrell-Bond argued that official assistance programmes, which placed refugees in controlled rural settlements, largely failed in Sudan as in most other countries to integrate them into the host country or make them self-reliant. Comparative evidence was drawn from those refugees (in fact the majority) who stayed outside official settlements and from countries where refugees were allowed to manage the use of aid themselves. She argued that refugee needs have been outweighed in mainstream programmes by the preoccupations of donors and host governments with control and security and by misplaced presumptions of the incompetence and untrustworthiness of refugees and local officials. The study found the refugees often had valuable skills and represented a pool of potential creativity, capable of responding to the stresses and opportunities in their new situation. This potential was stifled or inhibited by aid officials who considered themselves too busy, too knowledgeable and too worthy to need research on refugees' situations and activities or even to consult with the people they were supposed to be assisting. Harrell-Bond concluded that attempts to control, made from a position of ignorance and mistrust, produce severe negative effects for the refugees, in both frustration and dependency.

(C1) *Ethics of technical assistance and co-operation.* The refugees study has led us to issues in the actual operation of aid programmes, including the behaviour and lifestyle of aid agents, aid bureaucracies and their LDC counterparts. Aid personnel bid-up the local price of housing and introduce external consumption norms and the funds for some locals to acquire and practice them. Others make careers of *per-diem* luxury in the name of the poor. The enraged whistleblowing on UN agencies in Hancock's 'The Lords of Poverty' (1991) and Linear's 'Zapping the Third World' (1985) are rare examples, for literature here is limited by access problems and practitioners tend to be too busy, cautious and implicated.

A short story by Leonard Frank (1986) (perhaps an apt pseudonym, like Linear?) gives a glimpse. A UN project identification team visits the North-West Frontier Province in Pakistan. The team includes professionals from six countries; none have previously met. None of them has been there before, but many previous missions have, leaving reports. The team has four weeks to identify a project for around $30 million. Some team members are under extreme stress, caught between the demands of their actual job and their formal profession, others are committed to just one or the other – to 'the official world' or to 'the real world' (but perhaps with disagreements over which is which). A project is duly designed, on time, and with an eye to meeting the desires of donor and recipient agencies and to providing defences against critics.

(C2) *Emergency aid.* Whether on grounds of importance or interest or interconnections, we cannot exclude emergency aid just because it is sometimes defined as not 'development' aid. Much of the literature from cases like Ethiopia and Cambodia has, from the urgency of the events it describes, been pointed and holistic, not formal examinations of dense but narrow data, but thought-provoking accounts of decision-making with poor information and under pressure.

We earlier mentioned Shawcross's study of the US$ 1 billion-plus international relief efforts for Cambodians in 1979–83 and the ethical dilemmas in emergency aid. It records for example how the Cambodian government, still fighting a civil war against the Khmer Rouge and others, resisted and obstructed technical assistance to improve the inflow of food, ignored monitoring and reporting requirements and gave most of the food to government officials, soldiers and others not in greatest need – yet how this reduced pressure to extract supplies from rural areas. Many lines of international food supply emerged: including to border camps controlled by the Thai Army, Khmer Rouge or other Cambodian opposition groups, who diverted many of the supplies and to Cambodians arriving at the border, to distribute back inside the country, free of any conventional aid monitoring and probably subject to significant diversion. Shawcross concluded that, amidst the diversions, obstructions and confusions, food and relief still reached huge numbers of people in severe need and that conditionality to ensure no supplies reached unintended destinations would have meant that far less reached desired destinations.

HOW CAN WE ORDER THE DEVELOPMENT ETHICS FIELD?

The issues and literature on the ethics of aid are certainly extensive. The coverage in development ethics as a whole, as in Crocker's survey article or at IDEA conferences, is wider still. I have said little for example of the critiques and defences of utilitarianism and the rethinking of concepts of poverty, welfare and other ideas central in development discourse.

Crocker concludes his survey with unanswered questions on how to conceptualise, organise and engage in DE as a field of 'theory-practice', including its relations to other intellectual and practical fields. Such questions are themselves partly practical and political matters, not to be settled by purely theoretical analysis. The following reflections are simply suggestions, to help debate.

The previous section illustrated an approach that distinguishes between core, background and specialisation areas (C–B–S). We could extend this to cover more than the ethics of aid. DE as a whole draws on a number of standard fields and adds distinctive concerns in terms of topics (for example, rich–poor international relations in aid, trade, tourism and other areas) and of substance (because of distinctive conditions in poor countries). To refine use of the C–B–S model, one could look at how it applies in more mature fields of applied or practical ethics.

However, the model will not provide a definitive picture. There will be demarcation options and disputes in trying to use it and different views on what is the core. Let us identify some of the important disagreements, while remembering that there is unlikely to be one correct answer: why should core, background and specialisation areas be the same begs the question of whether this is a discipline or an inter-disciplinary field.

One area of disagreement reflects different opinions on the nature of ethics and hence whether DE is just 'applied ethics', or instead, using Crocker's term, 'theory-practice'. Another area concerns the scope of 'development', including whether DE's focus should be Third World, international or global.

The more one believes in universal principles of ethical theory that are universally applicable *and* still offer a lot of substantive guidance in particular cases, the more one will see those general principles as at the core of development ethics too. In effect DE will be one of the applied specialisation zones of a rather tightly unified and centralised ethics. For example, one might seek to establish 'first principles' through an abstracted thought-experiment on the lines of those that Rawls conducts and then apply the principles on various stages, including distant countries and international relations. (Rawls himself apparently held that his approach is specific to a 'Northern' context of relative affluence and diminished interindividual bonds and denied that it can be applied globally.)[9]

The alternative conception takes ethical theory as a necessary source of suggestions, principles and criteria, but not of hard and sufficient guidance. We find this pattern of work in the newly active areas like medical and business ethics. For any theory is inevitably simplified and has implicit assumptions and limits to its relevance. Experience tests the conceptions' adequacy and helps reveal what they omit. Similarly, general concepts, including general values, have limited specification and power. The practical issues prove richer than the concepts. (Work on gender and environmental ethics, for example, may modify various previous general assumptions and categories. And some readers may well feel, at least on first examination, that the most rewarding pieces outlined earlier were those, such as the books by Shawcross and Harrell-Bond, not written by philosophers or economists!) Codes of practice, if and when feasible and relevant, must be prepared by concerned practitioners, in contact with those they affect, not alone by philosophers.

Some writers accordingly prefer the term 'practical ethics' to 'applied ethics', for the latter suggests one only needs to apply already conceived principles. The more one thinks instead in terms of somewhat context-specific 'theory-practices', the more one sees general ethical theory as key background material, but not something to conclusively apply in every field of concern.

I suggest that DE is a swathe of 'theory-practice(s)' that is likely to be loosely articulated, internally and externally. My approach has reflected a traditional DS focus on poor countries, which tries to ensure emphasis on issues relevant to them. Some recent work, calling for a globally-focused rather than a Third-World focused development ethics, is likely to see core, background and specialisation areas in another way. (Believers in strong universal ethical principles will also tend to see a single global field.) This recent work proposes that in today's 'one world' we must look at the issues of international justice, growth, environment and security as an interconnected set, where sustainable solutions may require worldwide changes in ethics, culture and perceptions of identity. It attractively highlights responsibilities in rich countries, common intellectual and practical challenges, and our interdependencies and shared humanity.

These discussions about coverage in development ethics parallel earlier ones in development studies. DS has traditionally looked at the South and North–South relations and presented to the South some aspects of the North's experience (especially the strengths). The questions it tackles have led it towards seeing countries in their global context, while trying to respect the specific conditions of each; and, for many practitioners, to going beyond Eurocentrism. Overall, it has moved towards a more integrated and relevant social science. So we find DS also in the South, in many institutes, journals and training programmes; it is therefore not just the North looking at the South. (We find work called development ethics in the South too, and, one judges, not merely due to Northern trends.)

Some examples suggest a (re-)emergent DS of the North. Seers and others found it fruitful to apply DS ideas to Europe, given a concern with poorer areas that live in the shadow of richer ones and DS's broader approach and longer-term perspective than much other social science. DS will contribute to understanding the new Eastern Europe as it struggles to adjust structurally to the West and cope with Western assistance and incursions. And DS concerns with structural change are relevant to Europe as a whole, in the face of structural unemployment and reorganisation (Hettne, 1990). Some development journals have begun to publish not only on the South. However, a big gap remains between having some more integrated social science and having a unified social science. Of the latter there is no sign.

Besides the experience of DS, the sociology and philosophy of science suggest the likelihood of specialisation and differentiation. This applies to development ethics too, internally and with respect to general or global ethics. We could then have both global and development ethics, as related enterprises, and distinguish, as Crocker sometimes does, between 'development ethicists...[and] those involved in other forms of...global ethics' (1991b, p. 170). The latter term functions here as an umbrella, under which we can move around, without having to say that the areas spanned are all one.[10]

Within such inter-disciplinary fields, some shared frameworks and areas of theory, cross-fertilisation and co-operative areas of work are both feasible and desirable. To take one example: 'An important task of the emerging field of development ethics will be to grasp and assess Sen's proposals' (Crocker, 1991a, p. 466). This focus will appeal to a variety of people in DS, philosophy, economics, social administration and aid, given the range and force of Sen's writings, from famine to fundamental critique of utilitarianism. It can strengthen the theoretical basis for later work, in a more focused way than by reviewing tomes of philosophy, and it requires no close agreement on definitions of DE.

CONCLUSIONS

(1) DE may be seen as work on 'the ethical and value questions posed by development theory, planning and practice'. It has boundary-definition problems, both internally and externally, which partly reflect problems in defining what are 'development' and 'development studies'. If one sees 'development' only as all desirable change, there is a danger of endless diffusion of DE. Even with a more delimited view of 'development', as fulfilment of some of the modern era's potential for major improvements in welfare in poor countries, the scope of DE is very great.

(2) Amongst other stimuli, right-wing and free-market challenges to development aid and its associated conventional wisdoms have forced a salutary probing of ethical assumptions and led to a considerable extension and deepening of analysis.

(3) DE work has proceeded on a variety of levels, topics and theoretical tracks. On aid, analyses of past events affect present stances, but clear implications are hard to draw. Other ethical studies on aid have drawn out the value issues in: allocation of responsibilities (domestic/foreign and private/public/NGO); analysis of effects (who benefits? which effects to consider? how to interpret weak data? whose views are heard?); and conditionality (the balance of accountability against fostering independence). Special topics in aid ethics include technical co-operation, though this has rather little literature, and more thriving areas like environment and emergency aid (whose interest and importance demand its inclusion).

(4) While the upsurge of work is encouraging, the literature remains limited, sometimes in depth or quantity on key issues and in its organisation and availability. We need in addition to close the gap between abstracted philosophical work and the worlds of development practice (a stated aim of IDEA).

(5) Distinguishing between core, background and specialisation areas can be useful, but will be done differently according to the interests and perspectives of participants, in what is likely to be a multi-disciplinary field more than an actually or potentially unified (sub-)discipline. Trying to subsume DE in a wider field, such as global ethics or a unified ethics, has attractions but also significant problems. The parallel experience in development studies suggests there is valuable scope for globalisation of approach, but a continuing role for differentiation and narrower foci. Cross-fertilisation and co-operation between related streams of work can still proceed.

Overall, boundary-definition problems in DE probably neither can be, nor need to be, resolved presently. More important now is simply to promote interchange between relevant lines of work and to inject more good philosophy into development studies and more practical experience and awareness into ethics. I hope that an unusual form of literature survey will help in this, an unusual area.

Notes

1. Another pioneer, Peter Berger, defined DE as political ethics applied to social change in the Third World (Berger, 1977).
2. I argue there that recurrent features in much New Right anti-egalitarian argument are absolutised values and, as an offshoot of individualistic psychology, a preoccupation with blaming: being to blame, or not being to blame. I con-

sider too the constraints and consequent scale and types of obligation of the individual within his/her society, for example the developmentalist dispensing advice and also official funds, but perhaps not his or her own.

3. Riddell sometimes uses 'moral' to mean 'not implied by self-interest'. Elsewhere I take 'moral' and 'ethical' as synonyms.
4. Blaug notes that, having 'deliberately eschewed [discussions on values, economists] have largely denied themselves the analysis of value judgements as a fruitful area of research, [and are accordingly] rather poor at assessing other people's values' (1980, p. 149).
5. For example, he describes utilitarianism as if it calculates in terms of need-fulfilment, rather than utility maximisation (1987, p. 21) and describes Rawls's theory too as if it weighs basic needs rather than basic rights (Rawls, 1971). Thus he then introduces theories about the rights of the poorest, as if something further to the Rawlsian view (p. 23). See for example Sen (1981).
6. Similarly, Riddell identifies these two views: (a) 'National interest considerations are fundamental in foreign policy decisions' (1987, p. 65); and (b) a Nozickian position that 'there are no obligations for citizens or for governments to meet the needs of other citizens or to alleviate suffering either within national boundaries or abroad' (p. 66) because everything is instead to be left to mutually agreed contracts. But view (a) can be held by many non-Nozickians and be rejected by Nozick-style libertarians who stress only individual interests.
7. 'Ethics and International Affairs' appeared from 1987 with a much wider scope than aid and a different emphasis than development. 'Alternatives' often contains DE-type articles.
8. See Gasper (1986) for further comments; and Frankena (1977) and Hare and Joynt (1982) on the moral status of national boundaries.
9. Some writers disagree with Rawls on this, but his deliberate ignoring of most of the specifics of persons' situations might be less appropriate, or less widely acceptable, when applied in other contexts or across wider social and cultural ranges. Indeed it has been rejected by women commentators for his own 'Northern' context.
10. We can expect some correlation between answers to the three questions: (i) universal or contextual ethics? (ii) global or development ethics? and (iii) unified discipline or inter-disciplinary field? But the questions are not reducible to one, and various patterns of response are permissible.

References

Adelman, I. and C. T. Morris (1973) *Economic Growth and Social Equity in Developing Countries* (Stanford: California University Press).

Aiken, W. and H. La Follette (eds) (1977) *World Hunger and Moral Obligation* (Englewood Cliffs: Prentice Hall).

Aman, K. (ed.) (1991) *Ethical Principles for Development: Needs, Capacities or Rights?* (Upper Montclair, NJ: Institute for Critical Thinking, Montclair State).

Arrow, K. (1978) 'Nozick's Entitlement Theory of Justice', *Philosophia*, vol. 7, 265–79.

Bauer, P. T. (1975) 'N. H. Stern on Substance and Method in Development Economics', *Journal of Development Economics*, vol. 2, 387–405.

—— (1981) *Equality, The Third World and Economic Delusion* (London: Weidenfeld).

Berger, P. (1977) *Pyramids of Sacrifice* (Harmondsworth: Penguin).

Blaug, M. (1980) *The Methodology of Economics* (Cambridge: Cambridge University Press).

Cassen, R. et al., (1986) *Does Aid Work?* (Oxford: Oxford University Press).

Chenery, H. et al., (1974) *Redistribution with Growth* (Oxford: Oxford University Press).

Crocker, D. (1988) 'Towards a Development Ethic', mimeo, (Boulder: University of Colorado, Department of Philosophy).

—— (1991a) 'Toward Development Ethics', *World Development*, vol. 19, 457–83.

—— (1991b) 'Insiders and Outsiders in International Development', *Ethics and International Affairs*, vol. 5, 149–73.

DeMarco, J. and R. Fox (1986) *New Directions in Ethics – The Challenge of Applied Ethics* (New York and London: Routledge).

Douglas, J. (1983) *Why Charity?* (Beverly Hills: Sage).

Dore, R. (1978) 'Scholars and Preachers', *IDS Bulletin*, vol. 9, no. 4.

Dower, N. (1983) *World Poverty: Challenge and Response* (York: Ebor).

Engel, J. R. and J. G. Engel (eds) (1990) *Ethics of Environment and Development* (London: Belhaven).

Faaland, J. (ed.) (1981) *Aid and Influence – The Case of Bangladesh* (London: Macmillan).

Frank, L. (1986) 'The Development Game', *Granta*, vol. 20, 229–43.

Frankena, W. (1977) 'Moral Philosophy and World Hunger' in W. Aiken and H. La Follette (eds), op. cit., 66–84.

Gasper, D. (1986) 'Distribution and Development Ethics – A Tour' in R. Apthorpe and A. Krahl (eds), *Development Studies: Critique and Renewal* (Leiden: Brill).

Goulet, D. (1971) *The Cruel Choice* (New York: Athenaeum).

—— (1977) *The Uncertain Promise: Value Conflicts in Technology Transfer* (New York: Athenaeum).

Hancock, G. (1991) *Lords of Poverty* (London: Mandarin).

Hardin, G. (1974) 'Lifeboat Ethics: The Case Against Helping the Poor', *Psychology Today*, vol. 8, 1223–6.

Hare, J. E. and B. Joynt (1982) *Ethics and International Affairs* (London: Macmillan).

Harrell-Bond, B. E. (1986) *Imposing Aid: Emergency Assistance to Refugees* (Oxford: Oxford University Press).

Healey, J. and C. Clift. (1980) 'The Developmental Rationale for Aid Re-examined', *ODI Review*, vol. 2.

Hettne, B. (1990) *Development Theory and the Three Worlds* (London: Longman).

Hoksbergen, R. (1986) 'Approaches to Evaluation of Development Interventions: The Importance of World and Life Views', *World Development*, vol. 14, no. 2, 283–300.

Honderich, T. (1979) 'Distributive Justice' in T. Honderich and M. Burnyeat (eds) *Philosophy As It Is* (Harmondsworth: Penguin).

ILO, (1976) *Employment, Growth and Basic Needs* (Geneva: ILO).

Kitching, G. (1982) *Development and Underdevelopment in Historical Perspective* (London: Methuen).

Kurien, V. M. (1981) 'Life and Death Through Foreign Aid' in *Struggle Against Death* (Kottayam: The Kottayam Group, Baselius College).
Lal, D. (1976) 'Distribution and Development: A Review Article', *World Development*, vol. 4, 725–38.
—— (1978) *Poverty, Power and Prejudice* (London: Fabian Research Series 3340).
Lewis, J. P. (1980) Chairman's Report, in OECD Development Assistance Committee, *Development Cooperation* (Paris: OECD).
Linear, M. (1985) *Zapping the Third World – The Disaster of Development Aid* (London: Pluto).
Mosley, P. (1987) *Overseas Aid: Its Defence and Reform* (Brighton: Wheatsheaf).
Nelson, W. (1981) 'Human Rights and Human Obligations' in J. Pennock and J. Chapman (eds), 281–95.
Nozick, R. (1974) *Anarchy, State and Utopia* (New York: Basic Books).
O'Neill, O. (1986) *Faces of Hunger – An Essay on Poverty, Justice and Development* (London: Allen & Unwin).
Paul, J. (ed.) (1982) *Reading Nozick* (Oxford: Basil Blackwell).
Pennock, J. and J. Chapman (eds) (1981) *Human Rights* (New York: New York University Press).
—— (1982) *Ethics, Economics and Law* (New York: New York University Press).
Rawls, J. (1971) *A Theory of Justice* (Oxford: Clarendon).
Richards, D. A. J. (1982) 'International Distributive Justice' in J. Pennock and J. Chapman (eds), op. cit., 275–99.
Riddell, R. (1986) 'The Ethics of Foreign Aid', *Development Policy Review*, vol. 4, no. 1, 24–43.
—— (1987) *Foreign Aid Reconsidered* (London: James Currey).
Seers, D. (1983) 'Time for a Second Look at the Third World', *Development Policy Review*, vol. 1, no. 1, 35–46.
Segal, J. (1986) 'What is Development?', Working Paper DN-1 (Maryland: Institute of Philosophy and Public Policy, College Park).
Sen, A. K. (1981) 'Ethical Issues in Income Distribution, National and International' in S. Grassman and E. Lundberg (eds), *The World Economic Order* (London: Macmillan).
Shawcross, W. (1984) *The Quality of Mercy – Cambodia, Holocaust, and Modern Conscience* (London: André Deutsch).
Singer, P. (1977) 'Famine, Affluence and Morality' in W. Aiken and H. La Follette (eds), op. cit., 22–36.
Streeten, P. (1976) 'It *is* a Moral Issue', *Crucible*, July/September.
Sumberg, T. (1973) *Foreign Aid as a Moral Obligation?* (Beverly Hills: Sage).

10 The Decline of Food Aid: Issues of Aid Policy, Trade and Food Security

EDWARD CLAY[1]

INTRODUCTION

After the 'world food crisis' of 1972–4 international agreement was at least partially obtained on measures to increase the developmental effectiveness of food aid and to strengthen international food security. But changing circumstances since the mid-1980s, in particular the 'African food crisis' and its aftermath, raised questions about the effectiveness of these international arrangements to cope in future with an extremely serious and widespread period of food insecurity. Coping with shortfalls in local food supply was made more difficult by sharp price variability in world markets for cereals and other foodstuffs and by barriers to food security imposed on developing countries by the world agricultural trade regime. The combination of the volatile cereal markets and budgetary tightening in the late 1980s, especially in the United States, underscored the real opportunity costs of food aid as a developmental and humanitarian resource transfer.

Recent trends suggest relatively, if not absolutely, smaller levels of food aid during the 1990s. These transfers will be more closely managed and internationally co-ordinated as the balance shifts between developmental and humanitarian objectives within the constraints of the wider agricultural trade regime and development assistance budget. Whether food aid will be even less relevant to the development process in the 1990s than it was in the 1980s will depend to a substantial extent on the policy changes associated with the availability of food aid.

A TIME FOR REASSESSMENT

During the 1980s food aid became increasingly prominent as the most visible form of humanitarian and developmental aid from rich countries to the poor, hungry and displaced. Yet during that same period food aid declined in significance as a share of world food trade, imports of developing countries and official aid. These apparently paradoxical trends and a combination of more specific reasons justify a closer examination of the relationships between food aid and food security in developing countries. First, the Uruguay Round process could lead to agreements on agricultural trade policy that would have profound effects on the availability of food surpluses. Secondly, since 1989 food aid has provided a substantial part of the initial response by the European Community and the United States to the 'food problems' associated with rapid political and economic change in Eastern Europe and the former Soviet Union. In addition to the implications for those countries, there is the issue of potential competition with the Third World for aid resources. That concern was heightened as drought in 1991–2 brought massive food import problems for southern Africa.

In the years following the world food crisis of 1972–4, international agreements were at least partially based on measures to increase international food security, and changes were made, particularly at the international level and in bilateral food aid programmes. These developments included the Food Aid Conventions which since 1980 have guaranteed a minimum of 7.6 million tonnes of cereals food aid, the enhanced international emergency programme of WFP (World Food Programme) including the International Emergency Reserve and FAO's Global Information and Early Warning System. Most bilateral donors also revamped their programmes, particularly making more flexible provision for emergency aid.

Then circumstances changed dramatically during the 1980s. The experience of the African food crisis and its aftermath raised questions about the effectiveness of international arrangements to cope with an extremely serious and widespread period of food insecurity. The problems of shortfalls in food supplies could be compounded by sharp price variability in world markets for cereals and other foodstuffs and the barriers to food security imposed on developing countries by the world agricultural trade regime. Developing countries cannot count on the willingness of donor countries to seek efficient means of providing reliable food supplies to their population. The combination of firmer cereal markets in 1988–9 and budgetary tightening, particularly in the United States, which provides about half the commodities shipped as aid, underscored the real opportunity costs of food aid as a developmental and humanitarian resource transfer.

If evidence were ever needed that policy problems repeat themselves in cycles, it is amply provided by the debate over the role and effectiveness of food aid. Although food aid in the 1950s was primarily a surplus disposal mechanism for the United States, the monsoon failures on the Indian subcontinent in 1966 and 1967 sharply raised the opportunity costs of providing such aid precisely when it was most needed. Surpluses and surplus disposal returned in the 1980s, and disappeared yet again during 1988 with the US drought, only to reappear with the 1990 harvests. Just what is food aid for – surplus disposal, development assistance, or humanitarian relief? Is it a wonderful instrument that meets two or three objectives with just one expenditure? Or does the actual role of food aid change as its costs to donors and benefits to recipients shift with the international market?

The historical record suggests a complicated and changing answer, and trends since the early 1970s document a rising commitment to meeting humanitarian needs. But the volumes of food aid provided still reflect opportunity costs to donors as much as needs of recipients, and the changing composition of commodities – cereals, dairy products and vegetable oils – reflects these opportunity costs as well. More important, concerns about the effectiveness of whatever quantities of food aid are actually shipped have led to efforts to manage the resource more carefully. Such care sometimes takes the form of closely managed project support rather than more general and less accountable programme support, and sometimes provision for food resources to non-governmental organisations (NGOs) with more effective grass-roots capabilities. Most surprising, perhaps, is that food aid no longer necessarily originates in a donor country for shipment to the recipient. Innovative programmes to purchase supplies in second countries, or even in the country in need, raise questions about the boundaries of food aid relative to other forms of assistance. Such questions can only be healthy. Food aid has long suffered from its containment within a self-reinforcing network of food aid officials, recipients, agencies and analysts. Forcing the question of the effectiveness – even appropriate definitions – of food aid onto more open and general ground will help end this isolation, and may well contribute to raising the effectiveness of the resource itself.

FOOD AID OR FINANCE FOR FOOD IMPORTS?

Most writing on food aid is concerned with an aid transfer from a developed economy to a developing country. The commodity is a foodstuff that a developed country agrees to provide on a concessional basis, which, under the OECD's Development Assistance Committee (DAC) reporting definitions, involves concessionality of at least 25 per cent. It is an 'aid' transfer, because the transaction is mediated by an aid organisation – bilateral, international or NGO – and, therefore, is intended to have a developmental or humanitarian objective. In practice, most of the literature on food aid has also been concerned with 'cereals' aid, ignoring the substantial flow of dairy products, and so on. But this common-sense definition of food aid has become problematic because of developments which blur the distinction between on the one side food and financial aid and on the other food aid and subsidised commercial exports.

A substantial proportion of what is officially recorded as food aid, 8–10 per cent of cereals aid between 1987 and 1990, was acquired by donors in developing countries through purchases with convertible currencies or through a barter or 'swap' trade arrangement (Clay and Benson, 1991). Approximately three-quarters of those commodities were targeted on Sub-Saharan Africa (SSA), and half of the cereals were acquired within that region. In addition, perhaps a quarter of these transactions by volume in SSA also involved local purchases in the aid recipient country without any linked trade flow. This partial breaking of the link with trade has led to the suggestion that such transactions are not food aid, but aid for food. Such transactions, which still fulfil donor commitments under the Food Aid Convention, are usually an alternative to a normal food aid programme involving exports from a developed country. These purchase and barter arrangements raise operational concerns of cost-effectiveness, management efficiency and appropriateness, as compared with conventional food aid. In addition, questions arise with regard to development concerning the 'source' economy or region in which the commodities are acquired (Martens, 1990).

Three other forms of food related aid blur the distinction between food and financial aid. At least one donor, the European Community, has introduced a substitution arrangement whereby financial assistance is provided from the food aid budget if changed circumstances make it inappropriate to provide food aid after this has been committed (Franco, 1988). The IMF allows countries to draw upon its Compensatory Financing Facility (CFF) for additional food imports, and some bilateral donors are providing balance of payments support to finance at least part of food import requirements.

Large-scale soft credit and export programmes which involve substantial concessionality are not officially recorded as food aid. But by the late 1980s perhaps a third of wheat trade involved some form of export subsidisation. Since 1975 the US Department of Agriculture has used these credit sales rather than credits under the PL 480 food aid programmes as the major instrument of surplus disposal and market development. The EC has used export restitution to manage markets. Since 1989 the EC has also funded food aid to Eastern Europe and the former Soviet Union as an additional aid measure under the budget lines for these agricultural export programmes.

GLOBAL TRENDS IN FOOD AID

Food aid declined sharply during the early 1970s in the period of the so-called 'World Food Crisis'. The quantity of cereals provided has never returned to the record levels of the mid-1960s, when approximately 18 million metric tons were shipped, largely supplied under the US PL 480 programme. Nevertheless, food aid rapidly recovered to a level of around 9–10 million tons of grain or wheat equivalent in the late 1970s. In the mid-1980s, the coincidence of the African food crisis and a period of excessively depressed world markets resulted in annual levels of shipments moving slightly higher, to around 11 to 12 million tons in 1984–5. These higher levels were sustained up to 1987–8, but with a tighter market situation and the potential for reduced emergency requirements in SSA, total aid to developing countries declined to 11 million tons during 1988–9, and 10 million tons in 1989–90. Levels began to rise once more in 1990–1, with easier market conditions and the responses to fresh emergencies in SSA and the crisis in Eastern Europe.

The third Food Aid Convention in 1980 emphasised burden-sharing within the donor community and the desire of donors to avoid a recurrence of the negative consequences of a sharp fall in food levels in 1972–4. Minimum tonnages of 7.6 million tonnes of 'wheat equivalent' were agreed, resulting in relatively stable, institutionally determined levels of food aid.

Overall, there has been a secular decline in the significance of food aid as a share of international trade and the imports of developing countries. By the late 1980s, cereal food aid amounted to only around 0.7 per cent of global production, 3–4 per cent of cereal stocks and 5–7 per cent of world cereals trade compared to over 10 per cent in the early 1970s (FAO, 1991).

There has been a geographical reallocation of food aid to 'least-developed countries', particularly to Sub-Saharan Africa, which has had further implications for costs as well as programmes. The concomitant shift in allocations from programme aid for sale on local markets to emergency aid, and to a lesser extent project aid outside SSA, also involved donors meeting both a higher proportion of non-commodity costs and higher per ton non-commodity costs. This is, in part, because of the less favourable terms regarding shipping costs for least-developed countries. There are higher total costs of shipping commodities to landlocked destinations, particularly in SSA. Emergency assistance and project aid which are largely for direct distribution to beneficiaries involve higher administrative costs. The growing volume of acquisition in developing countries has not affected this upward cost trend, since evaluations show that commodity purchases have clustered around the import parity price levels of recipient, often landlocked, countries (Hay, 1989; Relief and Development Institute, 1987). The overall trend, from the viewpoint of those agencies, is for food aid to become more completely a full-cost transfer attributable to aid budgets and for non-commodity costs to grow.

A further complexity for economic analysis in recent trends is the rising importance of non-cereals food aid. The trends in non-cereals food aid are different from those of cereals transfers, having increased over time, and now accounting for around 10 per cent of total quantities, but 30 per cent by value of donor food aid costs. These commodities are typically considerably more costly per tonne both to acquire and ship. Since the mid-1970s, the European Community has been the second most important food aid donor, either in terms of physical quantities or costs as accounted by donor agencies. During a period of twelve years, from the mid-1970s, non-cereals, which were virtually all dairy products, contributed more than half of the accounted costs of EC food aid. An economic analysis which focuses on cereal aid, conceptually and empirically the easiest commodities to study, provides little insight into the impact of the increasingly important non-cereal commodities.

Overall, there is a growing lack of congruence between what is the most widely reported official statistic for food aid, total cereal tonnage shipped, and the scale and form of related resource transfers. The cost of food aid transfers, either in financial terms for aid budgets or in terms or real resource costs, may well have been higher during the mid-1980s than in the apparent peak period of the 1960s. The focus on cereals ignores the increased importance of non-cereals. A substantial part of food aid since the mid-1970s has not been drawn from surplus stocks of developed countries available for export but has been financed by donors under their commitments for the Food Aid Convention, including, as mentioned above, acquisitions in developing countries.

The upward trend in food aid costs also implies that it would be timely to re-examine the cost-effectiveness of food transfers and also the implications for the scale and balance of commodities to be provided for different purposes. Where these costs have been examined, then 'doubly-tied' aid shipped from donor countries is typically found to be less cost-effective as a resource transfer than the provision of financial assistance to enable recipient countries to organise their own food imports (Saran and Konandreas, 1991).

DEVELOPMENTAL ISSUES

The crucial test for aid is the extent to which it strengthens the capacity of developing countries to improve human and material conditions. Assistance to improve the ability to *produce* food would score higher marks than just *providing* food. In some situations, however, the supply of food may be a pre-condition for sustainable development even in a longer-term perspective. Such a role for food aid has typically been the rationale for 'projectised' food aid, such as food-for-work programmes, dairy development, and nutritional projects for building human capital (see, for example, Singer, 1987).

Programme aid is more commonly seen as relaxing balance of payments constraints on growth, or more fashionably structural adjustment. The difficulty is that exporter interests find the *explicit* objective of displacement of commercial exports unacceptable. Therefore, food aid is presented formally as *additional*, filling a *food gap*. But additional imports, by implication, could compete with agriculture in the importing country. Hence, for more than a decade, the declared objective of food donors has been to make food aid an instrument to promote, rather than hamper, agricultural development. In particular, the intention has been to contribute to increased food security by integrating food aid into national strategies for food security in recipient countries, especially in SSA. Measuring programmatic success or failure against such a vast and complicated objective is bound to be controversial and subject to many uncertainties and provisos.

Generating Resources for Development

From a macroeconomic perspective (programme) food aid does not differ in principle from other types of commodity aid. It is usually tied to procurement in the donor country, often double- and even triple-tied, that is, the product and even the producer are identified. Food aid saves foreign currency (improves the balance of payments) for the recipient if the government would have imported anyway. Alternatively, the food aid provides an additional supply of food if the government (or private trade) would not have imported the food. The criterion for assessing the impact of food aid provided for balance of payments support must be the performance of the whole economy, because of the fungibility of such assistance.

The effects of programme food aid are, therefore, highly dependent on the policy orientation and priorities of the recipient government. If the effect of food aid, in the first place, is to ease the balance-of-payments constraints of the recipient economy, then its effects on development will depend on how additional foreign currency is used. The food is usually sold on the domestic market, as are other forms of commodity aid. The developmental effect of the local currency generated is then determined by how these funds are allocated by the Ministry of Finance. This uncomfortable reality is fundamental in the aid relationship. The provision of balance-of-payments support and additional budgetary resources are logically alternative, but linked, consequences of food aid. Governments can allocate one or the other of these resources, not both independently. But the practice of considering these effects sequentially and independently in both impact assessment and policy prescription remains widespread.

Where food aid provides even partial balance-of-payments support, a donor entering into a policy dialogue about the uses of revenue from all local sales is seeking to influence the allocation of the government's *existing* revenues. Most donor governments insist on their declared policies that food aid is provided to satisfy food needs and promote sustainable development, often specifically of the agricultural sector or rural development. But the opportunities for legal or parallel trade open up possibilities for alternative outlets, which dampen the direct effects. Additional cereal imports may promote parallel trade of domestically produced food into a neighbouring economy, leaving foreign exchange in the private sector. In addition government intervention in domestic food aid in freeing foreign exchange may be positive in relaxing constraints on economic growth. Alternatively, these resources may provide a cushion for 'bad' non-development policies.

To forestall the diversion of aid from its intended use, donors have tried to exert greater control. Both bilateral and multilateral agencies have sought to *target* aid for the poor, variously defined as specific groups (women, children) or even regions, and to some extent, that explains the continued growth of projectised aid in the 1980s. Programme food aid is not particularly appropriate for this purpose of directly targeting the poorest, or even supporting agricultural development, except via control over government expenditures. The attempt by donors of programme food aid to influence the uses made of funds has been apparent in the 1980s, as they sought multi-year programming agreements and specific programmatic uses of counterpart funds to meet local costs of development projects or to facilitate change in economic policy (Maxwell, 1992). Programme food aid, as with projectised and emergency assistance, thus has been part of the trend for food aid to become a more closely managed resource transfer. There have been an increasing number of multi-year agreements with conditionality in terms of local currencies and policy changes, both on a bilateral basis, as in the early PL 480 Title III agreement in Bangladesh, and the proliferation of multi-donor common counterpart fund arrangements in Sub-Saharan Africa, including Mali, Mauritania, Senegal and Madagascar.

On both theoretical and empirical grounds, analysts are sceptical of the capacity of food aid to be an efficient resource for development. Roemer (1989) has restated the economic analysis, demonstrating that counterpart funds are not a real resource in any sense; such funds simply allow reallocation within a planned budget or permit inflationary finance for new projects. Empirically, only a relatively small proportion of imports is accounted for by staple cereals, except in a few countries in food crisis or in a chronic near-crisis food situation. Where food aid agreements are contemporaneous with improving sectoral performance (Mali) or general economic performance (Ghana and Jamaica), food aid has been part of a broader package of financial and commodity assistance, economic conditionality and domestic economic policy.

'Monetised' food aid, for example in the case of NGO projects supported under US PL 480 Title II, involves sale of some imported commodities to meet local currency project expenses. This process is a roundabout way of obtaining the beneficial economic effects of a resource transfer, and a financial transfer would probably have done the trick more easily. The 'second-best' nature of such food transfers underscores the crucial importance of the additionality question – whether food aid adds to total resources available to poor countries or merely displaces other financial aid – and continuing interest in cost-effectiveness of food transfers. Since the United States has changed its funding process for food aid, it is more likely that during the 1990s food aid will compete at the margin with other elements of the aid programme. Therefore, both the record of food aid and the options for its use are likely to be more closely scrutinised in the future.

The Economic Impact of Food Aid

The debate on the impact of food aid on the economy, and agriculture in particular, has been inconclusive. It has been difficult to determine the extent to which a food transfer provides foreign exchange savings or budgetary support. In the former case, there is only a substitution of concessional for commercial imports, usually precluding direct price effects on domestic markets. Methodological problems persist in assessing the direct impact of imports on food production and consumption and the role of other associated agricultural policy measures.

Evaluation models used by economists typically require that most variables in the analysis be held constant while only food aid levels, for example, are permitted to change. More flexible and robust modelling efforts, such as computable general-equilibrium models, require a functional understanding of sectoral interlinkages, which is difficult to acquire even in developed countries and is particularly slippery in developing economies with poor data, imperfect markets, and rapidly changing institutions and economic structures. It is not surprising then, that these more ambitious modelling efforts have produced few solid conclusions.

Impact of Cereal Aid

The potential effects of food aid, particularly in the form of cereals, cannot be accurately assessed in isolation, most obviously because of interaction between production and consumption, and also because of the dynamics through time of general economic activity and the evolving forward and backward linkages of the food system. Where quantitative economic analysis has been attempted, the overall impact on the economy and the agricultural sector varied considerably among countries, as the impact was heavily determined by the specifics of national food policy: the segmentation of markets, separation of consumer and producer prices, and overall investment policy (Cathie, 1991; Maxwell, 1991).

A further question on the economic impact of food aid is the overall implications of food imports of developing countries. The greater part of cereal imports is not provided as food aid. A substantial part of these 'commercial' or 'non-food aid' imports has been financed under soft credit programmes of the United States and export subsidisation programmes of the EC. An assessment of the impact of export programmes of developed countries, which would be comparable to the early studies of the impact of the PL 480 programme in India up to 1970–1, ought now to take into account programmes such as the Guarantee Market Supply (GMS) and Export Enhancement Programmes.

Impact of Dairy Food Aid

Food aid in the form of dairy products is, if possible, even more controversial than cereals food aid. Yet, these transfers have been relatively neglected in the food aid assessment literature. The findings of the programme of research at the Institute of Social Studies, The Hague, on Operation Flood in India, however, suggest that analytical and policy issues raised are broadly similar to those for cereals aid (Doornbos et al., 1991).

FOOD AID AND FOOD SECURITY

Food security for a country requires both reliable supplies and effective demand. A task for a country's long-term development effort is to create the reliable purchasing power or capacity to produce that generates effective demand for food by all households. The review above suggests that food aid has a marginal role, at best, in this effort. But because food security requires food supplies, many donors, recipient countries and analysts have argued that food aid could play a much more effective role in helping countries implement their shorter-term policies designed to stabilise food supplies and prices (Franco, 1988; Singer et al., 1987).

The Inverse Relationship: Price and Availability

In general, allocations of food aid by donors have been closely related to their minimum contribution levels under the Food Aid Convention. Nevertheless, overall food aid levels, because of the behaviour of a few large donors, have remained sensitive to price movements and relative tightness of markets for most commodities (Taylor and Byerlee, 1991). As a result of the practice in the United States of budgeting the PL 480 programme on a fiscal year basis in financial terms, the actual physical allocations and shipments have been sensitive to short-term price movements – downwards in fiscal year 1979, upward in the mid-1980s, downward again in 1989 and 1990 and upwards again in 1991. A close analysis of the short-term movements in allocations by some other food aid donors, Australia, Canada and the EC, also indicates that allocations are sensitive to prices and the level of stocks available for export (Clay, 1985).

Food aid is *not* a counter-cyclical element in the world food economy, buffering the effects that market movements have on recipient countries. Overall, the aggregated consequence of donor decisions is to leave food aid still significantly pro-cyclical in the level of allocations and shipments. Bearing in mind that the greater part of food aid is now targeted onto least-developed or low income countries, the dependence of food aid supplies on aggregate food availability is a serious weakness of the existing international arrangements and reflects negatively on the policies of some large donors. In retrospect, it now appears only fortuitous that the African food crisis coincided with a period of overhanging surpluses. The response might have been more limited, and possibly even more tardy, if there had been a tighter market situation than that which prevailed during 1983–6.

The Limited Role for Food Aid

The international agreements that made food aid an instrument of international food security, have not been, however, a complete failure. The commitments under the Food Aid Convention have resulted in cereal food aid levels fluctuating at around 90–120 per cent of the target of 10 million tons established by the World Food Conference of 1974. There is still a clearly procyclical pattern of fluctuations, but it is much less severe that experienced during 1972–6. That success in committing cereals aid, on however modest a scale, ought to be considered in the light of recent developments and possible scenarios for the 1990s.

Food aid cannot be considered a significant instrument of food security for countries, such as India, that might require import levels that are non-marginal in relation to world cereals trade. Secondly, the transitory problems of food security of countries that are in turn non-marginal in relation to overall food aid levels, such as Bangladesh, cannot be assured through food aid. Food aid can be, in fact, a significant instrument for food security at a national level, or regionally, only in countries that are marginal in terms of their potential import requirement in relation to world cereals trade and also to internationally agreed upon minimum food aid levels. Consequently, when a food security crisis is regional, as in SSA during 1984–6 or again in Southern Africa in early 1992, an exceptional co-ordinated response to needs that cannot be satisfied within initial annual food aid allocations is required. This response is problematic because additional resources have to be negotiated within donor agencies and with national treasuries as well as internationally in terms of burden sharing. The risk is of responses that are too little and too late and which divert resources from other longer-term developmental activities involving food or financial aid.

EMERGENGY AID: FOOD CRISIS IN AFRICA, 1982–86

The African food crisis has been the most important test to date of the credibility of the food aid system as reconstructed after 1974 (Borton and Clay, 1988). That experience demonstrated what could be achieved by co-ordinated action and the risks inherent in the current incomplete international arrangements for combating international food security or a major food emergency.

A large number of countries moved almost simultaneously into increasing deficit of staple foods. The crisis began with the onset of drought in the Sahel. Subsequently, the drought became more widespread, including many countries of east and southern Africa in 1983–4. The severity of the drought was also aggravated by the enfeebled condition of many poorly managed economies severely hit by the second hike in oil prices. There was growing recognition in 1982 and thereafter that agriculture in many SSA countries was moving towards crisis point. Nevertheless, the monitoring of events and articulation of a coherent strategy for responding to that crisis, as it came to involve a large number of countries, was both tardy and, initially, unsatisfactory. But, once the situation was seen as quantitatively different, a continent-wide crisis, there was clear increased response.

During the 1980s, emergency and developmental programmes appear to have been partly competitive alternative outlets for cereal food aid within a total that was largely institutionally determined. The only clear exception is 1984–5 when both emergency and programme assistance to SSA and the rest of the world increased simultaneously. The lagged response to the crisis, however, resulted in much of the additional emergency food arriving after many lives had already been lost and in some instances when it was no longer required. With favourable rains, production rose nearly to record levels year to year in many of the most severely affected countries, particularly in the Sahel during 1985 and 1986. There is some evidence of possible disincentive effects in Sahelian countries, the Sudan, and, as Maxwell (1991) hints, in Ethiopia.

The massive relief operations were successful in saving lives and limiting distress and economic disintegration in Ethiopia and other affected countries. The scale of food aid operations was such that for many countries food aid became temporarily a large part of overall development assistance (30 per cent of all aid from OECD countries to the most affected countries in 1984).

The severity of logistical problems pushed donors and governments closer together in co-ordinating food aid programming and delivery through information-sharing and attempts at consistent scheduling of shipments at regional and national levels. At least temporarily, effective local liaison groups involving governments and donors emerged that could have played a valuable continuing role in effective planning of food aid in a post-crisis situation. Once the crisis had passed, however, donors and governments appeared to have lapsed back in some cases to more bilateral, less co-ordinated relationships. Information-sharing at an international level for food aid to many countries was unprecedented and encouragingly indicative of agencies coming to terms with more complex multi-donor food aid systems.

As with the earlier crisis of 1972–4, a traumatic set of events appears to have been internalised as 'lessons' for administrative practice within donor agencies and recipient country governments, as well as NGOs. Firstly, the crisis generated considerable interest in early warning systems, in effect, a trigger for emergency food aid. Resource flows to such activities have continued at high level, even if some of the plethora of voluntary initiatives have faded away. Secondly, food aid donors re-examined their emergency procedures and changed regulations in order to streamline responses. Thirdly, donors also appear likely to respond more rapidly to appeals for international emergency assistance in order to avert the costs in terms of human distress, as well as in terms of the political fallout, of a repetition of the Ethiopian and Sudanese famines of 1984–5. Fourthly, the model of local liaison groups involving government, donors and NGOs, and in some cases a UN co-ordinator, has been followed in subsequent crises. Emergency assistance has come to have a relatively higher profile and priority within food aid.

A problematic consequence of that change of priority is that, as noted above, there appears to be substitution between emergency and developmental food aid, which probably reflects the new priority accorded to the fluctuating scale of requests for provisional emergency aid. If developmental programme food aid has become, in effect, a residual category, that would appear to restrict the potential for a positive impact on development. At best, it would limit the scope for multi-year programming and linking of monetised resources to particular development activities, as envisaged in the 1980s in many proposals for reforming food aid (see for example Singer, 1987). At worst, it confirms the danger that some bilateral food aid programmes serve mostly as all too useful ministerial slush funds for responding publicly to disasters the world over.

More Flexible Responses

The lagged response to the African food crisis again drew attention to the cumbersome, slow procedures of many donors. The programming decision process is slow. The mobilisation of commodities and the organisation of processing and delivery result in total response time from request to delivery, even for so-called emergency assistance, of several months and in many cases more than a year. When food aid is provided in an reactive mode, such inflexibility limits its use in responding to problems of food insecurity and substantial, unanticipated variability in food supply. Recognition of that inflexibility has also stimulated a variety of attempts to make food aid more responsive to varying food situations at regional and international levels.

The use of food aid to build up or finance food security or emergency stocks directly in individual recipient countries has been attempted, with patchy results. Nevertheless, such reserves at a national or regional level, financed by donors, continue to find favour in recipient countries. Food aid donors and international funding organisations are concerned about issues of food system management as well as costs.

The pre-positioning of relatively small stocks in convenient shipment points for rapid emergency responses could reduce the post-decision lead times for emergency actions. Apart from very small World Food Programme stockpiles in Amsterdam and Singapore, little has been attempted, and there has been loss of interest on the part of donors in establishing such stocks. Instead, 'borrowing' from development projects by drawing upon in-country stocks or re-routing ships has become the pragmatic, lower-cost response. But such an approach again risks sacrificing development objectives to meet immediate, overwhelming humanitarian priorities.

Rural works or nutritional supplementation projects that can rapidly expand or contract according to the food and economic situation play an important role in providing a food security net, particularly in South Asia as well as southern Africa (Clay, 1986; von Braun, 1991). In some African countries multi-purpose projects have been designed with an element of budgetary flexibility to allow a response to unforeseen emergencies (World Bank/WFP, 1991).

There appears to be an increased awareness of the problem of commodity appropriateness and of the need for more general flexibility in the acquisition of food aid commodities, particularly as a result of recent experience in Africa. The inappropriateness of distributing wheat and rice in rural economies that are based on coarse grains and tuber crops has stimulated triangular, local purchase and swap operations. Several donor agencies have modified their procedures to mandate at least a limited programme of commodity acquisition in developing countries, and such practices have to become more commonplace in food aid operations.

One final doubt must remain concerning the food aid response to the African emergency. The crisis occurred in a large number of countries whose aggregate consumption of staple foods is relatively modest compared with that of the large, densely populated countries of Asia. The food aid response involved only a maximum 20 per cent increase in cereals food aid during a period when world markets were overhung by large stocks and when exporters were competing with increasing intensity for markets. The response to that crisis, therefore, provides little indication of how the food aid system would have coped with a large-scale food crisis that might plausibly have been linked to a rapid rise in world market prices. The coincidence in 1992 of huge food import financing problems in the republics of the former Soviet Union, a massive drought in southern Africa and firmer grain prices is potentially just such a test of the donor commitment and capacity to respond effectively to a crisis of global magnitude.

FUTURE FOOD AID POLICY

Perhaps a majority of the general public in high income countries believe that food aid is an effective vehicle for assisting poor countries; it seems the one form of aid that resolves the paradox of food surpluses in the world of hungry people. Disillusionment among professional development specialists with the actual record of food aid in feeding hungry people in the short run and making them less vulnerable to natural and political disasters in the long run has not translated into sharply diminished political enthusiasm for using food aid whenever possible. The initial attempts to support reform in Eastern Europe and the former Soviet Union with food aid underscore all these problems. In 1990, Poland received more food aid from the EC than from the whole developing world; but this was only to find these imports exacerbating a situation of excess supply, as domestic markets were deregulated and subsidies to consumers removed (EC Court of Auditors, 1991). During the winter of 1991–2 presidents and ministers were only too anxious to be recorded for television seeing off the first transport planes in the emergency airlift to Russia.

Governments of donor countries are, however, sensitive to the charges that food aid has not benefited the poor or helped the development process. The response typically is to mandate further controls on who may receive food aid, in what quantities, and how it may be used in the recipient country. Negotiations for providing programme food aid are, increasingly, conducted as part of a broader policy dialogue, with food commitments conditional on changes deemed desirable by the donors. This increased managerial control and monitoring has raised the cost of providing a unit of aid in the form of food, as opposed to simple financial resources, and food aid has become a relatively smaller element of overall development assistance. There would seem to be a strong case for concentrating this limited resource on a small number of practical goals and in the neediest countries.

Emergency aid to food-insecure low-income countries and to assist the victims of natural disasters and conflict would command general support as the highest priority. Experience since the mid-1980s suggests that in any year between 2 and 5 million tonnes of commodities may be required for direct relief, especially to those affected by conflict and drought. Unless additional resources are available to respond to the needs of larger disaster-affected countries or regional crises, then emergencies are likely to absorb up to 40 per cent of food aid in some years, severely curtailing the scope for developmental uses of food aid.

Practical experience during the 1980s has underlined the need for greater flexibility in resources and the way these are provided for relief. Some of the recent changes in arrangements for international emergency food aid indicate the direction in which donors would need to move. There are too many agencies with overlapping mandates involved in emergencies, and so UNHCR and WFP have sought to rationalise at least their roles by WFP becoming primarily responsible for acquisition and delivery of relief food supplies. There has been a modest deconcentration of responsibility from headquarters within WFP and UNICEF, allowing country offices to make an immediate response drawing upon whatever resources are locally available. Rapid and appropriate responses may involve local purchases of food, organising of logistics and storage. In 1991, donors also agreed to WFP establishing a modest emergency cash fund. The bulk of emergency food aid continues to be commodities which typically require six months and more from commitment to delivery. This food can only replace in-country stocks already drawn down in the first phase of a crisis or sustain relief operations over a more extended period.

Supporting structural adjustment in the poorer African economy might be another effective use of food aid (Franco, 1988; Singer, 1991). This strategy implies that integrating food aid into the overall package of balance of payments assistance to countries engaged in adjustment would be justified where it increases the overall resources available, cushioning the austerity effects of adjustment. Programme food aid contributes balance of payments support, and project aid can be focused on social groups which may be particularly adversely effected in the adjustment process. Structural adjustment is providing a specific and contemporary policy framework for restating the more general arguments commonly made for developmental use of food aid.

Proponents of food aid argue that a much more powerful case could be made for increasing food aid flows substantially. The most recent comprehensive reviews of food aid needs all suggest that even a doubling of present levels would be required to maintain the approximate share of food aid in the imports of developing countries (National Research Council, 1988; Alexandratos, 1988). A World Bank/WFP (1991) report concluded that food imports for Sub-Saharan Africa will at least double on trend during the 1990s. But these are studies of projected food import financing requirements, not food aid requirements.

Food aid may be used to help the most vulnerable countries pay for the rising volume of food imports that has been projected. Inability to finance important imports will constrain the development process, and extensive malnutrition can be addressed only by expanding aggregate food supplies faster than foreign exchange constraints will permit. For example, Mellor (1987) has emphasised a considerable range of complementary opportunities for using increased food aid effectively both to finance the development process and to be used directly in labour-intensive rural investment, even in Africa.

There are several practical difficulties awaiting these substantially more ambitious direct uses of food aid for development. The recent record in many least developed countries, particularly in Africa during and after the food crisis, underscored the difficulties of programming aid-financed imports in those economies that have highly variable import requirements. How is development to be financed in years when food imports are not needed? In addition, conventional food aid does not provide appropriate cereals for many economies that are based on coarse grains and tubers.

The arguments in favour of greater flexibility and use of cash to finance food in emergencies, as well as the limitations of food aid in a developmental context, imply a still more important role for financing the acquisition of commodities of food aid operations in developing countries. There is a further argument in favour of using finance for food in this way to promote south to south agricultural trade. The pervasive role of export credits indicates the extent to which trade is inextricably linked with financing arrangements. There is an infant industry argument for using food aid interventions to overcome complex non-tariff obstacles to inter-regional trade and to encourage improvements in the logistical infrastructure, often required for increased trade flows. The evidence available suggests that commodity acquisitions in developing countries are no more costly than conventional food aid (Relief and Development Institute, 1987; Hay, 1989). On the negative side there are all the now well rehearsed problems of administered trade, especially when organised in an ad hoc manner to provide temporary financial support to the country that has transitory surpluses. The interests of the importing economy also need to be taken fully into account. The possibilities and the practical difficulties of encouraging south to south trade in this way are most apparent in Sub-Saharan Africa where agriculture in most potentially export surplus producing economies is vulnerable to large weather-induced fluctuations, markets are extremely thin and concerns about domestic food security may impede the growth of trade.

What are the realistic prospects for policy developments along these lines? Historically those donors which provide finance for food – Nordic countries, northern members of the EC, and Japan, as well as international organisations largely using the resources provided by these same donors – have been the most flexible (Clay and Benson, 1991). The EC, despite its large surpluses, has been drawn in the same direction. The implementation of the Single European Market involving also EFTA states will potentially untie more bilateral aid. These changes might increase Third World acquisition from under 1 million to at most 2 million tonnes a year. But that would be the upper limit, unless some internationally negotiated agreement were to draw the traditional cereal exporters, USA, Canada and Australia, into a more flexible procurement policy. That possibility might exist in the context of what these countries would regard as a successful resolution of agricultural trade negotiations within the Uruguay Round.

Two longer-term trends in food aid have been stressed. Firstly, there is the unquestionable relative decline of food aid as an aspect of aid and agricultural trade over the last two decades. Secondly, food aid has also become an increasingly complex phenomenon, as aid agencies and importing countries have sought to make more effective use of the resources that are available.

Increasing the role of food aid in compensating for the effect of crises and financing the development process implies that food aid is less costly than financial aid. Even if the juggling of agricultural and aid budgets makes that appear to be so for some donors, the economic resource costs for developed countries are now probably not lower, but higher, than financing food imports or supporting rural development directly. If food aid is provided in increasingly flexible ways, with purchases in developing countries and monetisation rather than direct distribution, the distinction between food aid and financial aid would gradually disappear in the face of such flexible arrangements. Then the food debate would no longer need to be distinct from the overall debate over the magnitude and effectiveness of development aid in general.

The alternative, more pessimistic prognosis of Falcon (1991) is to envisage that about 10–12 million tons of food aid will continue more or less within its existing set of institutional and economic supply constraints, with perhaps more resources being provided as relief, and the remainder being spread more thinly and with commensurate reduced impact amongst the countries of what was the 'Third World'. This ultimately unacceptable scenario is the primary reason for the international community to seek more flexible, better resourced arrangements to finance food problems in low-income developing countries.

Notes

1. This paper summarises findings from a workshop involving members of the DSA Study Group on Food Aid published as *Food Aid Reconsidered* (Clay and Stokke, 1991) and concludes with speculations on food aid in the 1990s. The central sections of the paper covering trends, developmental impacts and food security are adapted from Clay (1991) 'Food aid, development and food security', Chapter 8 in C. Peter Timmer (ed.) *Agriculture and the State: growth, employment and poverty in developing countries*', copyright © 1991 by Cornell University. Used by permission of Cornell University Press, Ithaca, NY. The contributions of Olav Stokke and Peter Timmer to those earlier papers is especially acknowledged.

References

Alexandratos, M. (ed.) (1988) *World Agriculture Towards 2000. An FAO Study* (London: Belhaven Press).

Borton, J. and E. Clay (1988) 'The African Food Crisis of 1982–1986.' in D. Rimmer, ed. *Rural Transformation in Tropical Africa* (London: Belhaven Press).

von Braun, J. et al. (1991) 'Labour-Intensive Public Works for Food Security: Experience in Africa', *Working Paper on Food Studies*, no. 6, (Washington DC: International Food Policy Research Institute).

Cathie, J. (1991) 'Modelling the Role of Food Imports, Food Aid and Food Security in Africa: A Case Study of Botswana', in Clay and Stokke (1991).

Clay, E. J. (1985) 'Review of Food Aid Policy Changes since 1978.' *WFP Occasional Paper 1*, (Rome: World Food Programme).

—— (1986) 'Rural Public Works and Food-for-Work: A Survey', *World Development*, 14(10–11), 1237–52.

—— (1991) 'Food Aid, Development, and Food Security', in Timmer (1991).

Clay, E. J. and C. Benson (1991) 'Triangular Transactions, Local Purchases and Exchange Arrangements in Food Aid: A Provisional Review with Special Reference to Sub-Saharan Africa' in Clay and Stokke (1991).

Clay, E. J. and O. Stokke, (eds) (1991) *Food Aid Reconsidered* (London: F. Cass).

Doornbos, M. et al. (1991) 'Dairy Aid and Development: Current Trends and Long-Term Implications of the Indian Case', in Clay and Stokke (1991).

European Community Court of Auditors (1991) 'Annual Report Concerning the Financial Year 1990, Together with the Institutional Replies', *Official Journal of European Communities* C324 (34), 13 December.

Falcon, W. P. (1991) 'Whither Food Aid', in Timmer (1991).

Franco, M. (1988) 'Food Security and Adjustment: The EC Contribution' *Food Policy* 13(1), 90–7.

FAO (1991) *Prospects for Food Aid and its Role in the 1990s*, Committee on World Food Security, 16th Session, 11–15 March, Rome.

Hay, R. et al. (1989) 'European Community Triangular Food Aid: An Evaluation', (Report to the EC Commission), (Oxford: Food Studies Group, Queen Elizabeth House) December.

Martens, B (1990) 'The economics of triangular food aid transactions' *Food Policy* 15(1), 13–26.

Maxwell, S. J. (1991) 'Disincentives to Agricultural Production', in Clay and Stokke (1991).

—— (ed.) (1992), 'Counterpart Funds and Development', *IDS Bulletin* 23(2) April.

Mellor, J. W. (1987) 'Food Aid for Food Security and Economic Development' in E. J. Clay and J. Shaw, (eds) *Poverty, Development and Food.* pp. 173–91, (London: Macmillan).

National Research Council (1988) *Food Aid Projections for the Decade of the 1990s* (Washington DC: National Academy Press).

Relief and Development Institute (1987) 'A Study of Triangular Transactions and Local Purchases in Food Aid', *Occasional Paper* no. 11, (Rome: World Food Programme).

Roemer, M. (1989) 'The Macroeconomics of Counterpart Funds Revisisted.' *World Development* 17(6), 795–807.

Saran, R. and P. Konandreas (1991) 'An Additional Resource? A Global Perspective on Food Aid Flows in Relation to Development Assistance' in Clay and Stokke (1991).

Singer, H. W. et al. (1987) *Food Aid: the challenge and the opportunity* (Oxford: Oxford University Press).

Singer, H. W. (1991) 'Food Aid and Structural Adjustment in Sub-Saharan Africa', in Clay and Stokke (1991).

Taylor, E. and B. Byerlee (1991) 'Food Aid and Food Security: A Cautionary Note', *Canadian Journal of Agricultural Economics*, 39, 163–75.

Timmer C. P., ed. (1991) *Agriculture and the State: Growth, Employment and Poverty in Developing Countries*, (Ithaca: Cornell University Press).

World Bank and World Food Programme (1991) *Food Aid in Africa: Agenda for the 1990s*, (Washington DC and Rome).

11 Two Views of Food Aid

H. W. SINGER

We may distinguish two schools of thought. One view is that the case for food aid is tied to emergency situations where it is justified for direct humanitarian reasons. Outside emergencies, there is no real case for food aid since it is fungible with, and usually inferior to, financial aid. I shall call this position the 'British view' since this broadly represents the long-held view of the British government and those associated with British NGOs.[1]

The other view is that, on the contrary, food aid should be directed at the real roots of poverty of which the acute emergency is more a symptom than a cause. On this view, food aid should be directed at creating situations in which emergencies either do not occur or can be coped with without the hectic Geldof-type humanitarian appeal. We will call this view the 'Dutch view' since it was presented as the underlying rationale for Dutch food aid policy at a 1986 workshop in Wageningen, and directly contrasted with the 'British view'.[2]

In part, the difference between these two views can be reduced to a different definition of 'emergency'. The British view is based on a relatively narrow definition of an acute emergency with imminent or actual deaths from starvation. This rouses the humanitarian instincts of the Western public, especially when pictures of starving children appear on television, and provides Western governments with the necessary political support. In such a situation food aid becomes truly additional to normal aid including voluntary private contributions. Moreover, such a situation of acute emergency is usually associated with supply problems like drought, floods, civil wars and so on; hence, in the absence of local food supplies, direct use of food as aid without monetisation becomes acceptable and appropriate. In the British view, the emergency appears as a definable, visible and transient situation.

The Dutch view, by contrast, is based on a wider definition of emergency, going much beyond the acute threat of death from starvation. On this view, the emergency is part of the general process of impoverishment rather than an exceptional situation. It starts well before the acute phase: absence of local reserve stocks, drop in local income and employment, deficiencies in the transport and other infrastructure needed for maintaining food supplies, and lack of efficient national and local administration convert what would otherwise be a preventable and absorbable situation into an acute emergency.

By the time the emergency becomes acute, the harm will already have been done. People will have left their farms and collected in refugee camps, whereas earlier aid could have kept them on their farms and tided them over a difficult period. Similarly, after the emergency there is a need for rehabilitation which merges into restructuring and general development.

It can be seen that this 'Dutch view' is linked with a demand-side view of an emergency where the emergency appears as a breakdown of entitlements (in A. K. Sen's terminology) which is really part of a long-term deficiency of entitlements (Dreze and Sen, 1989). Given this emphasis on the demand rather than the supply side of food insecurity, there is also a definite affinity between the Dutch view and an emphasis on the advantages of monetisation: that is, selling the food and using the cash proceeds rather than using the food directly to feed hungry mouths. The spreading use of monetisation of food aid also weakens the element in the British view that normally – that is outside emergencies – food aid is conceptually inferior to financial aid and represents a less efficient form of income transfer. The use of counterpart funds provides programme food aid given in substitution for commercial imports the combined advantages of efficient income transfer (since the money saved on commercial imports represents fully fungible financial aid) and the desired targeting on food and the poor. In the British concentration on emergencies, there is no inherent emphasis on monetisation, although this may be obscured by the fact that in the absence of major food surpluses UK food aid often takes the form of 'triangular transactions', for example buying maize in Zimbabwe for distribution in Zambia.[3] This can be considered a form of monetisation, at least from the viewpoint of the British budget, although it is not directly related to whether the aid to the ultimate recipient should be in food or in money.

Such a comparison of the British and Dutch views, making them hinge upon different definitions of emergency, makes it clear that there is no necessary and absolute contradiction between them. One could adhere to the Dutch view that food aid should be developmental in the broad sense in which it includes prevention of emergencies, building up the means of absorbing emergencies, rehabilitation and reconstruction after emergencies, and building the infrastructure for sustainable systems free of emergencies. Such food aid would be normally monetised. At the same time one could still argue in favour of the British view that in the case of the failure of developmental food aid, as evidenced by the existence of an acute emergency and absence of local capacity to cope with it, the humanitarian case for food aid associated with direct distribution of food and utilising the advantages – both political and budgetary – of strong popular support by an aroused public could be brought into play.

Another way of contrasting the two views is by relating them to different concepts of what is 'humanitarian'. In the British view, a distinction is made between humanitarian emergency food aid (acceptable) and more generally developmental food aid (questionable). This distinction disappears in the Dutch view when the developmental food aid is assumed to be geared to the humanitarian purpose of reducing poverty or more specifically to the purpose of anticipating, preventing, coping with and rehabilitating after emergencies. Ultimately, we may see behind the two views on food aid two different views on aid and indeed development: is it to build viable and progressive economies or is it more directly to reduce poverty? Just as these two views of aid and development are interrelated and reconcilable, so are the two views of food aid. But also, just as the two different views of the development objective may lead to different composition, direction, volume and organisation of aid and other supporting action, so may the two different views of food aid suggest different composition, direction, volume and organisation of food aid. To point out that the two views are interrelated and can be reduced to different definitions of 'emergency' and 'humanitarian' is not to deny that the differences between the two views are important and that they shape the actual food aid picture.

Edward Clay (1991), dealing essentially with what is called here the 'Dutch view', concludes:

> Conventional double-tied food aid would gradually disappear in the face of such flexible arrangements. Then the food aid debate would no longer need to be distinct from the overall debate over the magnitude and effectiveness of development aid in general.

This projection, if correct, would certainly represent progress in the direction of rationality and even honesty. The present line of division, not only between food aid and financial aid, but also between food aid and trade in food, is a murky distinction which leads to many misconceptions and unintended side-effects. At the same time, however fictitious the present category of 'food aid' may be, and however misleading the figures attached to it, at least it has the advantage of cashing in on what is still a good deal of popular and political support for food aid. Even if one can agree that this support for a separate category of food aid is partly misconceived and partly a side-effect of the harmful protectionist agricultural policies pursued in the EC, US and Japan, yet it has the effect of making food aid at least partially additional to financial aid.

At any rate it can be shown that on the whole the correlation between financial aid and food aid is positive rather than negative.[4] This is especially true in the US where food aid and financial aid are financed from different sections of the budget (as distinct from the UK where the two forms of aid come out of the same aid budget). In rationalising the present food aid picture and gradually merging food aid with other forms of aid, we should be careful not to lose this precious element of additionality. Merging is good provided it does not mean overall reduction.

Having said this, one must agree that the present distinction between food aid and aid for food security is obsolete and confusing. Much of what is presently called food aid is in fact direct balance of payments support, replacing commercial food imports and thus setting free foreign exchange for other uses. At the same time, much of what is labelled financial aid helps to support food imports and could therefore be regarded as 'food aid'. The food surpluses accumulating as a result of the Common Agricultural Policy in the EC and corresponding policies in the US and Japan have a depressing effect on international food prices; this could legitimately be considered as food aid for net food importing developing countries (although at the expense of net food exporting countries). In the absence of counterfactual evidence it is difficult to be precise about how much higher international food prices would be in the absence of these overhangs of surplus stocks. But broad guesstimates would lead to the conclusion that this form of what is really food aid – although not included as such in the statistics – is more important than the official category of 'food aid'. This is particularly true if other and even more hidden forms of subsidies for food exports to developing countries are included, such as trade credits – very widespread in multiple forms.

This issue will also come up in the Uruguay Round of GATT negotiations where reform of agricultural policies and reduction of export subsidies are key items. Everybody is agreed that 'genuine food aid' should be exempt from such agricultural reforms, but the issue of how 'genuine food aid' should be defined has not been clearly tackled. One suspects that there is a general feeling that it is better to leave it vague – lest the much bigger cause of agricultural reform and a successful conclusion of the Uruguay Round (still in the balance at the time of writing) should founder on the rock of a definition of 'food aid'.

Notes

1. The most widely illustrated example of this position was in Jackson (1982).
2. The direct juxtaposition of a 'British view' and 'Dutch view' will be found on p. 69 in the presentation by A. P. J. M. Oomen, Dutch Ministry of Foreign Affairs in ICFSN (1986).

3. See for example Borton (1989).
4. See Saran and Konandreas (1991).

References

Borton, J. (1989) 'UK Food Aid and the African Emergency 1983–1986' *Food Policy*, vol. 14, no. 2.

Clay, E. J. (1991) 'Food Aid, Development and Food Security' in C. P. Timmer (ed.), *Agriculture and the state* (Ithaca: Cornell University Press) pp. 202–36.

Dreze, J. and A. K. Sen (1989) *Hunger and Public Action* (Oxford: Clarendon Press).

International Courses in Food Science and Nutrition (ICFSN) (1986) *Targeted Food Aid: Criteria for Commodity Choice* (Wageningen, The Netherlands: ICFSN).

Jackson, T. (1982) *Against the Grain* (Oxford: Oxfam).

Saran, R. and P. Konandreas (1991) 'An Additional Resource? A Global Perspective on Food Aid Flows in Relation to Development Assistance' in E. Clay and O. Stokke (eds), *Food Aid Reconsidered: Assessing the Impact on Third World Countries*, (London: Frank Cass).

Index